A Road with Memories

BY

JOHN WELDON EVANS

(Author of Songs and Stories of a Digger's Son)

TABLE OF CONTENTS

MOST UNFORGETTABLE CHARACTERS

LOVE

HOPE AND DESPAIR

FAITH

REDEMPTION

DEDICATION

To my 'big' brother Lamb (Hubert M. Evans)
who always loved a good story and could tell
the funniest jokes.

INTRODUCTION

(For what is life? It is even a vapor that appeareth for a little time, and then vanisheth away...James 4:14

Man is like a mere breath; his days are as a shadow that passeth away...Psalm 144.4)

If not for stories, written and/or told, real or imagined, human experiences could not be captured and preserved to inform, instruct, and entertain. Our coming forth and going hence would indeed be like vapors and shadows here for a little time and then vanished forever. In a story, however, a human experience can live on and be retold until the end of time. There are countless examples of fragile humanity existing throughout time, just as there are countless grains of sand or molecules of air, and no one (Except God) can know or witness them all. Here are forty-one stories I have written and assembled before my vapor, too, vanishes and my shadow passes away. In them, I tried to illustrate some of the themes and characteristics that are common to our fragile humanity: fear of the unknown, triumph over adversity, dreams and illusions, love, hope and despair, faith, sin, and redemption.

Some are based on facts, and some are fiction; all are intended to hold the attention of the reader and entertain him/her for a short period of time. This is a book of stories with fictional names given to most of the characters, and any similarities to real people are coincidental, except for those cases where the stories are derived directly from the writer's own life experiences. The first four are about facing the unknown: **The Blizzard** tells of events in the life of James Dixon, who braves one of the worst snowstorms in the northeast while attempting to travel home to Deer Park, L.I., from New York City. The second story, Mephistopheles, is about the fear of dying and losing one's immortal soul. It is a tale within a tale told by a sly old boozer who captivates the attention of a group of Satan believers and nonbelievers, and in it, if the storyteller is to be believed, Satan is outsmarted. The third story, **Russian Roulette**, is about a game of life and death by sudden violence. It depicts either bravery or human stupidity. The reader can judge. Two fools tried to test each other's courage with a pistol with one bullet in it.

The next group of eight stories deals with triumph over adversity. Unconquered is about a paralytic who managed to overcome impossible

1

odds and perform a feat of extraordinary heroism and bravery. **Fighting Fire with Fire** is about two unhappy people who act un-neighborly towards their neighbors, engaging in extreme anti-social behavior to the extent of resorting to sorcery and mystical rituals (obeah) to control others. **The Ghost** is a story about a poor family moving into their own 'piece of heaven' (a house in the suburbs) for the first time and taking on a formidable paranormal entity, but persevering to overcome it, of course, with a little help from experts in the field of paranormal science. The Little Black Box is a story about the Whittlings who moved into the Wexford Terrace apartment building in Queens, N.Y. and were, at first, victims of the most vicious gossip machine run by a neighbor, Mrs Dingman. Life for them was unbearable until they found a way to overcome this adversity and end the harassment. Sheppe is a pet dog that is the real hero in the next story. He overcomes every challenge and every obstacle put before him and finds a way to solve the problem of his confinement to a pen when all he wanted was the freedom to run around the backyard. Not only did he escape each time when no one was looking, but he went back into the pen before anyone could discover his trick. I spied on him one day and saw how he did it. I could have sworn that he had the human intelligence to be that smart for a dog. But the most important thing I remember about Sheppe is the debt that I owe him for saving my family's lives early one morning when we were asleep. It is still a mystery to me, up to this day, how he was able to accomplish that. Was it by canine or divine intervention that a certain disaster was averted that morning? I will never know the answer, but I shall always be grateful to *Sheppe*, my amazing dog. **"A-we-may-we"** is the name of a remote resort in the bushes of Negril, Jamaica, and this story deals with the weird experience a couple had and what it took for them to overcome that frightful and nearly fatal night in the wildest bushes.

The next group of stories deals with dreams and/or illusions and how they affect the characters' lives. **The Man Who Had Everything** is about a young man named Edward Giles who was well off but was not satisfied; he dreamed of becoming richer by gambling heavily in Atlantic City. He was disappointed by the vision revealed to him by Madam Saadi, the fortune teller. **Satan's Palace** is a tale of Atlantic City that led to a frightful awakening for one Jim Forbes, which he will never forget. My Father's Dream in **"Arraijan"** is a story about a dream my father had of transforming a piece of land in the bushes of a place called "Arraijan," the Republic of Panama, into a residential paradise, but it was never realized. Though disappointed, he later settled for a more modest version somewhere else in a place called Parque LeFevre that brought marital peace and harmony. **The Old Sailor** is a story about the ambition or dream of a young man which was deferred to care for his ailing mother. The dream was further deferred when he got married and devoted himself to caring for not only his mother but also his wife and children. As he got older, he still did not abandon his childhood dream, which stayed with him literally until his last dying breath. **Richard Graves** is the story of a mature man who had a delusion about relationships and a penchant for pursuing much younger women, which led to repeated disappointments. **Iceman and Ruby** is a story about two special people, an illusionary mighty Adonis, whose false prowess is about to be exposed, and an adroit and disappointed sex goddess, Ruby. Somehow he was saved by the intervention of local law enforcement one critical night in her boudoir. They say that dreams are illusions. In this story, **Maria's Dream**, the dream came true, however, and brought with it heartbreak and sadness in the life of a newlywed on what should have been her happiest and most glorious day. **The Fountain Pen** is about a fountain pen sold to Alan Ferguson in an ancient-looking, antiquated store on Hillside Avenue, Queens, N.Y., by two eccentrics, two weird-looking old ladies who appeared to be from another time and dimension. The purchase led, for Alan Ferguson, to his experiencing a brief period of writer's euphoria, followed by pain and disappointment, which he attributed to the pen.

The Missing Seven Hours is the next story. The mysterious thing about these 7 hours is that they cannot be explained or accounted for by John Bascombe, and when he tries to find the answer, it only leads to more questions and an unresolved dilemma. **The Reunion** is a tale of five former college buddies who died during WWII but had made a blood pact before leaving college that they would have a reunion on a specific future date, 25 years after graduation, no matter what their future circumstances may be. The only way this could have taken place, however, was by supernatural means, and three roving little boys found what might be the only material proof that it did. The story of **James Baker** is about an illusion of a life fulfilled, which was the last and happiest dream James Baker ever had in his life. **The Bus** is a story that attempts to depict a cross-section of ordinary people brought together on a passenger bus and their interactions with each other while traveling at nighttime. The illusion is so real that the reader might be disillusioned by the way the story ends, which injects a final touch of realism into the conclusion.

The next group of stories concerns the theme of Love. **Julia** is a love story filled with passion, remorse, and regret where love is affected by the corruption of big city life that often ruins too many young people who venture there from out-of-state small towns. They grow to hate it like Julia, who has to face the consequences. **Nadia** is a love story clouded by

3

intriguing possibilities when a mystery tests the faith and hope of one Phillip Richards. He fell in love with Nadia, who returned his love and swore to love him forever, although she mysteriously appeared one day and less than a year later also mysteriously disappeared; however, Phillip would not give up his faith that she would return and that one day he would see her again. **The Organ Music** is a story about a love triangle. It begins with a strange experience that one of the characters, Fred Ames, had when he thought he heard organ music playing in an empty church. On another occasion, at a social gathering when he learns about the most tragic story he has ever heard of, a love triangle of love and hate that ended in a double homicide involving three choir members of the same church, that story gave him such an eerie feeling that it brought back his memory of the organ music. **The Man Who Hated Love** is a story about a man who had no faith in love but found it in the charity of a blind beggar and an old lady, both of whom he had despised. Through them, he found the true meaning of love. **Reunited** is another love story of a young man who abandoned his young bride on the day they were to be married, and she, without revealing to him that she was pregnant, was planning to do so on their wedding night. The family was humiliated when he ran away on the day of the wedding, and Druscilla Harley, the bride-to-be, was shamed. She was sent away to another state to live with relatives, where she gave birth to twins and raised them to adulthood as a single parent. Many years later, Karl Stevens regretted his action. **The Ring** is about a mother's love, the greatest gift next to God's love. It tells about a mother's love for her son. **The Lovers** is a very heartbreaking story about two young lovers who died in a murder-suicide tragedy. The young man, Shakeem, was murdered, and Kumarie, his lover, committed suicide to join him in death forever. The families were close and friendly to each other, unlike the Montagues and Capulets, though the commitment of love between Shakeem and Kumarie was very much the same as that of Romeo and Juliet in William Shakespeare's tragedy.

The next group of stories deals with Hope and Despair. **Jackie's Christmas Present** is the story of a homeless and destitute little girl named Jackie who was found lying unconscious in the snow by a very kind and generous family who took her to their home nearby. When she had lain in the snow just before losing consciousness, the last thoughts that she had were of a cozy, warm place, a Christmas tree with ornaments and lights, and a warm dinner on the table. With the love of the Mason family, this story had a happy ending. **The Pigeon Lady** is a story about a lady who had lost her will to live after her only child was murdered in the apartment when she left her at home alone one evening. She had gone out on a date hoping to find a husband and a father for her child after her common-law husband had abandoned her. The tragedy destroyed her will to live, and she climbed to the roof of her building one night, intending to leap eight stories to her death, when a miracle took place. **Karla** is another sad story about two lovers, Karla St. Clair and Raymond Denis, who were planning to be married in the spring and were filled with happy expectations. She would meet him every day at the subway stop at 179th Street and Hillside Avenue, Queens, N.Y. Almost every day, she came to be with him in his apartment a block away from the subway station, but, as fate would have it, just a few weeks before they were to be married, one evening when she came to meet him turned out to be the last time they saw each other on this earth.

The next group of stories deals with Faith. **Angelique** is a story of a truly blessed individual whose faith was so strong that when you met her, you could feel the spiritual aura that she possessed. I can say now, with certainty, that she was a child of God in every sense. The catalyst that brought her to life in the church may have been an experience she had when she was a teenager. Innocent and vulnerable, she was a victim in a relationship in which she was deeply hurt and deceived beyond her ability to cope with it. She turned to God for help, and from that day, she gave her heart, soul, and mind to Christ. She left Martinique and came to Brooklyn, N.Y., to live with the Martins and later moved to Houston, Texas, where every minute, hour, and day of her life was spent in the service to God and the Christian Mission Church until her passing. **The Wooden Horse** is a story about childhood and the faith of a little boy.

The last two stories in this book are about redemption and/or divine intervention. **The House of the Lost** is a story of twelve lost souls from twelve different walks of life who converge in a place of disrepute, seeking escape from demons that tormented them, seeking oblivion in a bottle or a pill or other source. **Amazing Grace** is a story about two individuals, one is good, and the other is bad or lost. The good one dies, yet he lives, and the bad one lives, yet he dies. It's a miracle how redemption works. He, who seemed to be damned, turned out to be God's instrument and became a great preacher. This, in essence, is the story about two boys, Mark Andrews and Robert Patterson, who grew up together heading in opposite paths, one to perdition and the other to God. When Robert dies in his youth, however, Mark becomes what Robert had intended to be, and he fulfilled God's plan. Strange how God works in our lives!

FEAR OF THE UNKNOWN

THE BLIZZARD

On Friday afternoon, February 11, 1983, James T. Dixon sat in the Ziegfeld Theatre on 54th Street, New York City, engrossed in the movie, "The Life of Mahatma Gandhi." No doubt the life and achievements of this saintly man, who is recorded in history as one of the greatest human beings of his time, made a deep impression on James Dixon. As he sat engrossed in the movie, the unceasing downpour of snowflakes outside in the streets was the farthest thing from his mind. Finally, however, at the conclusion of the picture, he left the theatre and found himself confronting the reality of the blistering weather outside. He walked in the streets of Manhattan, stumbling and plodding through the mounting white stuff on the ground, making his way to the municipal parking garage on 54th street, and could not imagine what a never-to-be-forgotten experience that night would have in store for him.

It was 8:10 p.m. when he got into his car and drove out of the garage heading towards the east side along 54th Street. He intended to go down 2nd Avenue South to the midtown tunnel, to the L.I.E., and continue east until he reached Deer Park, Babylon, L.I., where he lived 50 miles from New York City. In case one might think that that was foolhardy (in view of what happened later), he had traveled in bad weather before, even with lots of heavy snow and ice on the ground, and he had always managed to make it home however long it took.

By now, it was about 9:15 p.m., and he had somehow managed to make his way to the midtown tunnel entrance at 34th Street and 2nd Avenue, traveling at about five mph when he was moving at all, as the steady downpour of snow kept piling up on the ground. He thought of turning back several times when the prospect of getting stuck crossed his mind, but as he turned left down the entrance to the midtown tunnel, he realized that that option was no longer available to him. Anyway, he figured, as long as he was moving, time was not important - after all, he had a full tank of gas, and his car, a '78 Buick Regal, was holding up quite well. He wasn't discouraged yet, but it wouldn't be long before his confidence wavered.

When he got on the L.I.E. just a little distance from the tunnel exit approaching Queens, he saw the first batch of stalled cars, some on the right side of the road, some on the left, some in the center, some near exits, and like other fortunate drivers he carefully passed to the right and left and around those stationary vehicles mired in the snow. He thought:

"Well, now, I'm in the soup, so I'd better keep moving and praying if I am going to get through this night!"

He was moving slowly through the thick snow and trying not to think about what lay ahead. He knew he couldn't get off the parkway now, for all the exits were impassable, and many drivers who tried that got stuck! At least on the parkway, the cars in front of him were making tracks that he could follow, except now and then when the car in front stalled, then he had to somehow drive around it. For that reason, he stayed behind a most formidable-looking medium-size truck with heavy traction snow tires. That way, he succeeded in reaching a good distance somewhere in Fresh Meadows, Queens. By then, visibility was poor at best as the downpour kept falling, and the wind kept blowing the snow about. The windshield wiper was on high speed, and he kept the heater on out of necessity.

He was approaching the Francis Lewis exit on the expressway going east when the traffic up ahead suddenly came to a dead stop -- the worst thing that could happen. Sometimes after stopping too long, car tires get stuck in the thick snow where the traction is poor, and just skid deeper and deeper in it till you can't move! He was hoping that that wouldn't happen as he waited for the traffic to move again. But he waited for a heck of a long time, not knowing what was going on up ahead. After a while, he ventured to get out of his car to see if he could find out what was wrong. As it turned out, a huge trailer truck had stalled across the expressway and was blocking the road. Now it seemed like he might never get out of there. He got back into his car and had the bright idea to shut off his headlights, radio, windshield wipers, heater, and finally, the engine. "No use in wasting good gasoline," he foolishly thought. About twenty minutes later, the traffic slowly started to move again. Apparently, the problem was solved. He pressed the accelerator pedal and turned the ignition key to start up again, but instead of a turned-over engine, he heard a dull clicking sound, and after a little while, he heard nothing at all! He tried it again and again, the same result! He waited for another fifteen minutes and tried again, but it was useless. It was clear by then that the battery had gone dead, cold dead! He sat in the car for another ten minutes thinking what to do as his heart kept sinking and he was freezing, and then he turned the ignition key again. It was no use; his car had become a roadside casualty. He, too, was now a roadside casualty.

He tried not to panic, but it was cold, and the falling snow gave no sign of abating. The ground was so thick with the white stuff that only snowshoes could keep one from sinking two or three feet in certain places. His tall boots allowed him to sink without getting his feet wet. He was out of his car now, trying in vain to wave at anything moving to stop for him, but other motorists were too busy trying to keep moving and to rescue themselves. It was no use! Somehow he didn't blame them. One thing he knew, he had to find shelter…but where? He struggled on foot through the snow near the Francis Lewis exit, trying to get to the service road. He looked up the embankment beyond the service road, and everywhere was deserted or closed up tight and in total darkness. As luck had it, he saw the lights of a theatre, the Fresh Meadows Theatre, about five hundred yards away still burning, and he fought his way against the wind and snow drifts till he reached his hoped-for place of refuge. It was about 11:45 p.m., and he was half frozen.

As he entered the lobby, a flicker of hope that he could spend the night there was shattered when the attendant promptly informed him that the theatre was closing in 15 minutes! He pretended not to hear him as he took a seat and watched the last 15 minutes of the movie, "Beverly Hills Cop," thawing out from the freezing cold at the same time. Besides himself and the attendant, the theatre was virtually empty. At twelve sharp, the movie ended, and the attendant came over.

"Sir, we are closing up now. You will have to leave," he said.

"Sir," said James, "my car is stalled on the Parkway; I live in Babylon, Deer Park, and unless you have a better suggestion, my only chance of survival is to spend the night right here, even if you have to lock me in!"

He softened his attitude and showed a little bit of compassion then and suggested that James call the local precinct for them to send help. He had nothing to lose; besides, the police business was rescuing citizens, and he was a taxpaying citizen. The attendant gave him the number, and he called the precinct. The desk officer at the precinct answered the phone.

"I am sorry, but there is no way we can get help to you - you'll have to stay where you are!"

"But, Sir," said James, "I am in the Fresh Meadows theatre, and it is closing now, and there is no place that I can go!"

"Perhaps there is," replied the officer, "go out of the theatre and walk east on the service road for about a quarter of a mile. You'll come to an all-night diner on the other side of the parkway. There you can get warm food, and at least you can sit there until morning."

"Thank you, officer," he replied and hung up.He didn't know why he took his advice and why he didn't just stay in that damn theatre and dare anyone to remove him or come and arrest him! He had absolutely no control over the events that were to follow, and he would soon reach almost to the point of panicking. He left the theatre with an uncomfortable feeling and went out into the blizzard once more. As he walked eastward along the service road, he remembered a story written by Jack London about a traveler on the Yukon trail who had to keep moving in sub-zero weather to keep from freezing to death, and when he finally stopped to build a fire (with his last match!), the wind blew it out! You know, that story only made him feel worse, especially when he reached where the all-night diner was supposed to be, according to the informed police officer, and there was no diner! In fact, there was no place in sight that wasn't closed tight and in total darkness! He felt abandoned and lost. He was too cold and numb to feel anger. He fought desperately against fear and kept walking eastward on the L.I.E. service road with no conception of what he was doing, what lay ahead, or how far he would get before collapsing, for he certainly wasn't going to make it all the way to Deer Park on foot! Yet, unexplainably, he was compelled to continue. He kept walking in the snow, both gloved hands in his coat pockets, at the mercy of the elements and an unknown destiny. He had a strange feeling as if this wasn't happening to him, as if he were an actor in a play and at the same time as if he were a spectator, an audience of one watching the play unfold, wondering how it was going to end. Real panic never came, though it should have, as he walked another mile eastward. He was walking in the middle of the service road when he looked back and saw two headlights coming straight toward him. He remained in the path of the car as it forged through the snow behind him. He made no effort to move out of the way, and the driver barely avoided hitting him and pulled up beside him. It was a black man in his thirties, and the car was a small, old Chevy model. He must have thought that James was crazy, but James thought that he was a miracle as he opened the door and said:

"Where are you going? Come on, get in!"

James got into the car and sat down beside him, and they began to introduce themselves. His name was Paul. James told him he was going to Deer Park, Babylon, N.Y.! In good humor, Paul responded.

"You'll never make it!" His benefactor looked at him and continued, "I am going to Hempstead; God willing, I could take you that far."

As if he had a choice, James said, "Hempstead sounds good enough to me; yes, I'd like to go there," shivering with cold as he spoke.They kept up a conversation mostly for conversation's sake, to take away the edge off of what fears they were feeling. James told him all about his unfortunate car breakdown on the L.I.E. in Queens and how he came to be walking to nowhere in the snow and was lucky when he came along. Paul kept very quiet while James talked about what happened to him, and when he was through, he simply said:

"This old Chevy is going to get us to Hempstead. Don't you worry about a thing!"

They were two crazy men driving in a snow blizzard in a small, old Chevy on the L.I.E. heading east to Hempstead. The storm was raging, the wind howling, and snow falling, but somehow James had no more fear of danger, even as they seemed to be driving blind through the blizzard. Who or whatever was controlling his destiny that evening, he did not know, but he would see the hand played out. As they drove along, the car seemed to glide over the thick snow like a snowmobile instead of sinking or sliding in it as so many other abandoned vehicles did. He was amazed at its performance! Even the wind didn't bother it! They must have passed over a hundred stalled or abandoned cars by the time they reached the exit to take them to Hempstead. James didn't even know how Paul saw the exit sign, if he did any at all, but figured he must have traveled this way many times and had some way of knowing. They cut right off the parkway into a pile of snow over what seemed to be two faint car tracks that some other brave souls had made before them. The car hit the trail without even hesitating or sticking, and they kept forging forward. Not more than a hundred yards in front of them, they suddenly saw two headlights coming directly at them in their path! There's no way two cars could pass on this trail unless somebody reversed. On the right and left, the snow drifts were high. You could hardly tell whether you were driving over the road or over a ditch the way the snow covered everything. Anyway, just as they approached each other, both cars managed to sidestep each other and stopped momentarily alongside. James heard the other driver say something as he lowered his window.

"Turn back! Turn back! You'll never make it! It's over 8 feet deep!...and a gully! Turn back!"

Paul and James both knew, instinctively, that they were just saved from a fate that was not meant for them, and the warning was more than fortuitous! They couldn't make a U-turn, so they reversed all the way back to the L.I.E. and continued east to the next exit that they could barely see, Glen Cove Ave. West (Exit 39 So.). They got off the parkway and traveled mostly by instinct for almost an hour when they arrived in the town of Hempstead. It was covered with a blanket of snow, and nothing was moving in the streets. In fact, the streets were barely passable. They arrived in Hempstead at about 3 a.m. Saturday, February 12th. They were driving on Fulton Street, and James made a comment.

11

"Only two more miracles left! If I could only find a place to eat and if I could find a place to sleep!"

But that was resolved shortly when they saw perhaps the only diner that was open on the entire island at 3:00 a.m. that morning, with its sign barely visible but lit up, "Ambassador Diner!" They pulled up and went in. He couldn't express how wonderful it felt to be in a warm shelter with warm food and friendly people - it didn't matter if he were in a foreign country at that moment! He was happy and would have paid them any amount they asked for a hot cup of coffee and hot food.

He and Paul sat at a table and ordered two huge breakfasts, for which he later picked up the tab. While they ate, the two of them talked about their lives, their families, and the strange circumstance that brought them together. They were there for nearly an hour in the warmth and comfort and had finished eating when James looked out the window, and the cold realities of the night returned.

"Paul, I can't ask you to do any more than you have already done. I know you must be anxious to get home to your family, so you can leave me here; I'll be all right now!" He said to Paul.

"Nonsense," replied Paul, "we have to find you a place to sleep! Look here. Let's go down a few blocks. I think there might be a motel there. You can't just sit in the restaurant!"

Sure enough, they drove three blocks west on Fulton Street and came to a Holiday Inn. The Inn was surrounded by snowdrifts as high as 12 feet! He got out of the car in the middle of the street. He thanked Paul again and even offered to give him some money for all he had done, but it was not for money that Paul rescued him on the L.I.E. Of course, he refused, and James felt embarrassed for having offered it. They said goodbye, and Paul drove off in the snow while James climbed over the snow banks up to the motel lobby. Inside the Holiday Inn, to his surprise, there was a crowd of stranded people drinking in the bar and making noises. He went up to the front desk and asked for a room. The desk clerk informed him that there were no more rooms available. They were all booked up! He walked over to the bar and bought a drink, and sat there wondering.

"What next in this unfolding adventure?"

Just then, a hotel floor man touched him on the shoulder and told him the front desk wanted him. He went over to the desk clerk again, who informed him that he was lucky because he had one room left, but it had a problem, something was wrong with the lock, and there was no key for him. They could let him in, however, and in the morning, if he called them, they would come and let him out. Now, he didn't care about any problem. All he wanted was a room with a bed and a telephone, so he took it even though he knew they were scalping him when they charged him $60.00, and if he didn't check out by 12:00 noon, another $60.00 would be added. The floor man took him to the room and locked him in. He called home and spoke to his wife. He told her not to worry, it was a long story, but he was safe. He made it as far as Hempstead and would be home as soon as the weather had cleared up, possibly by the next evening. In any case, he would call again later. By then, it was 4 a.m., and he was too sleepy to contemplate about tomorrow or yesterday, for that matter. He awoke at about 11 a.m., showered, and flashed on the T.V. The news was on.

"The entire city of New York and suburbs are paralyzed by the worst blizzard since...," said the news commentator, "...as much as 26 inches of snow has fallen in some places. All railways, airports, and surface transportation are shut down. You are advised to stay put wherever you are and not try to travel...Stay off the roads!"

Then it dawned on him where he was, that for twenty-four hours he hadn't been home; that he was caught in a blizzard last night and his car was still stuck in the snow on the L.I.E. somewhere near Fresh Meadows, N.Y. He realized, too, that the plot or drama that was carrying him forward had still more to unravel. He was no spectator now, he was the central character, and he was becoming concerned. It was almost 12 noon! He quickly called the desk to come and unlock the door! As he stood at the lobby desk checking out, a tall brown-skin "sister" came up beside him--apparently, she was also checking out of the motel. After checking out, he went across the lobby to the restaurant to get a cup of coffee and a sandwich. He sat at a table and the tall, better-than-average looking "sister" came into the restaurant and sat down beside him. They began a conversation about the prospects of getting out of their snowed-in predicament, and in the course of the conversation, she confided that she lived in New York City, she was stranded in Hempstead, where she works, and was anxious to get on the road and drive back to the city. She convinced him that she was sure she could make it, but she was looking for a driving companion. He agreed to drive back with her.

"By the way, where is your car?" he asked her.

"My car is in the parking lot across the street," she said, "it broke down on me, though!"

"It did what? Did you say broke down?" he asked as he looked at her a bit suspiciously.

"Yes, but AAA is on their way right now to give me a boost!"

"Then don't you think we should be over there where they can see you when they come?"

She agreed, and they went across the street by a fire station next to the parking lot and stood in the foyer of the station to keep warm while looking out for the AAA truck. They must have been standing there for about an hour, and no truck came!

"Are you sure you gave AAA the correct address?" He asked her.

"It wasn't I who called them, I telephoned my girlfriend in New York City, and she called them for me."

"How is that now?" he asked her, "Don't you think you should call them again yourself and confirm this? You don't even know if she gave them the correct address - if she ever called them."

So she went back to the motel to call AAA again while he waited for her to return. About twenty minutes later, she returned, and he spoke first.

"Did you get them?"

"Yes, they are on their way," she replied.

"What was the address you gave them?" asked Jim.

"Fifth and Market Street!" she said.

He looked up at the signpost at the intersection where they were standing, and it said, 'Clinton and Fulton Street.' He suddenly got some funny vibrations, and his instincts told him not to continue to play this part, that this script was not for him. Something told him to return to the motel lobby at that very instant, so he told her he had changed his mind about going to the city with her, but he wished her a lot of luck, and he returned to the motel.

As he walked into the motel lobby, as if by perfect timing on the part of the scriptwriter, who should be walking from the opposite direction directly towards him? Yes, it was Paul! When he thought how he was sidetracked, and a few more minutes he would have missed Paul completely, he knew for certain that some unseen power had a hand in this!

"James, I came to get you," Paul said, "come on, we are going back to New York City!"

James was overjoyed! He didn't question him at all. He wasn't even going to mention the news bulletin he heard that morning. After what they had come through the night before, he wasn't going to worry about their chances.

As they got outside and approached Paul's car, another gentleman got out to greet them.

"James, I want you to meet my brother, Andrew. Andrew, this is James, whom I told you about."

"Yes, I am pleased to meet you," said Andrew.

They got into the car, and Paul picked up the conversation as they drove off.

"You know, Andrew is a preacher. He has a church out here in Hempstead. He wanted to come in case we needed help. He even brought a shovel; we are going to need one."

As they drove westward along the expressway, James reflected for a while. He had seen what it was like to face the unknown, and he tried to describe the experience. It is like a parenthesis, like a pause in which you traverse the darkness between two lighted spaces, and to traverse it blindly, you must do so only with faith, and it gives you a great awareness that "there are unseen forces that play a major role in our destinies. There were three strangers whose lives came together because of a blizzard. Was it chance? Did they make it happen?

It seems that on the highways, snow plows had started cleaning up by now. Actually, they were trying to clear a path as best as they could so that the highways could be passable. As Paul, Andrew, and James traveled west, the road was a bit treacherous, but they negotiated it well. Paul kept pointing to huge mounds of snow on either side, some 8 to 12 feet high.

"There's a car snowed under! There's another one and another one!" said Paul.

"I don't see any cars, how do you know?" James asked.

"Every one of those mounds is an automobile covered over. See how the snow plows are being careful to avoid those mounds!" replied Paul.

Just then, James thought about his car, wondering if he was going to be able to find it at all! Cars were buried along the expressway; not one was visible, only mounds! In some instances, he saw people digging out their cars, that is, if they were lucky to know exactly which mound was theirs. By now, it was late afternoon, about 4:30 p.m., February 12, 1983, the sun was shining, and the city was busy recovering from last night's blizzard. Three total strangers from just 14 hours before were now driving in a little, old, blue Chevrolet toward the city. They were approaching the Cross Island Parkway exit, exit 30, and James knew that Springfield Blvd. exit was coming up soon. He began to get anxious because he knew they couldn't be too far from where he left his car. He was counting the mounds of snow on the eastbound side and looking far ahead for Francis Lewis Blvd. and 188 St. Exits. Somewhere along there, he hoped, was his car. He thought they were going to have to get out soon and start digging mound after mound until they found it! Andrew asked him if they should stop or go on further, and just as he was about to tell Paul to stop and start digging mounds, he looked further down the parkway as the sunlight reflected on a shiny, burgundy object. He couldn't tell himself that what he saw was real because he thought he was imagining it. What he saw so dumbfounded him that he yelled out: "It's a miracle! It's a miracle! There it is! There it is!"

They pulled up on the westbound side of the divider next to his car. It stood in the sunlight, bright and shiny, not a drop of snow! Not a speck! It looked like it had just come out of a car wash, so clean! Why were all the other cars covered with snow, and his didn't even have a speck? They brought two shovels all the way from Hempstead, but they didn't need them. He was so excited he tried to jump over a mound of snow and fell, then got up, then fell, then got up again, climbed over the divider, got to his car, and kissed it.

"Here it is," he said, "here it is, not even a speck of snow! Not even a scratch!"

Paul and Andrew came over the divider and tried to calm him down, but they, too, were dumbfounded. It's as if no snow fell on his car or anywhere near where it was standing.

"You're going to need a push or a boost to get started," Andrew said soberly.

"After what has happened so far, maybe not," James said to Andrew and Paul, "what's another miracle, anyway?"

He said this jokingly, opening the door to his car. He got in, put the key into the ignition, and turned it once. The most beautiful sound you ever heard came from the engine. It started up like it was just waiting for him to touch it! It purred like a cheerful kitten! He was so happy he didn't know what to do. He got out of the car and thanked Paul, and Andrew must be a dozen times. He took their names and telephone numbers and promised to visit Andrew's church one day. They seemed almost as happy as he was because they, too, had witnessed something unusual, and somehow they knew that the events of those past 14 hours would have a permanent impact on their lives. Three strangers then drove away, one to Deer Park and two to Hempstead, with a common bond -- a most unforgettable experience.

M.E. PHISTOPHELES

One evening, many decades ago, in Brooklyn, N.Y., some believers and non-believers in demons and devils gathered in a certain local bar and were trying to convince each other about the powers of the dark side. They cited many strange happenings, disappearances and deaths of people that appeared in the Missing People's columns in newspapers and to this day have never been solved and they swore it had something to do with the occult. Some said that Satan was responsible, that he was the most powerful of all demons and was in fact the supreme ruler of evil in this world. Some said that he was once the highest-ranking angel in Heaven second only to God and that he was banished from Heaven by God because he challenged the Almighty and rebelled against Him. They all finally agreed that he was responsible for all the sins and evil in the world; he turns some people into monsters and preys on many human beings on earth by tempting them to make choices that lead them down the dark path to Hell and eternal damnation.

These demon debaters, however, couldn't agree on two things. First, some had the notion that outside of Heaven itself, Satan was more powerful even than God because too much evil exists and seems to corrupt and dominate everything and everyone on earth; but some, on the other hand, said that that's impossible since no creature can be as powerful as, or more powerful than, its creator either in Heaven or anywhere outside of Heaven, period. They had no answer, however, as to why God allowed so much sin and evil to exist in the world except that He must have cursed mankind a long time ago and allowed Satan to run wild among humanity to add to man's punishment and miseries. Then they argued that no human could stand up against Satan's powers, let alone outsmart the master trickster himself, although many have tried. But one wise old man, who was sitting quietly in a corner of the bar waiting for his opportunity, when he heard those words took exception to that argument. He interrupted them and said to them that he knew of someone who did, and he bet that right now Satan was still fuming hotter than ever down in Hell over it. So, they all took him to task and demanded that he reveal to them this unheard-of mortal who accomplished such a feat as to outsmart Satan himself! Maybe they could learn something from him/her. They insisted and the old man, a consummate storyteller and a notorious boozer, who now saw that he could weave his tale with maximum effect over them and for maximum benefit to himself, said, if they wanted him to tell them anything, he would have to have something to wet his palate first. They knew exactly what he meant and gave him a fifth of good scotch to get him started, and after a couple of mighty good swallows he began to tell them the following story:

"Most of you young bucks weren't born yet or were too young to know anything," he said, "but it happened about thirty years ago, right here in Brooklyn. I remember because it was getting close to the Christmas season and there was Christopher Springer, who used to live right here on St. Marks Ave. near Brooklyn Ave., and he was so desperate because he could not face his wife and children to tell them he had lost his job and there would be no money for Christmas presents, not even enough to pay the rent which was now one month in arrears, and there was little money to put food on the table. Whatever little nest egg he had he already used up most of it and it would soon run out. He was already over his head in debts, was behind in some payments, and was barely squeaking by, and now, with all that, he lost his job besides." *(The listeners began to get anxious because just as they were waiting to hear how this poor fellow was going to extricate himself from his predicament, that's when the old man stopped to take a couple more swallows from his glass. Their body language said, 'Get on with the story, Pops', and he finished the last swallow.)*

"Well now, as I was saying," he continued, "several days went by and Christopher Springer could not face up to telling his family the truth. He would leave home in the morning and return in the evening at the same time as he did when he was working. There was no way he could bring himself to tell them, at least not right away, not until he had had a chance to think things out and figure out how he was going to manage. So, this last evening he came home again as if nothing had happened and told his wife he was tired and would lie down awhile before supper. As he lay in bed his mind was working feverishly. What was he going to do? He had used up almost all his savings. How was he going to pay the rent, feed his family, and pay his debts? Time was running out, he thought, as his wife Mary called him to come and eat supper. At the dinner table, as he watched the faces of his three children, and his wife, knowing the holiday was all the children were thinking about, he felt sad and defeated inside, but he pretended otherwise as he listened to them talk about their Christmas wish list, you know how children are. That night he went to bed terribly sad and broken in spirit, though he kept his feelings to himself."

(The listeners were all thinking the same thing: What kind of fool was this, Christopher Springer? Why didn't he tell his family sooner rather than later? But each man deals with his crises in his own way. Maybe Chris was hoping that in the meantime something would turn up, after all, he was out there pounding the pavement, trying to call in some old favors, and maybe cash in

some old chips. Here the storyteller took another brief pause to take a sip before continuing.)

"The next day," he continued, "Chris left home as if he was going to work as usual, as he had done several days before while hoping that the problem would disappear or some miracle would happen. Maybe today would be the day that he would find a job before he ran out of options or out of time. He spent this day like the previous ones, trying to find a job by calling on all the personnel managers in all the companies he could think of, and by stopping by every workplace and business to apply, but with no success. Everywhere they were laying-off workers, too, or had filled all their temporary vacancies, so jobs were hard to come by. Things looked bad! It was now less than a week before Christmas and he knew he could not go home again and pretend any longer. He called home that Monday evening around 5:30 p.m. and told his wife he would be coming home late, not to wait up for him, he had overtime work at the company. Instead of going home, he hit all the dives and bars trying to bury his troubles and frustrations. He ended up in a dive somewhere on the lower Eastside of Manhattan."

(Pausing here again to take a couple more sips while his impatient audience was waiting for him to continue, the old man looked around and saw that their interest was at its peak and they were deathly quiet with anticipation of what he was going to say next.) He continued.

"Chris was sitting on a bar stool at the end of the bar drowning his sorrows when he observed a gentleman with a goatee, long moustache pointed at the ends, thick eyebrows and sharp, beady eyes sitting alone at a table in a corner of the bar."

(The audience all seemed to nod their heads when they heard that description and some of them thought that they, too, were sure they had seen such a person somewhere, sometime in their lives. Their imaginations were awakened.) The old man continued.

"The goateed gentleman called the waiter over and told him something. Shortly after, the bartender gave Chris a complimentary drink and said it was from the gentleman sitting at the far table. Chris took the drink and looked over at the table to thank his benefactor. The gentleman smiled and made a sign for Chris to join him.

*(Just then someone in the audience shouted: "**Don't go, you fool**, don't go; **that's Mr Slickster, the devil himself!**')* The old man ignored this interruption and continued.

"Chris accepted the invitation and as he sat down, they introduced themselves to each other. The strange gentleman spoke first."

"My name is Dr M. E. Phistopheles at your service."

"And mine is...." Chris started to say, but Dr Phistopheles finished it for him.

"Christopher Springer! Correct?"

"Yes, but how did you know?"

"That does not matter, really, what does matter is that I have the solution to all your troubles."

"What do you mean?" replied Chris.

"I know all about your situation," Dr M. continued, "but how I know is not important. What would you give me in return, let's say if I could make you a rich man by Wednesday night, around this time, so that you would not have to work for anyone again, and you could buy your family all the things they wanted, pay off all your debts and never have to worry about money again?"

(Here the audience mulled among themselves about the craftiness of that devil, Satan, for he knew how desperate Chris was. They couldn't decide what they, themselves, would do if they were in Chris' place, whether they would take the offer or tell Satan to go to Hell. They seemed to be evenly divided.)

"You're crazy," answered Chris, half wanting to believe and disbelieve at the same time.

"I am far from crazy! But you didn't answer my question!" said Dr M. E. Phistopheles.

"Just for argument's sake," said Chris, "If you could do what you said, I would give you anything, anything in this world, but I doubt you could do it!"

"In any case in your predicament what have you got to lose?" said Dr. M. E. Phistopheles.

"I said I would give you anything, didn't I?" retorted Chris.

"Well," said Dr Phistopheles, "would you give an arm?"

"Yes!" replied Chris.

"Would you give a leg?"

"Anything that would save my family!" answered Chris.

"Then would you give me your immortal soul in exchange for, let's say, eighteen million dollars?" said Dr M. E. Phistopheles with a seriousness that Chris believed he meant every word of it.

(It was here that many in the audience started to think seriously if they could put a price on their own immortal souls what that price would be. Eighteen million dollars seemed like an awful lot of money to pass up! It's possible that some of them would have even given theirs for far less.)

Chris pondered for a second.

"If I said I would give you anything, that's what I meant!"

"Good," said Dr Phistopheles, "I propose we go to my office a block away from here and finalize the details of our agreement."

They left the bar together at about 10 p.m. and walked a few blocks to an abandoned building to which, it seemed, Dr Phistopheles must have had a key because they had no trouble entering. Somehow, in that abandoned building there was a well-furnished office and a desk behind which Dr. M. sat and lit a lamp with a flame from his index finger as he looked at Chris from behind the desk, then pulled out a partially completed written agreement which said that he, Christopher Springer was agreeing to give up, for the sum of 18 million dollars, his immortal soul on the blank day of blank...etc."

(Among the doubters and believers who were gathered in the bar some were saying, 'Take it! Take it, you fool! Who cares what happens after you're dead; with that money you and your family can live like rich people for years and have no more worries. You can buy happiness. Take the damn money, you fool!)

Chris and Dr. M. haggled over the remaining details such as the missing date whereas Dr. M. conceded latitude in time and allowed 4 months, so the date was set for Easter Sunday of the coming year. The agreement then read:

"Whereas I, Christopher Springer of sound mind and body, do agree to relinquish to one Dr. M. E. Phistopheles, for the sum of 18 million dollars, my immortal soul at exactly midnight on the third Sunday of April (Easter Sunday) of the coming year, this agreement becomes binding upon my signing the same."

But before Chris signed, he made him include a clause that the contract would be null and void if either party did not stick to the terms agreed to to-the-letter. Dr. M said he was a gentleman about such things and agreed to those terms.

"There is one more thing," Chris said. "How will I receive the payment?"

(It seems like most of the audience agreed with Chris' decision and would have done the same thing. At this point, the old man's glass was nearly empty and they were most eager to fill it back up for him so he wouldn't have to keep stopping to refill his glass himself. Now they made sure that that glass would never again be more than half-empty. The old man continued to speak.)

Dr Phistopheles then took out a piece of paper from his pocket.

"On this piece of paper," he said, "are written the six numbers that will play in the N.Y.S. lottery two days from today, on Wednesday.

All you have to do is purchase the ticket with these numbers and you will be the sole winner; if not, you are under no obligation to keep the agreement we made."

He made sure, however, that he did not give Chris the numbers until after Chris had signed and he, Dr Phistopheles, had countersigned in blood. Then Chris left the building, but as he was leaving, he could hear behind him a weird diabolical laugh echoing from the building, "Ha-ha-ha- ha-he-he-he-he…" He hurried to the subway and went home to Brooklyn, N.Y. to his family. He felt uneasy about the whole thing and for a while wasn't quite convinced that it had really taken place, or that he wasn't too drunk to realize it, but, in his pocket, he had the six numbers.

(Not everyone in the bar, however, agreed with what he did, for there were still a few who thought it was not a good idea to bargain away one's soul, even for such a large sum, $18 million, because hell and eternal damnation are worse than death, at any price. Poor Chris did not realize the magnitude of the bargain he made; he was only thinking of his family. Still, if he was a God-fearing man, he would not have done it.)

The next day, Tuesday, he bought the six numbers, and, on the strength of it, decided to spend whatever credit he still had as well as the balance of the unpaid rent money they were saving although it was already overdue. He bought a few presents and a fat capon for Christmas dinner! Somehow Christmas arrived, even though tenuously, at the Springers' apartment that year. They had a wonderful Christmas day, and that night, Wednesday night, without a doubt Chris sat glued to the TV set as, lo and behold, the six numbers came out just as Dr. M. Phistopheles had said they would. Chris was a millionaire! They were so happy that most of the night they stayed up celebrating and finally after 2 a.m., they went to bed.

Their lifestyle drastically changed after that. They paid off all their debts, bought a home in the suburbs, bought a brand-new car, new furniture, and clothes, and took a vacation in late January. They even shared some of their wealth with relatives and friends. They were the happiest family!

(As the agnostics, atheists, and Satanists in the bar heard this they were overjoyed for Chris, saying, 'See how the rich live in this world. With money, you can buy everything, even happiness. Who cares about the next world, the only thing that matters is here and now. Chris did the right thing, even if he loses his so-called soul.)

By now Chris had forgotten all about the agreement; however, February, March and April came around very quickly. It was now April 25th and he realized that within 24 hours there would be a reckoning for his sudden good fortune. His wife observed his changed mood and tried to find out why a man who had everything in the world he wanted was pacing the house like a man with troubles. That is when he confided in her.

"Mary," he said, "all this good fortune didn't happen by chance. There's more to it that you don't know about! I tried to keep it from you just like I did about my losing my job, but now I don't know!"

"Don't know what, Chris? You didn't keep anything from me as you say, I had known about your lay-off, but I didn't say anything because I knew sooner or later you would have told me. I just thought it was a God-sent blessing when we won the lottery. What, then, is this thing you don't know how to tell me?"

And he confided in her the whole story of how he met this Dr M. E. Phistopheles that night in December and the contract they had signed. She asked him to show her his copy of the contract, and she read it through carefully.

"I want to be by your side tomorrow night," she said, "when this Dr M. E. Phistopheles comes if he dares to come here!"

The next night, Sunday, April 26th Chris and Mary sat up in their living room waiting while the children were all in bed sleeping. It was very late and Mary tried to console Chris by telling him not to worry, they'd face it together; in any case, he might not even show up! Just as she said those

24

words, Dr Phistopheles appeared before them in the living room looking most satisfied with himself.

(The old man's glass was getting empty again and he got a quick refill and was told to continue, not to stop talking for any reason, and that he can sip while he is talking...which he did.)

"You know, Christopher," said Dr M, "I was most generous with you; I get most of my clients much cheaper. Yes, sir, it is midnight and as we agreed, I am here now to collect; shall we be going?"

Just then Mary jumped in between the devil and her husband and spoke to Dr. Phistopheles.

"Going where? Where are you going with my husband? Look here now, you Mr Phesto or topless or what your damn name is, what business you have with my husband?"

"Why, Mrs Springer, I am afraid you don't understand," said Dr M. E. Phistopheles, "but I'm sure your husband must have explained everything to you about our contract. You know, a bargain is a bargain is a bargain, and I always keep my part. So must your husband!"

(All eyes and ears were now glued to the old man because this was the point of no return if anything was going to happen. And the old man never disappointed them; but first he insisted that they must open another bottle of scotch, for the first one was almost empty. And up came another bottle, his glass was filled one more time and after a few big sips and swallows, he hit them with the punch line.)

"Well now, hold it one moment there now," said Mrs Springer, "what business you got coming into my house at one o'clock Monday morning, April 27th? Do you hear me? I read your so-called agreement, and it said nothing about one o'clock."

M. Phistopheles' face started to get redder and redder as he saw that this wasn't going to be easy at all.

"What's this about one o'clock;" he replied, "its midnight, midnight, midnight. You can't cheat me, its midnight!"

"Oh no you don't, not so fast," said Mary, "You never heard 'bout Daylight Saving Time? I see you are not as smart as you think you are. It's way past midnight, you're one hour late in fact. It is now 1 a.m., Monday, April 27th,

25

therefore you broke the terms of the contract. You got no case, so gone 'bout your business!"

And the devil, seeing that he was outsmarted, started to rant and rave and curse and swear as he stormed out of the house because he never thought any human could have tricked him like that. Good for Chris he had such a wife who was very wise to have thought about Daylight Saving Time.

And as the old man concluded the story his listeners didn't know what to make of it, nor whether to believe him or not. In any case, they had plenty of food for thought; and the old man got himself some good top-shelf free whiskey to boot; and the moral questions still remained in dispute among the believers and nonbelievers: "What would you give in exchange for your soul?" and "What does it profit a man to gain the whole world, and forfeit his soul?" I guess that is why the Bible said in Matthew 3:12: "His winnowing fork is in his hand, and He will thoroughly clear His threshing floor, and He will gather His wheat into His barn, but He will burn up the chaff with unquenchable fire."

RUSSIAN ROULETTE

On Wednesday nights business was a little slow in Harry's bar. Usually when there was a slow night Ceci, the bar mistress, didn't mind if the guys told stories, played a little poker in the back room, or messed with the game machine. In fact, she would join them herself, sometimes, to kill the time, since she was fun-loving by nature. You never met a woman more fun-loving, uninhibited, loose-tongued and crazy! She would do and say the craziest things; it's a good thing no church-going, righteous people were around to hear her sinning the way she did! She would swear up and down the alphabet, with more 4-letter words than you can imagine; and it wouldn't be past her to expose herself if that would bring a wave of excitement! Actually, her body parts were always over exposed anyway, so a newer revelation by her never caused too much stir. Whenever the guys told yarns, she always had a bigger one so as not to be outdone. On Wednesday nights, therefore, it wasn't unusual to see her and her regulars tossing coins to see who could match heads or tails, throwing darts, even throwing dice from a cup onto the bar, arm wrestling, or whatever diversion they thought up whereby they could wager on the outcome. They used to test each other out by doing little tricks like staring at each other to see who would blink first while a match or lighted cigarette lighter was held between their faces; holding each other's breath to see who could hold out the longest; holding a bottle of liquor to their heads to see who could gobble it down straight in one gulp without stopping!

Ceci never took a back seat to anyone, man, woman, or beast. She had nerves like steel and wasn't scared of anything. Anybody dared her, she would take them up on it, "Fearless Ceci", they would call her, and she had the size to back her up at that! She weighed close to 190 lbs with large biceps for a woman. In spite of her size, she was pleasing to look at, however, and had a nice-looking face. Anyway, the regulars loved to hang out there because with her something exciting was always happening.

That brings me to the Wednesday night in May of 1984 when Big Red walked into Harry's bar. Big Red was the kind of person who was always loaded with a big bank roll although he never had a job. He never worked a day in his life for an honest living, but he drove big cars and dressed sharply, and he loved to gamble. He remembered the last time he was at Harry's; Ceci had beaten him out of $200 and he wasn't too pleased about that! He sat down at the far end of the bar counter and asked for his usual bourbon and water.

"Hi, Big Red," said Ceci, "how's tricks?" as she poured the bourbon.

"Everything's cool," responded Big Red, "how's everything with you, big mamma?"

"Everything is fine, just killing some time with the fellows on a slow night, you know what I mean!"

Before she finished talking to Big Red one of the guys called out to her to come and finish the game of coin flipping 'cause they had a bet going; she reacted.

"I am taking care of my customer, besides you guys have to think of something new, coin flipping is too tame for my blood! Ain't that right, Big Red?"

Big Red didn't say a word, but slowly he reached into his coat and took out a 38 revolver and placed it on the counter. Everyone in the bar got quiet, eyes wide open looking at the revolver. Ceci spoke.

"You ain't thinking of holding up the place, are you B.R.?"

"No, nothing like that," replied Big Red. "You said you wanted excitement."

"Yeah, I ain't scared of nothing! A little piece of 38 doesn't frighten me! What you got in mind, B.R.?"

Big Red picked up the gun and pointed it straight at Ceci. Everybody else in the bar ducked down below the counter or took cover under a table, but Ceci just stood there because she could bluff and she was damn sure he wasn't going to pull the trigger. She was right, he was just testing her.

"You got a lot of nerve all right, woman!" said Big Red.

And as he turned the gun away from her he started to empty out the bullets from the chambers onto the bar counter except for one lone bullet; then he spun the barrel around a few times and set the gun back on the counter in front of Ceci.

"I got a new game for you! Ever heard of Russian Roulette?"

"Yeah, I heard about it, what do you want, to play Russian Roulette?"

"Maybe."

"Well, I'm game if you are! I bet you the $200 I won from you I beat you at that, too! Is it a bet?"

Big Red nodded his head.

"Its a deal," he said.

Ceci picked the revolver up in her hand, spun the barrel, and pointed it at Big Red menacingly.

"Should I pull the trigger, B.R.?"

"No", said Big Red, "that's not how the game is played!"

But Ceci knew, so she turned the revolver, pointed it to her head and pulled the trigger before anyone could wink, "click"... an empty chamber! A sigh of relief went up across the room as she handed the gun to Big Red.

"Your turn, brother man!"

Big Red looked at her and looked around the room; then he looked at the revolver and slowly held it in his hand. He pointed it to his head and again the room became deathly quiet with all eyes transfixed on him. He hesitated a few seconds then he pulled the trigger and again the hammer struck an empty chamber, "click!" and B.R. and everyone in the room breathed a sigh of relief as B.R. wiped the perspiration off his forehead.

"Blow your head off, sister, it's your turn!" He said to Ceci.

Ceci still showed no sign of cracking even though the tension in that room by then was excruciating! It was her turn and she wasn't going to back down, no sir! She spun the barrel then pointed the revolver at her brain and, as if she didn't want to prolong the agony and suspense, pulled the trigger without hesitating, "click"... again nothing happened!! Meanwhile Big Red was squirming as in his own mind he started to wonder if it was worth it to risk his life for $200. How many more times can he do this before his luck would run out; better let that crazy woman win! But if he did that the whole purpose for which he came there would be defeated, besides he would lose face! He picked up the gun, and spun the barrel, perspiration flowing down his neck and forehead as he held the nozzle to his temple and his hand began to tremble a little, then the hesitation, then the tenseness, then dead silence as he squeezed in full view of everyone..."click"..., and you saw the utter relief that came over him as his body relaxed. He laid the gun down on the counter once more for Ceci.

"Its all yours, baby!" he said.

"Thanks for nothing," replied Ceci.

She picked up the revolver wondering where that illusive single bullet was. Was it in the next chamber...she wondered after she spun the barrel... was it waiting for her this time... or could she draw a blank once more? For the first time in her life, Fearless Ceci felt a little uneasy. Were her nerves finally giving out on her, she wondered. Was this her last trick? She spun the gun barrel. She hesitated...then she held the revolver to her temple.

Everyone in the room became deathly still, many of them with fingers crossed, fear and tenseness gripping them to witness this death-defying spectacle by two maniacs! One more instant and either brain would go flying across the room or else death would be cheated one more time. Which would it be? Ceci looked in the mirror... then she looked at Big Red... then... calmly... she pointed the gun at her temple and pulled the trigger... "bang!!!" the gun went off!!! It was no blank this time!!! The explosion filled the room... the echo resounded... but Ceci was still standing!! Her brain cells were still intact!! What happened? ...At the very last second, it seemed, a sixth sense made her aim the gun at the mirror, shattering it into a thousand pieces!!! Better that than her brains, she thought. Then she walked over to Big Red handing him the emptied revolver.

"I think my life is worth more than 200 lousy bucks; here is your g.d. 200 bucks. Now we're all even, Big Red!"

TRIUMPH OVER ADVERSITY

UNCONQUERED

Martin Theodore Anderson was born with a fighting spirit, the will of a warrior, and the heart of a champion. It was hard to imagine that anything could destroy him. After all, if the human spirit is indestructible and true to a higher power, what does it matter that the flesh decays or the body is mangled? What will the angels say of a mortal who overcomes the most severe adversities through sheer strength of will and spirit? The flesh must die, but the spirit when tested is another matter. It is that that concerns this story, the struggle of mind over matter, spirit over flesh, and human will in the face of adversity.

Our story begins as Martin sits in a wheelchair, an inseparable extension of his body, trying to deal with his emotions, and with his thoughts that at times are his tormentor, and at times his incorporeal wings! He was trapped inside a shell, inside a twisted, loathsome prison, inside a machine that no longer worked for him the way it used to, no longer responded, and no longer bowed automatically to his will. He was trapped inside a relic, inside a broken mannequin-like form without motion or reflexes, looking out at the world of perpetual activity helpless to impact objects around him or to divert the trajectory of even the slightest particle, let alone a fly or insect, whose path his helpless form obstructed. The process of disciplining the mind, in such a circumstance, to think without being able to manifest thought into action, except through others on whom there is a marked dependency, was not only humiliating for him but was formidable, to say the least. How was he going to cope with this tragedy? How will he survive? As he sat in his wheelchair reflecting on the past, he remembered with clarity previous near tragedies in his life, and how each time when it seemed that the grim reaper had come for him he managed to survive and come back from Death's door. There was the time when he was driving alone on the highway and his car skidded off the road into a river near a treacherous crossing and he almost died because no one was supposed to remain in a submerged car trapped for at least a half hour underwater… and live! But he did, by breathing the trapped air in the back of the car somehow and holding on until rescuers, who happened to be nearby when the accident happened, came and got him out. He had spent months convalescing from a broken leg before making a full recovery. It was a near miracle!

And then there was the time in New Jersey when he was working for a chemical company, and, while mixing chemicals in a warehouse full of volatile substances in the manufacture of paint, he swore he was going to see his maker when someone dropped a match or lighted cigarette that set the place on fire, but a sixth sense warned him to get out fast when he saw Death in the form of a sea of flames envelope the whole warehouse. With only seconds to act he had run for his life, yes, run like the dickens through a blazing fire to get to the nearest exit, and half of his body was covered with flames in the process. How he survived that, even he can't explain it to this day. Nevertheless, he suffered from it with 45-degree burns over his entire body and the ordeal of undergoing severe burn convalescence and multiple skin grafts. It took him three years to heal from that encounter, and even then, he lost the use of one hand that was too badly burned, and he still bore other scars from it as well.

He had really thought that God was through testing him after he faced the severity of that ordeal, for it was more than ordinary men could cope with and survive; but who was he to judge God's purpose? No, as it turned out, after that his trials were not over, for in the summer of '88, he recalled, in the fullness of his manhood and with prospects for a successful career in business and real estate, having put behind him the setbacks of the past and having mustered all his energies of intellect and physical strength to regain largely his health (except for a scar or two and a few permanently crippled fingers), it was in that summer that the worst disaster yet suddenly struck. One morning without warning he was felled by a severe stroke that left him in a coma for several weeks. The only question at the time was, would he live, for it seemed like the end and if he lived, would he be a vegetable?

Yes, he remembered these things, and he remembered, too, regaining consciousness in the hospital and seeing the world for the first time through the eyes of a man paralyzed from the neck down.

"What does God want of me?" he asked himself, "Surely, if He wished to destroy me, He could have done so already with a mere thought, and I would be no more! But instead, why condemn me in this way?"

And he remembered hearing a voice from nowhere speaking to him.

"Take heart, Martin Theodore Anderson, and use your greatest gift!"

Then he looked around to see who was in the room and queried:

"Who said that? Who said those words?" and seeing no one, he lay there silent, wondering what those words meant.

Again, he recollected, the same voice spoke in his ear.

"You've been tested three times, and you shall face yet an even greater test!"

33

Martin lay in his hospital bed, not sure if the voice he heard came from his own subconscious mind or imagination or somewhere else; but it did not matter, as he thought of it over and over, trying to understand what it meant. He remembered saying to himself at that moment that he only knew one thing: He had to start life all over again as if he had just been born. So there he was, six months later, sitting at home reflecting, a post-stroke paralytic, trying to grasp fully what it meant that all physical activity and even intense mental strain for him were ruled out, that there'd be no more working around the house, no more outdoor strolls, no fishing trips, no getting around, no dancing, no playing chess, no physical sports, in fact, just going to the bathroom would require assistance, and to move an arm or a leg would take a Herculean effort. But, gradually, ever so slowly, he dealt with it, day-by-day, month-by-month, even taking great pride in every little accomplishment trying as best to recover.

In all the ordeals that Martin faced, the one person, the one true faithful companion, Aida, his wife, was his strength, his constant support, ready to give of herself, her heart, her every hour to care for him, standing by his side and ministering to him whenever he allowed her to, for she knew that helping him meant being careful not to hurt his pride for within that shell, within that tent, there still lived a proud, fighting spirit! Even Martin, however, had enough sense to know that he could not survive without Aida's help. If he was indomitable, then, surely, she was courageous.

So, it was that he started to read, for short periods at first, and at times Aida would read aloud to him. One of his favorite pieces was the poem "Invictus," which she often read to him:

> "Out of the night that covers me,
> dark is the pit from pole to pole,
> I thank whatever gods may be
> for my unconquerable soul.
>
> In the felled clutch of circumstance
> I have not winced nor cried aloud,
> under the bludgeonings of chance
> my head is bloody, but unbowed.
>
> Beyond this place of wrath and tears
> looms but the Horror of the shade,
> and yet the menace of the years
> finds, and shall find me, unafraid.

It matters not how straight the gate,
how charged with punishments the scroll,
I am the master of my fate,
I am the captain of my soul."

He had her read this poem to him every single day and drew strength from it, for he felt a kinship with its author, Sir William Ernest Henley who had suffered amputation of one leg, surgery in the other leg and who was condemned to a life of crippling illnesses.

Life in Brooklyn, as in all the five boroughs of New York City, was fast, hectic, insane, overcrowded, crime-ridden, polluted, confined and impersonal. Two years after Martin's stroke, it was no longer desirable or practical for them to continue living there, especially in his condition. So, they moved to Durham, N.C., where he was born, to live in a house in the country, close to nature. There he would be at peace with himself; there he could breathe the country air again, and commune with nature; there time could stand still, and the pace of life around him would not be so hectic; there he could convalesce and gain some strength in his crippled body, and test his will on his own terms, until God was through with him. But he needn't have worried about that score, for God was not through testing him, not yet.

His final test came one year after they had returned, to Durham, N.C. and had almost gotten used to the small town, to the country life once more, the change having done him a world of good, although he was still crippled and bound to his wheelchair. It was on a Friday morning in the summer, Aida was upstairs taking a nap and Martin was downstairs looking at the news on television when the house suddenly caught on fire! He must have dozed off for a little while, but when he opened his eyes, he saw New Jersey all over again, he saw the warehouse go up in flames before his very eyes, only this time, it was his home and Aida, his wife, was upstairs sleeping!

He was alone. It was too late to send for help, and there was no one to turn to. He called out, "Aida!!!...Aida!!!..." But his voice was weak, she could not hear him, he could not scream any louder, he was helpless. He didn't care so much about himself, he could accept his own fate, in fact, he would welcome it, but not Aida, no, not Aida too! When a strong man, when a proud man is brought to such a state that he has nowhere to turn and must watch a loved one perish because he is helpless to save her, that, surely, is a test no man should ever be subjected to, no man should have to face. With tears in his eyes, his paraplegic body trembling, Martin reached to the depths of his soul and called out to his maker.

"O God, this yoke I bear is worse than death! Give me the strength I need, not for myself, but for my Aida!!.. I would gladly die to save her!!"

Smoke began to engulf the house; the fire was spreading and there at the foot of the stairs was Martin in tortuous emotional and physical pain with an insurmountable flight of stairs and an impossible task before him. He threw himself forward from the wheelchair and, on hands and knees, with the strength no paralytic in his condition should possess, painfully crawled up the stairs. Somehow, he reached her bed chamber that was filling up with smoke and managed to grasp, drag and carry them both down the stairs and outside to safety. There in the yard two hundred or so meters away they both finally lay in the grass now unconscious. How could this miracle have taken place? Aida was the first to revive and was in tears as she sat cradling Martin who was still unconscious when she called to him:

"Martin... Martin...Please... Speak to me! Martin... Martin... speak to me...!"

Words could not suffice for the emotions she was feeling as she called his name repeatedly.

Help finally arrived and found them lying together in the grass in front of the burning house. The ambulance quickly rushed them to the hospital. Martin was still alive! Thank Heaven!! And would survive this greatest ordeal yet that defied all earthly explanation. No one understood, no one, not even Aida, how it was that they managed to get out of that burning house alive; but when she saw Martin in the hospital bed fully awake, and she looked into his eyes and saw the smile that beamed from his beleaguered face, it was as if to say:

"You see, I'm still a fighter, God willing until He puts me in my grave!"

Then Aida knew, though it seemed impossible, without a doubt that it was Martin who had miraculously saved them both from the burning claws of death.

FIGHTING FIRE WITH FIRE

The Midland Gardens is a seven-story apartment building, just like Wexford Terrace, in Jamaica Estates, Queens, N.Y., that had gone co-op many years ago. In the 80's when the real estate market skyrocketed, and co-ops were not selling as well as before, some units were rented out under one–and-two-year leases with options to buy. 6F was one such apartment. In apartment 7F lived an old lady, Mrs Olewitch, who, along with her husband, had fought the landlord when he was converting the apartment building years ago to a co-op, and, using some mysterious influence they were able to keep living as the only renting tenants at the time of conversion, paying their same old rent besides. The landlord, it seemed, was too afraid to tangle with Mrs Olewitch and made a special accommodation for her. It was also true that in the building many residents, too, were afraid to cross paths with Mrs Olewitch, for, like her sister who lived in the Wexford Terrace apartment building a block away, she had become somewhat of a problem for her neighbors as well as the landlord. They could do nothing about her. She was always acting suspiciously and had a way that caused you to believe there was a sinister motive for everything she did or said. Although she was small in stature and frail in appearance, that was misleading and was one of her weapons to catch you off guard. You were more likely to be her victim than she was yours. She was vindictive, malicious, devious, scheming, in short, dangerous. In fact, she was a witch! Her face was dried up and if you looked closely, you saw that she had a few carbuncles, blood shot eyes, and yellow teeth (One or two were missing!). Her facial expression was constricted from years of frowning, ill will and evildoing, so that if she smiled it was at the risk of the facial tissues breaking up! Her skin was pale and jaundiced and when she spoke it was like a person speaking who could barely open their mouth. It seemed as if she suffered from some kind of neuromuscular malady that caused her to speak painfully and when she did it was with a grating, irritating sound.

When Henry Mitchell, a city clerk, moved into apartment 6F, below Mrs Olewitch, little did he know what he was in for! The first three weeks of grace things were fine indeed. He didn't even know who she was at the time, but that didn't last very long. He soon started seeing notes scotch-taped onto his door; then letters slipped under the door as well. This was her way of introducing herself to him, to let him know, it appears, who ran the building and how he must behave in his apartment if he wanted to continue living there. The notes insinuated that he couldn't play his radio, or hi-fi, nor TV after certain hours, nor above a certain volume anytime. He certainly could not play his piano at any time at all, day or night, according to her rules, for she hated music and all musicians as well. Once, she came down to his door ostensibly to complain, but perhaps more accurately to see what was in his apartment or who else was living there (She was a busy body, too, of course). She tried to intimidate him or test him out, warning him that she would take stern measures if she thought he would give her any trouble. Henry completely ignored her and turned her away from his door. He was sorely annoyed by her, her notes and her harassment. She didn't like the idea of his living there either for whatever reason, so, she stepped up her campaign to remove him. After the notes, then came the rotten eggs left outside his door, garbage, etc. When that didn't work, it appears she recruited a sister witch below him in apartment 5F to join the campaign. They must have successfully joined forces before for their alliance was formidable. They both were very busy night and day trying to achieve their objective of forcing him to move. Henry did everything he could for the sake of peace, even taking off his shoes whenever he entered his own apartment because they said he walked too hard (He only weighed 150 lbs. and wore rubber heels and slippers). He bought extra rugs, one thick rug under the piano and one heavy rug covering the piano and he played only between 5 pm and 7 pm a few times a week, sometimes a couple of hours on the weekend, but that wasn't good enough, so he stopped playing altogether. But they insisted they could still hear every movement he made in his apartment, even when he turned over in his bed, or got out of bed late at night to go to the bathroom, and that was disturbing because it woke them up. Even when he breathed and yawned, they could tell. They continued this attack for some time, and, when that didn't work, he started hearing strange sounds coming from upstairs as if someone was stomping and pacing the floor above him, chanting and uttering strange animal sounds. The old-timers from the Caribbean where Henry was born would say it sounded like a ritual of some kind (obeah in other words!). The sound and chanting would go on for hours at a time and it was spooking the apartment somewhat, spooking Henry, too, as a matter of fact.

One evening when he was coming home from work, a young lady, a Latina, who must have seen him coming and going into the building, stopped him on the street and spoke to him.

"Are you the new tenant in 6F, Midland Gardens?" She asked.

"Yes, as a matter of fact. Why?" Henry responded.

"Oh, my name is Maria Prieto. You see, I used to live in that same apartment before you moved in, but I had to move out. Thank God I did! I now live a couple of blocks away! I couldn't take it any longer; they hounded me and put me through hell! I am glad I left!"

Henry started to say, "What…" but she interrupted.

"That witch above you, Mrs What's her name, did she start writing you notes yet?"

"Yes," said Henry.

"Has she started stomping and chanting and putting garbage outside your door yet?"

Henry began to feel that it was not he that was the problem after all since someone else had the identical experience he was having. Maria continued.

"I got out of there before she cast some evil spell on me. You better watch out; I am telling you!"

Her remarks didn't do any good for Henry's peace of mind. Not that he really believed in witchcraft or such, but you must admit, being around certain negative and evil people can be disquieting.

In the days and weeks that followed, some of the things Maria said were confirmed by the super and several other tenants in the building. Their remark, almost without exception, was, "Is that sick lady at it again?" for they had apparently either had some unpleasant experience with her or knew someone who did. They empathized with Henry, but, although their empathy may have helped a little, it did not remove his fears and continued annoyance. The person who was the source of his annoyance had even written a letter to the landlord telling him lies, that Henry was some kind of criminal who brought drugs into the building, disturbed the peace, and was a threat to her and other tenants, and she wanted something done about it. Of course, the only other tenant she could be referring to had to be her cohort, or sister witch in 5F, Ms Bell, who, as was stated, was already part of her conspiracy. The landlord did not take her seriously because he knew her reputation, although he did warn Henry Mitchell that he was her target, and he should try to ignore her and watch his back! Things started happening to Henry like his car windshield being smashed twice within the same week, his mail being tampered with, strange threatening telephone calls coming in, the mess behind his door, etc. He was able to deal with those kinds of harassment, but obeah was another matter. He suspected that Mrs Olewitch and Ms Bell were getting together in their apartments and practicing witchcraft or some kind of voodoo ritual. It must have been having its effect, because he would awaken suddenly in the wee hours of the morning with cold sweat all over his body, shaking with fright, and would hear all kinds of strange voices and sounds like someone, or something, was calling out his name and telling him to leave the apartment. There was more than one voice sometimes and they would alternate or would be heard in a chorus.

"L-e-e-e-e-v-v-v-e....!!   L-e-e-e-e-v-v-e....!!   Before...something... terrible... happens ...to you. We...want...you... to...l-e-e-e-v-v-e!!!"

The poor man couldn't sleep at night, so he decided to fight fire with fire!

He made inquiries among his friends in the Caribbean community and was referred to someone versed in the art of making counter spells to fight off evil spirits. He was put in touch with one Miss Sarah, as she was called, who was a famous spiritualist (obeah woman in some circles) and got her to come to his apartment and work a powerful spell that would reverse what was going on.

Well, Ms Sarah came all the way from the island, and if the people upstairs did not know who they were dealing with, they would soon find out. She brought her paraphernalia of witches brew, incense, goat dung, witch hazel, monkey paws, witches dust, candles, etc. into Henry's apartment one evening to do battle. She set up her 'stuff' and while they were raising hell upstairs, she began her own counter spells. It was something to behold! Candles were lit in the center of the room, incense was burning, she had a shaker in her hand made from some kind of dried leaves, and she began to speak a strange tongue. Her whole body started to shake violently then she went into a voodoo chant while rhythmically stomping around the room, scattering obeah dust, rattling the leaves, huffing and puffing, dipping her head down then raising it up to the ceiling. At one point her chant sounded like she was saying, "Hummm, hummm, hummm, hummm, go back... to the one... you come from. Hummm, hummm, hummm, humm, go back...to the one...you come from," over and over. She chanted in the living room, in the bedroom, in the kitchen, and all over the apartment, and it is certain they heard her upstairs. Something was taking its effect already because at one point strange screams and gasps were heard coming from upstairs when their chanting suddenly stopped and only Sarah's could be heard. Sarah's spell seemed to get stronger and stronger, and she suddenly stopped and raised both hands toward the ceiling and gave a hideous cry like a curse: "Abulubulubulu." The floor above rattled, the room shook and then there was complete silence. A most wonderful, positive energy filled the room, a wholesome, peaceful atmosphere prevailed, and she turned to Henry after a few more minutes, shook the leaves over his head and all around his body, hugged him and said, "You will have no more trouble from those charlatans again!!"

Before she left his apartment she gave him some extra candles, incense, and an amulet which she said would protect him anywhere he went, because you don't know when and where evil spirits may attack. Whether you believe in witchcraft or not, from that night on Henry slept like a log and he never saw or heard any more from Mrs Olewitch or Ms Bell. After several weeks went by, he got to wondering, especially when he saw a huge moving van downstairs, and he asked the super about it.

"Ms Bell is moving out, man," said the super, "and you know, Mrs Olewitch is in a sanitarium. She went berserk! I don't think we will be seeing her around here anymore!"

A week later the landlord called him and asked him if he knew anyone who needed an apartment, he had a vacancy in 5F.

"By the way," said the landlord," are things any better with you lately?"

Henry said, "Yes, a lot, thank you!!"

But of course, the landlord knew what had happened and no one was happier than he was because he couldn't get rid of the witches, it took Sarah, the 'baddest' obeah woman in town to do it.

THE GHOST

Slowly he got up, clumsy and disoriented. He cleared his eyes and stretched his limbs as if trying to remove his lethargy. He had just awakened, it seemed, from a long sleep as he looked around, still dressed in street clothes, a bit disheveled, and then he heard a noise outside his bedroom. He opened the door. A little creature stared at him with big, bright eyes, petrified, and yelled, "Mommy, mommy," while dashing down the stairs still yelling. Descending the stairs in pursuit of the fleeing youngster, he tried to process the strange phenomenon and to grasp what he was experiencing. At the foot of the stairs, he saw another creature, a woman, then another in the living room. They were both busy, apparently, cleaning and moving things around. The house appeared to have been in disarray, and full of dust and cobwebs like it had not been used to such housekeeping. There were signs of broken furniture and torn drapes everywhere. A young man was taking the broken furniture out as the cleaning went on.

"Who are you people," he queried, "and what are you doing here?"

They seemed to ignore him and went on doing what they were doing. He went into the kitchen, a woeful sight of neglect, and there was someone there attempting to clean the levels of neglect from everything in sight. He opened the basement door, a few steps down he looked and saw several people cleaning, fixing what appeared to have been a finished basement at one time, but had become a home for dust and spiders, and crawling things.

"What is going on?" he asked.

Neither his voice nor his waving arms seemed to stir the dust in the room. They paid him no mind and went on about their cleaning and their attempts to rehabilitate this seemingly badly neglected place as if no one had lived in it for a very long time. The brain or whatever was in his head began to stir again.

"But how can this be?" he said to himself, "Who are these strange people and what are they doing in my house? Where are my wife, Bea, and my daughter, Cleo? Why is my house like this? How? Where? What?"

He left the basement and made his way through the kitchen, toward the front door through which people were coming and going, discarding things. As he went outside, he could see some of them removing boards from the windows to let sunlight in, for some of the windows were still boarded up, and the grass on the lawn was high from lack of mowing! Oh, he hated that! How many days and hours he had spent cutting the grass and cleaning up the yard, planting new grass and shrubs to make the lawn look decent…but this! How could this be? He stood on the stoop and looked at his house; looked at himself; looked at the strange people and what they were doing, and he yelled with all his might,

"WHAT THE HELL IS GOING ON HERE? WHAT IS HAPPENING? WHAT ARE YOU ALL DOING? …WHY? …WHY?" And he started to cry!

They say that many souls are doomed to linger in familiar places or to roam the earth after death, whether due to some unfulfilled desire, sudden and tragic circumstances precipitating a premature departure, or some rare mistake in transition from one state to another. He must have fallen asleep when the express that takes people to the other world was leaving and he got left behind, or maybe he was sent back for some reason or other, who knows; nevertheless, here he was and he still didn't quite grasp it. Whatever the explanation may be, each time a client showed interest or someone entered the property, the same ritual repeated itself as if for the first time. He would awaken as if from a long sleep and move about to see what they were doing, and as soon as the intruders were gone, he would return to sleep until the house was disturbed again. As it happened, no one was really interested in buying the damn property anyway, and no one even stayed there more than a few minutes before leaving, except in this case which was a much different matter.

He was sitting on the stoop sobbing when he overheard two ladies, a mother and daughter, apparently conversing. They were the interested clients, a family of four, a mother, daughter, son and granddaughter. The two ladies had sat down right beside him but didn't pay him any mind as if he weren't there, and went right on talking.

"You know," said the mother, "we were lucky to get this place so cheap, and it's not so bad after we finished cleaning it up a bit."

"Of course, we got it cheap," said the daughter, "this whole area has been run down. Nobody wanted to live here."

"Well, they're a bunch of fools," said the mother, "I like it. It's in the country ain't it? It's got trees. It's quiet. This is good land. I don't care what you goin' to tell me 'bout that landfill. The papers say they goin' to clean all that up."

"Yeah, but when? Anyway, I guess at one time it wasn't so bad out here. I hear the people who used to live in this house were a young couple with a daughter. That must have been about 20 years ago. That landfill wasn't there then, I suppose. You know, Ma, it wouldn't be such a bad place if they were to really clean that mess up. What do they need with a landfill so close to where people live anyway?"

"What was that you say, Janie, I mean about the people who used to live here?"

"Oh, I was saying that they were a young couple that lived here with a daughter. The husband was killed, murdered one day right here on the property."

"You always know the most awful things about people. Since you going tell me anyway, go on, tell me how he was killed."

"Well," said the daughter, "I heard they were not getting along and had sent their daughter down south for a while to stay with relatives while they tried to sort things out. They couldn't! They used to quarrel a lot and the poor wife was so unhappy with the way he was treating her, and for his many infidelities, that she couldn't take it any longer. He was a policeman, you know."

"What you say, the police what, honey?"

"I said, he was a cop(!)…and I don't believe he thought his wife was capable of such a cold-blooded thing!"

"She really killed him then?"

"Yes, he came home one day and after the usual bitter argument, he went up to the bedroom and must have laid his gun and his jacket down on the chair beside the bed and dosed off as he often did. While he was sleeping in his bed, his wife came into the room and took his gun and shot him dead!"

"Good Lord, I can just imagine how terrible that must have been! And what happened to her after that? They must have locked her up!"

"No, they couldn't. They said that after she killed him, she left the house in a hurry, jumped into her car and drove like a crazy woman onto the parkway and killed herself, too, when her speeding car ran off the road and crashed into a tree."

"That's a very sad story. I never heard anything so sad. How about the little girl? What happened to that poor little girl who was left without a mother and a father?"

"Yes, I asked about her, too, when I was asking about this place. It seems she remained down south and lived with her grandparents who raised her."

"What about the house? You mean to say that over the last 20 years, we are the first and only persons to move in here?"

"Maybe not; but it doesn't seem like anybody else ever lived here since until we arrived. I found out that after the tragedy, the relatives tried to sell the property, and I guess after they couldn't, they must have abandoned it. Anyway, the bank foreclosed it sometime later and sold it on bids to some developer. By that time the property value around here had gone down so low nobody wanted to buy it. Then the developer went out of business and the price of the house was reduced so low we were the only fools that wanted to take a chance and buy it!"

"You shouldn't talk like that, child, we got a good buy; furthermore, someday the value is going to go up again. You wait and see! I hear them talking and they say that that landfill has already been condemned and the county and the state have already taken steps to make them move it somewhere else, and this place is going to be like it used to be one day. Think of it as an investment. It's for you, you know, and your brother. Some day you goin' to thank me for it, you'll see! And that business you been telling me 'bout those dead people, that doesn't bother me, neither. This is my house now and we are moving in, and we are going to stay, tragedy or no tragedy, landfill or no landfill, so you better make up your mind and get used to the idea and get on and help me with it!"

Meanwhile, the cop, or the ghost, who overheard everything the ladies were saying, couldn't have been completely ignorant now about what had happened to him, after all, he knew his wife had plenty of reasons to hate him and that they fought everyday even up to the moment when he came home just before he withdrew to the bedroom to get some sleep and got his lights blown out. Maybe his state of mind, his questioning and his denial were because he just didn't want to accept what had happened like a good ghost and move on. Anyway, as far as these new occupants were concerned, he would have to conjure up some really good spells and haunting tricks if he was going to get them to move out, they were determined to stay!

Each day the ghost tried to muster all his psychic powers, but all he tried he could not communicate with the living, much less use physical force against

45

them. He retreated to a secret room in the basement to consider how to accomplish his goal, and in his spirit form he discovered something, if he concentrated all of his psychic energies on a single point, or a single object, small at first, he could get it to move, even levitate, or sail across the room. He practiced and practiced throughout the late nights and early mornings, and gradually he gained increased strength and was ecstatic, that is if at all ghosts can feel such emotions. Several weeks later he ventured to apply his new-found ghostly powers. Emerging from the basement late one evening, he went into the kitchen. There, he made the kitchen utensils, knives, forks, and spoons fly across the room and bang against the wall. Then the pots and pans started to fly. It was so much commotion it woke the family up. They came down in full force and turned on the lights to see what was causing the racket. To their astonishment, they saw the utensils on the floor and were just in time to see a dish or two go flying across the room. Mrs Jackson screamed and shrieked.

"What is going on here? Who… is making this happen? Stop it! Stop it!" she yelled.

Then it subsided and seemed to stop. They didn't know what to make of it, but picked up the utensils and pots, replaced them and went back upstairs. Naturally, they were scared, especially the son and daughter; but Mrs Jackson was a strong southern woman and was very determined. They went back to bed and there was no further incident the rest of that night.

The following night, however, sometime after midnight, the noises were repeated while the family cuddled together, all four in their mother's bed, scared and wondering what to do. After a while the noise stopped and it was quiet for about 15 minutes, then the piano in the living room downstairs started to play. He was such a lousy ghost 'cause he couldn't even play well, just made a lot of discordant sounds that hurt the eardrums Jane, the daughter, turned to her mother, her brother Mike, and her little girl Annie and spoke.

"We got us a ghost in the house for sure!"

"A ghost, mommy," said Annie, "must be that man I saw upstairs when we first came here. I thought I saw him come downstairs behind me and go toward the kitchen. He was strange looking though!"

"What, child," said Jane, "you mean you saw it and didn't say anything before this?"

"Why…I thought he was working with you all cleaning up the house. Anyway, I never saw him again."

46

"No, honey, he wasn't helping us, he must be the ghost! But how come you are the only one who saw him and nobody else did? What did he look like?"

"I didn't see his face really, because it was a little dark, but he had on a T-shirt with some red in the middle, and blue pants or something."

"Yes, that's the ghost alright, that's Mr James Holloway, the man who was murdered. I think he wants his house back!"

"Hell, no," cried Mrs Jackson, "he dead ain't he, and we alive... no way!"

"What are we going to do?" said Jane.

Well, Beatrice Jackson had made up her mind that she wasn't going to let any ghost frighten her out of her little piece of heaven that for the first time in her life she came to own.

"Children, you stay right here in the bed, I am going downstairs and giving that ghost a piece of my mind, or something."

She went downstairs with a broomstick and approached the piano with the broom brandished menacingly like a sword.

"Stop that damn noise so people can get some sleep! Stop it I tell you, stop it or else!"

She yelled while flailing the broom into thin air. Then, in the next instant, the broom flew out of her hands like it was yanked by someone or something and it went sailing across the room.

"Good Lord a mercy," she cried, "Jesus, Jesus, sweet Jesus, help us!"

And she ran back upstairs to recover from the encounter. Meanwhile, for some reason, the ghost was quiet as if he was relishing in his temporary victory and hoping that by the next day, they would decide to leave.

The next day when the family arose, although smitten and with little sleep, Mrs Jackson recovered sufficiently to want to seek a better solution to this ghost problem. Her daughter Jane said:

"We better seek help, ma, we can't live here with no ghost frightening us like this!"

"Yes, child," said Mrs Jackson, "and I know the right person to help us, too."

That evening she sent for one Ms Sarah, a famous obeah woman who was only too willing to come and collect a fee for what she thought was going to be a piece of cake. When Ms Sarah arrived, the family thanked her for coming, fed her and told her the whole story. Ms Sarah, who was from the island, spoke assuredly to them.

"Don't worry at all, chile, me got the experience. Although me never come up face to face 'gainst no ghost before, if me can fight off witches and obeah spells, me believe me can deal with this ghost creature."

So, after dinner, Ms Sarah proceeded to sprinkle every corner of the house with her "duppy" water and incense as a first step in her upcoming war against the other side. Mrs Jackson then showed her a room to sleep in or rest up until the wee hours when the ghost usually starts up. Sure enough, a little past midnight the "duppy" came up from the basement and started his racket. This time doors started to slam, chairs started to move, pots and pans started to fly, you name it.

Upstairs, the family regrouped behind Ms Sarah who led the way down the stairs to face the irrepressible ghost. Armed with her incense, witch hazel, monkey paws, and the rest of her paraphernalia, Ms Sarah came down chanting and humming and huffing and puffing and dipping her head down and raising it up to the ceiling while saying the following words to whomever or whatever it was she couldn't see.

"Humm, humm, humm, evil spirit, go way, go way! Leave this house tonight I say!! Evil spirit, go way go way!! Leave this house tonight I say!!"

It looked like the ghost was amused by all this, or at least entertained for a while, that is. Then, as if wanting to show who was in charge, he made all of Ms Sarah's things come loose and go flying around the room; then he picked up a chair and hurled it at her in fast succession till poor Ms Sarah didn't know what to do. She lost her grip and made a beeline for the front door, ran to hell away from the house and never came back again! In the meantime, the rest of the family was on the stairs leading up to the bedroom and when they saw what happened to Ms Sarah, they ran back upstairs into the bedroom and did not come out again until daylight. They hardly slept, while trying to figure out what they were going to do next.

"What are we going to do? What are we going to do?" repeated Mrs Jackson, "We must find a way!"

"Maybe there is something," said her daughter.

"Tell me what then…anything to get rid of that thing!"

"You mean ghost, ma."

"Yes, ghost! I even hate the sound of the word! Go on tell me what you were going to say!"

"Something like this happened many times before. I remember an instance that happened not far from here in Amityville, L.I., where there was this haunted house with strange things happening, and people were afraid to stay there. The people who lived there were so terrified that they hired a spiritualist to help them, but, in the end, they had to move out of the house. In fact, this story was in the papers about a month or so ago!"

"You mean in one of those weird, spooky newspapers that write about freakish happenings and weird people?"

"What difference does it make? We are not dealing with some ordinary thing here, we dealing with the dead, you know. In any case, that story was even in the New York Times when it happened, because it stirred up a lot of public interest at the time. Most of the other papers carried it, too."

"All right, all right, go on with your story."

"Anyway, a spiritualist is an expert on ghosts, with all kinds of special cameras and devices to see and talk to ghosts."

"Lawd", cried Mrs Jackson, "you mean them talk like people, like you and me?"

"No, not exactly."

"Well, how then?"

"You see, they have a séance in the house."

"A séance, what's a séance?" asked Mrs Jackson.

"It's a group of people sitting 'round a table holding hands…"

"I don't see what good that will do when chairs start to come flying at them."

"No, ma, it doesn't go like that. You see, the spiritualist must be a person they call a "medium", somebody who has a special gift for reaching out to ghosts so they can talk to us, using the medium's voice."

"Lawd, you don't mean that the duppy takes over their body and talks like a real person?"

"Yes, that's exactly what I mean, that way we can find out why the damn ghost wouldn't go away, what it is they want, and how to make them find peace and rest."

"Peace and rest, damn it, I wish they would give us some peace and rest."

"That's just it, ma, there must be a reason why ghosts still linger here in spirit form after they are dead."

"All right, so how it ends then; either we frighten the ghosts or the ghosts come and frighten all of us away?"

"No. All the troubled spirits want is to tell somebody the truth about their tragic deaths, the agony and the injustice they felt, and in most cases to reveal the identity of their killer or killers."

"And so how does that help get rid of the ghost?"

"They say that after they find the killer(s) the ghosts will never haunt the house again!"

"That's fine for them who lived in those other haunted houses where the ghost was kind enough to leave! How can we get a spiritualist to come here and get rid of our ghost? Now, you tell me, chile, 'cause I am ready to do anything for my peace of mind."

"I am going today to see if I can get hold of a copy of that newspaper. I might try the library, or I might go directly to the newspaper office itself."

So that day, Jane Jackson left the house on a mission to find a medium to solve their problem. She went to the New York Times office and sure enough, someone there remembered a story of a haunting and how psychics removed the entities. They were able to track down the article and find out the name and address of the spiritualist who spearheaded the ghost investigation. In fact, it turned out to be Professor Drackmar who was teaching a course in "Mysticism" at the university. He had been doing a lot of research on haunted houses and on paranormal activities connected with them. Fortunately, when she contacted him he was still looking for haunted places to do his research on the paranormal psyche to help him finish a book he was writing on the same subject. After Jane told him the whole story, he was naturally curious and agreed to come out to the house a few days later with a few of his students to study the phenomenon.

When they came, they brought with them spectroscopic equipment, energy sensors and heat detectors, audio spectrographs, special cameras, etc. They came in the daytime and set up their equipment and went about measuring and taking readings with their instruments. When they went down into the basement it was cold and damp down there and they came back up in a hurry. They met with the family and told them, yes, there is a presence in their house and it is probably observing them even as they speak; but not to be alarmed, it is probably just as curious as we are. Then the family started to ask questions, first Jane:

"How are you going to get it or him or whatever to leave? Aren't you going to have a séance?"

"That may or may not be necessary," said Dr Drackmar, "we do need someone or something present that was close to the deceased in life. That would help a great deal. The energy generated by the spirit being when someone close to them is present could cause a visual image or apparition of the entity."

"Oh, there is something else I remember!" said Jane Jackson.

"Yes, what is it?"

"When we first came here, one evening my eight-year-old daughter saw him following her down the stairs, but nobody has seen it again after that."

"That explains it! I am almost certain that he mistook her for his little girl and that was the cause of the temporary appearance. We would like to reconstruct that, but with his real-life daughter if it were possible. You told me her name was Cleo Holloway, didn't you? If you had her address or told me how I could get in touch with her I could take care of that for you."

The spirit must have overheard them because at the mention of his daughter's name a mysterious address book was found on the floor and it contained the name and address down south where the Holloways had sent their daughter to stay before the tragedy occurred. Dr Drackmar had one of his assistants copy the information and said he would get on it right away and, after everything was arranged, he would call them back in a day or two to let them know the date and time they would reconvene to proceed to the next stage.

During the next few days, Dr Drackmar contacted the grand-parents of Cleo Holloway in Myrtle Beach, Va. and found out that she had gotten married and had moved to Atlanta, Ga. where he eventually contacted her and arranged to go there immediately and meet her at her home. He tried to persuade her to come to New York City and help solve this mystery involving her deceased father.

"Why should I leave my family here in Atlanta to come with you to New York City? It's crazy! My father's been dead for almost 20 years! I don't see what good it would do. Besides, we can't afford it anyhow."

"Why Ms Holloway, I mean Mrs Claymore (her married name), can you imagine the torment and torture of a soul that for these past 20 years has not been able to find rest and peace in the afterlife? It is worse than death itself. Besides, he, I mean, his spirit is what led me to you, and there is every indication that you are part of the answer for him to find the peace he is seeking to move on. And consider your trip, a weekend in the Big Apple, an all-expense paid vacation for you and your husband. And before you ask why I am going to all this expense and what I will get out of it, let me say that in my profession I try to help souls that have died but cannot move on, as well as the living who are affected and the relatives of the deceased, to find closure. In the end, the knowledge that your father's soul is finally at peace should be a comforting one to you. I beg you to please consider my offer!"

Of course, he didn't tell her that he had gotten a large advance from the publisher and that he was charging the Jacksons a fee. Nevertheless, it was difficult for her to turn him down although she did not want to open up old wounds, she surely wanted to put closure to the plight of her father's tortured soul!

Mr and Mrs Claymore came to New York City that weekend as arranged by Dr Drackmar and stayed at the Pennsylvania Hotel. They arrived on a Friday evening and the following evening Dr. Drackmar escorted them to the home of the Jacksons on Long Island. They arrived at Jackson's home around 11:30 p.m. as prearranged. Dr Drackmar spoke first when they arrived.

"Well, Mrs Jackson, we have finally arrived to see if we can accomplish what we set out to do. First, let me introduce you to Mr and Mrs Claymore who came all the way from Atlanta, Ga."

"Welcome, welcome," said Mrs Jackson, "I am glad you could come, although I wish the circumstances were a lot different. I know you, Mrs Claymore, are not a stranger to this place because you lived here as a child. I only hope coming back here at this time is not too painful for you."

"In a way it is, but we are anxious to finish what we came here to do and put all of this behind us, which is what I am sure you want most of all, as well."

"Yes, Maam, I sure do! And bless you for coming!"

When they were inside, they gathered in the living room and sat in a circle holding hands. There was Dr Drackmar, Mr and Mrs Claymore, Mrs Jackson, and Jane Jackson, with two of Dr Drackmar's assistants manning their special spectrographic and paranormal equipment. The children were told to stay upstairs in their beds and not to go downstairs. At about 12:30 a.m., all the lights were turned off and only a lighted candle was left on the table in the middle of the circle. It was now time to invoke the ghost of James Holloway. Dr Drackmar asked everyone to sit still and not to break the circle no matter what. Then he called out for the ghost to appear.

"Ghost of James Holloway, give us a sign that you are present!"

He didn't have to wait long, for the candlelight flickered and grew very dim, then it flared back up and grew dim and flared back up again three times. Then, again he called out to the ghost.

"Ghost of James Holloway, reveal yourself, appear before us!"

But the ghost was invisible still. Then he asked Cleo to call his name and ask him to reveal himself. Cleo spoke to the ghost.

"This is me, Cleo, your daughter; please, Daddy, let us see you, let us see your face!"

And at that moment a surge of energy rushed into the room 'til everyone felt it and an image took shape in front of them all; but it was not James Holloway, it was another spirit…It was Mrs Beatrice Holloway, the wife, who had come back, for, her spirit, too, had been in limbo and could not go forward because of her violent death and her guilt for the murder she committed. She was wandering in the area and did not return inside the house before because of her guilt and fear of confronting the spirit of her husband whom she had killed. Now it was different, however, for her spirit was drawn back to the house because of the presence of her daughter, Cleo, and her longing to be with her in spite of her husband. Those present were amazed when they saw Beatrice's apparition which was sobbing and crying out:

"Forgive me…, forgive me… forgive me!"

And Cleo, too, began to cry though she did not break the circle. Not surprised, the spiritualist realized that there were two ghosts in the house and was counting on it! That way, the ghost of James Holloway would have his family back again. When he saw them both, Mr Holloway appeared in the room as clear as if in the flesh; and when he heard his wife begging for forgiveness, he realized that as ghosts, there was nothing to forgive, for she, too, had suffered, and he had wronged her as well. Then you heard two ghosts and a living person sobbing profusely, for all the anger and guilt were now gone, and in death, the two of them were finally reconciled. After that, there was nothing that needed to be said, as the two ghosts seemed to embrace their daughter, Cleo, or hover near her briefly then embraced each other, and hand in hand their apparitions gradually faded and soon disappeared. The ghosts, it seemed, were gone forever for they found the peace that they needed to move on. As for the Claymores, with this episode behind them, they found ways to enjoy the rest of their weekend in New York City. As for Dr Drackmar, he completed his research and wrote his book, "Psychic Phenomena in the Spirit World." As for the Jacksons, well, let's just say they found peace and quiet at last and slept well from that **day on.**

THE LITTLE BLACK BOX

In 1978 Mr and Mrs Whittling moved into apartment 6C at the Wexford Terrace, Jamaica Estates, Queens, N.Y., a building that had gone co-op many years ago but began renting some units, especially since the real estate market went sour a few years back. They had been living there only three months and although the rent was a bit high, $750, it was conveniently located near the subway, and it was a halfway decent neighborhood. Mrs Whittling was 44 years old, and Mr Whittling was 50. They had one son together and Mrs Whittling had a daughter by a former marriage. The daughter was 26 and the boy 19, but neither of them lived with their mother, though they visited occasionally. Mr Whittling worked as a construction worker for the City of New York.

Next door to the Whittlings, in apartment 6D, lived Mrs Digman, 55 years old. She lived alone although she was married. Her husband had left her 25 years ago and never returned. Unfortunately, she was never blessed with children.

Mrs Digman was the type of person who was always poking her nose into everybody's business and was given excessive gossip about her neighbors and people in general, always complaining about something or other, even when there was nothing to complain about. She did not have many friends and even the ones she had associated with her reluctantly. She never seemed to be happy except when spreading some juicy piece of gossip about someone. God knows she must not have been this way at one time, but life sours some people sometimes and they become unhappy and meddlesome and malicious like Mrs Digman. Most of the neighbors were really afraid to confide anything in her because no sooner they did that, the whole world would know about it. So they pretended to be her friend and usually lied to her or said very little.

It happened that, ever since the new neighbors moved next door three months ago, Mrs Digman had been trying to find out something about them to gossip about. She watched to see when they left and when they came home, who came to visit, what type of clothes they wore, and who they talked to. She even checked the garbage containers to see if she could learn anything about them including the kind of food they ate from the garbage they threw away, the kinds of things they read, including any letters or discarded mail, etc.

About two or three weeks later, in her eagerness and determination to learn about the Whittlings, she started listening through the wall, which was thin as paper, to learn Mrs Whittling's secrets and personal business. She listened to conversations between Mr and Mrs Whittling; she even listened to conversations on the telephone (the telephone was near the wall!). If it was possible for her to wiretap their phone, she would have done so.

One day she overheard a heated conversation in which Mrs Whittling called her husband a good-for-nothing drunkard and a slob, and he in turn called her a bastard and a prude. Well, it didn't take long before the whole neighborhood knew about that!

Then there was the time she heard Mr Whittling say that Mrs Whittling's daughter by a previous marriage was no good because she was pregnant and not married, and she didn't even know who the father was! And another time she heard his wife refer to him during an argument as an "ex-jailbird" before she met him. These pieces of news never failed to hit Mrs Digman's gossip circuit.

One day she was listening when Mrs Whittling received a telephone call and she heard Mrs Whittling laughing and carrying on, saying to the person on the other end, "Honey, you know how I feel, I want it just as much as you do. Maybe we can meet on Friday." And with that, the word got out that Mrs Whittling had a secret lover.

By now the gossip was catching up to the Whittlings because whenever Mrs Whittling went to the laundry room, her neighbors looked at her suspiciously and started whispering behind her back. Sometimes they put little notes under her door like, "Jailbird!" or "Bastard!" or "Stop trying to be uppity, you are no better than the rest of us, you and your jailbird husband aren't welcome here!"

Life was getting to be hell for them and although at first, they did not know who was behind it, they soon realized that there was only one-way people could know these things since they said them within the privacy of their apartment. So they decided on a plan to prove their theory. The following is a conversation that ensued as part of their plan. Of course, Mrs Digman was listening on the other side:

"Harry, what are we going to do with all this money? You know it isn't ours and if the investigators find it here, what will they do to us? You know they are coming here tomorrow, what are we going to do? At least if we hid it for a while, they can't find it here and when they are gone tomorrow, we could retrieve it and figure out what to do with it then."

"Yes, Mary, but what are we going to do with it in the meantime? Where are we going to hide it?"

"I know what we'll do," said Mary, "you see that little black box that the USPE items came in two days ago? We'll put the money in it and bury it!"

"But where are we going to bury it?" asked Harry.

"In the back yard, stupid, the soil there is soft and sandy! Wait until everybody is asleep tonight, around 2 a.m., and go out back and bury it in the little black box. Mark the spot, then we will wait until tomorrow night to retrieve it!"

"That's a very good idea, honey, I'll do it tonight!"

Now, in the meantime, Mrs Digman had her ears glued to the wall and heard the whole conversation. She decided she was going to sneak out before him at 1:45 a.m. and hide in the laundry room; then as he passed by she would watch where he buried the money, and after he left she would dig it up and all that money would be hers! At least that's what she thought.

So, everything was set! At exactly 1:45 a.m. Mrs Digman went down to the laundry room and waited. At 2 a.m. sharp Mr Whittling left his apartment with the black box under one arm and a small shovel in the other. He headed straight for the back of the house and found a good spot by a clump of bushes where he buried the box in the sandy soil and marked it carefully by placing three stones around it, each stone 1 foot from the center of a triangle, with the center the spot where the box was buried. He was satisfied. All they had to do now was to wait!

He headed straight back to his apartment to tell his wife that all had gone well. Mrs Digman made sure he had gone back upstairs and twenty minutes later went out back and dug up the little black box, put it in a shopping bag she took with her, and returned to her apartment with her stolen treasure. The Whittlings, meanwhile, were awake and they, in turn, sat quietly in their apartment waiting. At exactly 3 a.m. that morning a horrible scream was heard coming from apartment 6D that was so loud and frightening it woke the entire building out of their sleep!

Everyone wondered what had happened and if some terrible crime had been committed. Several people including the super rushed to apartment 6D to see what had happened. They banged on the door until the super in desperation used his master key and opened it to get inside. To their amazement and horror, they saw Mrs Digman standing petrified, white like a sheet, motionless and speechless! Then they saw the little black box on the floor. A three-foot snake had crawled out of it and was trying to find someplace to hide. It must have been scared, by Mrs Digman's screaming.

Well, the fact that it was a non-poisonous snake didn't matter; it served its purpose quite well. As for Mrs Digman, she never regained her speech and is still going to a therapist up to this day. If she ever talks again, it is certain she will never gossip or poke her nose into other people's business anymore!

Sheppe, My Amazing Dog

I remember when Sheppe was first brought home as a puppy. My wife had picked him out at the dog pound where many dogs and puppies were waiting to be adopted or to be put to sleep. His instincts must have told him this was his big chance, he crept out of his corner when he saw her and mustered all his courage, though he must have been in poor health, and wagged his little tail and managed a feeble puppy bark and a whimper, as if to say, "Here I am, please pick me, I'll be a good little dog, I promise!" He was the cutest thing with his furry brown hair and his pleading blue eyes as he stumbled towards the front of his cage. He was so convincing that the moment my wife spotted him, he won her over completely. She knew immediately he was the right dog for us and made her claim on him.

Sheppe was a pup of barely three months when he came home. A cross between a German shepherd and an Alaskan husky, he had big paws for his body, he was beige and brown all over, with a black nose and white underbelly. He was sick, though, and had to be taken to the veterinarian where they found that he had worms and was badly undernourished. We got him just in time!

With good care and nourishment, he got well and was frolicking all over the house and yard and adapted amazingly well to his new surroundings. He grew rapidly and was almost full-grown after his first year. He was playful and he loved to chase after balls of all sizes and sticks which he would catch in mid-air leaping or standing on his hind legs. He was very skillful at it and he looked forward to those hours of fun and exercise. He loved to chase after other animals that came in or near our back yard and once, I remember, one neighbor's kitten came over onto our yard, out of feline curiosity. The instant she got halfway across the yard, Sheppe dashed out from wherever he was hiding like a bullet and chased her up a tall oak tree. That's when I saw how swift cats can climb trees! Sheppe knew he couldn't go up after her, so he just sat down on his hind legs at the base of the tree knowing that sooner or later she had to come down and he was going to wait there 'till hell froze over or until she did. Darkness came and he was still sitting under the tree with a frightened cat out of reach between the oak tree branches. I think that he would still be sitting there today if I hadn't gone out and held him against his very strong protests and pulled him away to let the cat come down.

By now Sheppe was about three dog years (equivalent to 21 human years). He was still very frisky and playful. He and my adjacent neighbor's dog had a game they used to play. They would run up and down along the fence, each on his own side of the fence that separated our yard from our neighbor's. They dashed alongside each other in a mad race from one end to the other. As they ran back and forth, back and forth, they would frequently stop, first, one then the other, raise a hind leg and wet the fence on each other's side. I think in dog language this meant they were declaring their territorial claims so that there was no doubt whatsoever in each other's mind whose territory was whose. No wonder they drank so much water because they couldn't have much liquid left in their bodies after they were through laying claims. Every stump, every tree, every pole, every post bore their marks.

As playful as Sheppe was, and as much as he loved to chase other animals, and humans too, he never bothered with birds which were numerous in the spring. They would come near him, and he would just lay there quietly, occasionally following them with one eye. They even ate his food, and he didn't bother them. I couldn't figure this out for anything! Perhaps he understood their bird language and made a pact with them, or perhaps he was repaying them for their bird songs, or maybe he just figured that their wings gave them an unfair advantage and it was a waste of his time trying to catch flying birds. Whatever it was, Sheppe never moved a muscle when the birds came around.

By now, my wife and I felt that the backyard needed special care and that Sheppe should be confined to his own space so we could plant flowers and new bluegrass etc. So, I built a fifteen-foot square enclosure in one corner and surrounded it with a five-foot fence. Sheppe was not pleased with his new playpen and confinement, and it was not long before he communicated this to us. Towards the end of the first summer of his confinement I began to see gopher holes under the fence, but only on the sides leading towards the house! I didn't do anything about it at first, but one afternoon I watched to see what he was up to. I never saw a more intelligent dog than Sheppe! He would burrow under the fence like a gopher, run around the backyard when we weren't looking and after a while burrow under the fence again in the same place and go back into the pen as if he was there all the time.

Well, I found out his little game and put a stop to that right quick! I placed logs along the sides and even poured concrete in the earth under the gate so he couldn't get underneath. I soon learned about his indomitable spirit, for Sheppe proceeded to use his mouth and paws to lift the latch and open the gate to his pen. What a wretch! I bought a lock for the gate then, so he couldn't do that anymore! About a week later I saw a hole in the nylon wire mesh that covered the gate; he had torn it with his teeth and got out again! What was I to do now? I went to a fence dealer and bought galvanized wire and rewired the gate. I thought now that I had surely solved the problem and there would be no more of his tricks! I was dismayed when I later discovered that "Houdini" Sheppe had pulled another one on me and still got out at will! How did he do it? The fence wasn't torn, there were no holes under the fence, and the lock was secure. I was determined to find out and one Saturday morning I watched him from a hiding place because he never did mischief when he thought we were looking. I didn't have too long to wait! I saw an acrobatic dog climb a five-foot wire fence like a cat with the greatest of ease and run around the backyard as free as a bird. You know, I couldn't help admiring him! I didn't have the heart to scold him either! But I had to face his challenge and use my superior intelligence to find a way to stop him. The only solution that finally seemed to work was to tie him to a leash in the middle of the pen so he could not reach the fence again. That put a stop to his Houdini tricks for a while. Of course, I let him loose often when I was there to watch him and play with him, and also take long walks with him, but I think he came to realize that he had reached the end of his rope as far as "breaking out" was concerned.

At night we fixed a place in the garage for Sheppe to sleep. A door led from the garage, which is attached to the house, to the recreation room which in turn led into the kitchen on the first floor. He became accustomed to the garage and would cuddle up in there on a rug with his ears peeled for any unfamiliar sounds or footsteps approaching the house. His bark would signal that someone was approaching the house. This arrangement worked out fine, except that sometimes in the early morning hours, he might interrupt our sleep, and the cause may be a pedestrian walking in the street 90 or more feet away from our house - that's how keen his ears were!

One night two summers ago an incident happened that I will never forget. That night we were extremely tired and had gone to bed early so we were dead to the world. I sleep on my back and I remember my right hand was hanging out over the side of the bed. I was suddenly awakened at about 2 a.m. from what I thought was a nightmare as I was dreaming that some monster was savoring my hand before making a meal out of me. When I looked down I saw it was Sheppe licking my hand and gently tugging at it with his teeth. I got up startled, "Sheppe, what in blazes are you doing? How did you get in here?" Poor Sheppe only wagged his tail, gave a whimper, and started walking out of the room. I followed him down the stairs into the kitchen when to my utter amazement I saw the stove lit up and an aluminum pot on the burner - someone had left a pot of water boiling on the stove, and the water had boiled to vapor so that the pot itself had turned red hot from the intense heat and was about to burst into flames and would have if I hadn't followed Sheppe downstairs at that precise moment! I quickly turned the burner off and grabbed a rag, took the red-black pot by the handle and doused it in the backyard with a water hose -- a narrow escape! I put Sheppe back in the garage and tied him up again. Then I began to wonder, how did he get loose, open the garage door, and come upstairs? Did he know of the danger and come to warn me? I have no explanations - none whatsoever! To this day I can't explain it! For some time after that night, Sheppe enjoyed the status of a hero and got a lot of attention and was scarcely ever scolded. He was a good dog in many ways. We had come to regard him as one of the family and he, no doubt, must have felt that we were his relatives from the time he was a puppy. He loved a lot of attention. When he was in his first year we allowed him the run of the house, but as he grew older he did a lot of mischief when left alone inside the house. As a result, the only places that were not "off limits" to him were the garage and the "rec" room.

Sometimes we permitted him in the kitchen when we were in there to watch him. About the time he was two-and-a-half years old, I first discovered a weakness in his personality. He was upstairs in the den where I often did some writing and where occasionally I would let him stay for the night. Early one morning it had started to rain and the thunder and lightning kept rolling and flashing. When we awoke and I went to the den and opened the door, I found Sheppe hiding under the desk trembling with fear and the room was a mess! He had torn up the carpet around the door - it was ruined! The door was scratched so badly near the bottom it was almost in shreds! I couldn't understand at first why he did that damage because he had slept in the den many times and this never happened before. Then it occurred to me, he was mortally afraid of lightning and thunder! This was later confirmed when it stormed and thundered. He would shake like a leaf and act very crazy. He was never himself in that state.

On another occasion, I remember, he was sleeping in the garage when a storm broke out. He was not tied. From upstairs in the bedroom, I heard a racket issuing from the garage. When I went downstairs I found Sheppe tearing and eating away the garage door! The whole door frame was torn up; the doorknob which is metal was dented out of shape; the TV antenna wires running under the door were torn up; I couldn't believe it! From that time whenever it stormed I stayed in the den with him and tried to keep him calm till the storm abated.

Up to a year after that whenever we left Sheppe loose in the backyard he never tried to dig under or climb over the fence to run away. He only did that when he was in his pen, and he wanted to have the full freedom of the backyard. Then he would climb over the pen into the backyard and run loose on our property all day. Around the summer of 1982, he was loose in the backyard and the skies began to get cloudy, the lightning began to flash and the thunder began to roar! Sheppe went berserk! We looked in the backyard for Sheppe to let him into the house, but he was not there! We looked behind every brush, and in every corner, but he had disappeared! Later that day I saw him come scampering up the street toward our driveway. I called him and he ran towards me. He acted guilty but I didn't scold him, I opened the garage door and he went in and sat in his usual place and looked at me sheepishly, knowing that he had done something wrong. I realized then that we had a serious problem, for a pattern of behavior had developed over which we had no control.

In fact, it happened two or three more times after that. Each time, however, the prodigal returned after he had gotten over his fear. On the morning of Saturday, July 30, 1983, when my wife and I were away, my stepdaughter not realizing it was going to storm that day let Sheppe out in the backyard to play and run about awhile. Around 10 a.m. the sky suddenly became ominous, and the wind started to howl. Then the thunder grumbled, and the lightning crackled in the heavens. Our daughter, Lyndia, related later that when she looked out the back, she was just in time to see Sheppe climb the fence into the pen, then climb the outer fence away from the house and leap into the bushes! Whatever demon possessed him, or chased him, he never turned back, and we have never seen him since! Perhaps he was killed on the highway -- I have seen many dead dogs on the highway, but there's another possibility, someone may have stolen him. If that is the case, I hope and pray that he is being cared for and loved. I hope, too, that he has learned to live with his dreadful fear of thunder and lightning!

AWEMAYWE

The ad read: "Beautiful resort village surrounded

When we saw the ad Eva and I were both excited. We wanted to stay in Negril, and we wanted something reasonable. Besides, it was short notice, and the ad was convincing enough. When we called the number for verification, we were told that a villa was available, to mail the money and it would be confirmed by mail or phone.

We had been looking forward to this vacation for a long time and only now it was certain that we were really going. We had the plane tickets, prepayment for two nights was made by mail, confirmation was received, and all we had to do was pack our bags. We couldn't wait to get to Negril!

When we arrived at Montego Bay Airport there was no doubt we were in Jamaica, the "twang" hit you right in the face:

"Welcome, man, to the land of paradise, man, don't worry, be 'appy, man, let me help you man, want a taxi, want a guide, anything you want, man!"

There were all kinds of people offering their services including one man who seemed like he was in charge.

"Welcome to Jamaica," he said, "I am here to serve you. My name is Sam Turner, just call me Sam. I am the ex-mayor of Montego Bay. I am a lawyer, diplomat, real estate broker, taxicab co-owner, taxi cab driver, etc, etc."

"Mr Turner, we are very impressed," I said, "but all we want is a car to rent and we'll be fine."

I had to cut him off before he offered to sell us the whole island, and I believe he would have sold us that, too, if we let him. The moment I said rent a car he pulled us aside, showed us several cars in the parking lot, and asked us which one we wanted. He seemed legitimate, showed us credentials and he went across the lot to a booth that he operated from, got the contract and returned. We filled it out, paid him, received the keys to a medium size black Chevy, packed our bags into the trunk and took off for Negril.

The highways in Jamaica are something else! You never saw so many curves in your life and the roads are very, very narrow. In addition, you have to drive on the left side, which is the opposite of how we drive in the U.S., and, as if that isn't all, they have no passing lanes! On those narrow, curving roads you take your life in your hands when you pass another car, because you can't see what's coming ahead on account of the curves, but, believe me, that doesn't bother the natives; they zip in and out and around oncoming cars like daredevils and pass cars where even a mosquito would be scared to pass! How they don't have a high rate of accidents is amazing! I wondered how car insurance companies manage to survive there!

After about an hour of driving on the narrow, curved roads (and I was becoming an expert by then), we finally reached Negril and came to the resort where we were supposed to be staying. A sign said, "Welcome to Awemaywe"! Frankly, if you didn't see the sign you never would have known that that was the place. A sort of wood-framed shack stood at the side of the road. It looked, on closer scrutiny, like it could be a restaurant of some sort - the word restaurant was written on it somewhere. We pulled over in front of this structure and parked in a gravelly dirt area, beside an old wrecked, hollow shell of what was formerly a car. There were some local youths lounging on this convenient makeshift sofa. They looked at us suspiciously as if we were a new kind of misplaced specie, and seemed to be trying to figure out if we had any human intelligence. I walked up to them and asked if they could direct me to the reception office. Upon hearing this, they looked at each other sort of nonplussed then one of them turned to me and spoke.

"What office that, man?"

I saw that my words didn't ring a bell so I used a different tact.

"Is there a manager of this place by the name of Ms Mae Bell, and do you know where I can find her?"

That must have rung a bell because one of them, in no particular hurry, responded.

"She right there, man, just go in the place and ask for her!" as if to say, 'Where you come from, you should have known that!'

Inside we found Ms Bell who didn't wait for us to speak before she did.

"Yes, Mr Briggs, we have been expecting you, I know you prepay for 2 nights, but how many in all are you going stay, now?"

I looked at her and the surroundings and wondered if this shack was the reception office. Obviously, it was! I wondered also where the resort was hidden, for I didn't see it anywhere in sight. She read my thoughts and reassured me.

"This not the resort here, you know, man, the villas them are all across the street behind them trees and bushes there. It is in nature the place is, you know, for nature lovers. Thomas here will take you there after we finish checking you in."

I told her reluctantly we might be staying five days, but definitely two. She called Thomas who didn't look like much of a bellhop, but more like a country bum (or a transplanted beatnik), and told him to take us to Villa No. 3.

We got in the car and Thomas insisted that he drive because he knows how to maneuver the car over the road we had to take to get to the place. I didn't object. He drove a little way on the main road then made a right turn into what looked to me like a"bush", for there was no side street and I wondered if cars could drive through the "bush". He noticed the concern on my face and made some reassuring remarks.

"No problem, man, don't worry, be 'appy!"

And I swore he was going to wreck the rented car as the path was too narrow, and we were hitting branches right and left. He nearly hit a couple of large boulders in front of us, as the car bounced up and down and shook from side to side from the bumpy, gravelly terrain. Finally, we got to a small clearing when he stopped the car.

"We reach, man, there it is!"

I looked out and saw an abandoned, half-wrecked bamboo hut and uttered,

"What! Is that the Villa?"

"No man, not at all! That's not the one, man," he replied, "there it is straight in front of you. Now isn't that gorgeous, now?"

Well, gorgeous it wasn't, although it looked a lot better than the first hut. It was made of wood and bamboo, though, like the builders attempted to blend the structure in with nature. It was certainly not a modern-type construction.We got out and took our bags to enter the house as our guide, Thomas, tried to open the door. The door had no conventional lock, it had a padlock! We should have figured then that things weren't right and gotten the hell out of there, but the spirit of adventure in us made us ignore that in the same way that we had ignored some other things. Reluctantly, I thanked him for bringing us through the bush and gave him a couple of dollars (though I don't think he deserved it!)

"Y'all, enjoy your stay, now. Hope you like Negril!" He said as he disappeared into the bush.

We entered the hut, surrounded by wild, primitive nature, and started to explore our living quarters possibly for the next 5 days. There was no kitchen! Downstairs had a bedroom, a shower, and a little room with a waterbed. They must have added that as a modern convenience to impress visitors, but we weren't impressed. The bed (It's a good thing we didn't lie in it!) looked like it hadn't been slept in for 100 years and, foolishly (or wisely), I moved the sheet and pillow and discovered that underneath was a family of bugs and crawling things that must have made this their private residence. We vacated that room and considered it off-limits. In the other room with the water bed, the walls were made of bamboo and you could see from outside into the room, so I figured it must have been a peeping Tom's paradise! We had no intention of sleeping there, either.

There was a stairway leading up to a kind of loft, where we ascended, Eva and I, to see if there was any improvement there. There was a bed which we examined carefully and found that it was tolerable as a place to sleep; besides, it was high up and gave us some vantage in case anyone tried to break in. Before settling down, we thought about the place, the surroundings, the people, and the fact that there was no electricity, no refrigerator, no radio, no TV, no telephone, hardly any furniture, and we wondered if we were wise to stay there. But by now it was dark outside, must have been about 9 p.m. or later, so we thought we might as well stick it out for the two days already paid for, and then decide what to do.

We stayed up talking awhile and at about midnight, I came downstairs to use the bathroom. I heard footsteps around the hut outside like someone was scrutinizing and sizing up the place or its occupants or both. I kept still, and after a while the footsteps went away. In the dark, I tried to use the bathroom and hoped that my aim was accurate! When I flushed, however, nothing happened! There wasn't any water in the tank! I decided that in the morning I would take this up with the management. I certainly didn't want to further alarm Eva so I didn't say anything to her when I returned to the loft.

Eva must have been tired for she had fallen asleep. I, however, was contemplating the next disaster when about 1 a.m. almost in concert a herd of goats started "baaaaaaing" in the bushes. I didn't know if they resented our presence and were letting us know, but you try to sleep late at night with a herd of discordant goats singing in unison," Baaaaaa! baaaaaa!"

Almost as soon as the goats had finished making their point, at about 1:30 a.m. the local dogs started! Funny, we hadn't seen one dog when we arrived, but at this time of the morning, they let us know that they were around. It seemed that that was the time they come out to play or do whatever they do. It was one loud barking and howling one after the other. Eva awoke and complained that the noise woke her up! She's lucky, at least she was sleeping; I never did sleep!

When the dogs got tired and the noises subsided, we tried again to sleep. I was almost succeeding, too, when at about 3 a.m. the entire forest was aroused by the most grotesque screaming in the whole of God's kingdom! It sounded like a woman in terrible, terrible agony as her voice rose to an unbelievable pitch that I didn't think a human voice could reach and sustain for so long. Then it descended like a siren only to start up again but more gruesome and horrible than before. We awoke in shock and wondered what could have happened to cause a human being to sound like that! I was sure it was some terrible, frightful tragedy; and each time the screaming subsided, it started up again sending waves of terror and fear through our hearts. It continued for almost an hour. It was the most earth-shattering experience! Obviously, any notion of sleeping was now dispelled by us.

"Let's get to hell out of here!!" I said to Eva.

It was around 4:30 a.m. when we, like two Arabs, decided to make our escape. They could keep our down payment; we had had it with "Awemaywe". If the first night we were lucky to survive, I was almost certain staying another night would be pressing our luck too far. How I managed to drive the car through the bushes and trees is a mystery but drive it I did. I hit the main road and never looked back as we headed towards Montego Bay.

Later, when we reached Montego Bay we found a better accommodation, of course. And when I asked people there if they knew about "Awemaywe", they said there was no such place in Jamaica! We talked to people in the hotel business who should know, and they said the place just didn't exist. After that, we decided not to tell anyone else our story lest they think that we were crazy. I have a word of advice for the reader, however, "Beware of beautiful ads making offers too good to be true about fabulous places with strange sounding names like "A-we-may-we."

MR MAXIMILIAN

When I was a boy growing up in La Boca, C.Z., I remember Mr Maximilian, a disabled French West Indian "canal digger," who used to visit my parents about once every six months. I believe he would have visited more often but he had to come from very far. He lived in the country, in the "interior" of Panama "over the Ferry" we used to say, about 5 miles from the ferry on the west side of the Panama Canal. That was far because he usually walked, although sometimes he took the interior bus on its way from Chiriqui, Cocle and Chorrera to Panama City, and it would drop him off near La Boca, then he would walk from La Boca town limits to the apartment house where we lived, 1032 San Domingo Street. He was a skinny man of medium height, dark complexion, elderly, country or earthy-looking, always very plain and simple in attire -- He wore a marino (undershirt) like a regular shirt dress shirt. I remember he used to smoke a pipe, which he made from a section of corncob. The center of the cob was soft; he gouged it out and stuck a tube in the side of it for puffing the smoke. I think he grew his own tobacco, but I am not sure. I liked to watch him puff on his pipe, and sometimes when the fire was dying down he would draw frantically on the tube 'till the tobacco re-ignited and he could puff more easily to his satisfaction. He and my father and mother were friends from way back growing up in the old country, and they all spoke "Patois". My mother and he originally came from St. Lucia where they were born and where people speak broken French, called Patois. My father's mother also came from St. Lucia, but my father was born in Panama. Whenever Mr Maximilian visited, the three of them had a lot to talk about, especially since Mr Max was glad to be with company that his solitary life otherwise denied him… and he would often spend the night. How the Patois used to fly then!

Whenever he came, he would always bring a large "crocus" (burlap) bag sometimes filled with chickens (though I don't know how they were still alive), but mostly he would bring produce which he grew on his little farm in the interior. There was always plenty of "cocoa", yam, yucca, potatoes, "yampi", corn. Mr Max was one of those men, like my father, who loved the land, the feel of the soil between their fingers, the mystery of nature, and the art of extracting her secrets from her with their strong backs and hands, and patience. They also loved seeing and handling the products of their hard labor, and sharing them with others. Through their efforts, our family had plenty of fresh "earth food" and we didn't have to buy a lot of groceries. Sometimes when my father reaped his harvest (for he also had a little farm on "Far Fan Hill" on the West Bank, just across the ferry), he would travel to the interior and take a portion for Mr Max. Whenever Mr Max visited, we would give him a lot of provisions like salad oil, kerosene, rice, and sugar that we bought for him in the commissary since he didn't have commissary privileges. So it was a reciprocal kind of arrangement.

I always liked to watch Mr Maximilian unload his Crocus bag like Santa Claus unloading toys at Christmas. I was especially thrilled one day when he came to visit because he brought with him a special small box along with the crocus bag that he had carried over his shoulder. It seemed that there was a conspiracy between him and my father to surprise me on my ninth birthday because in that box was a little "puppy", my birthday present. You see, Mr Max also raised on his farm dogs, cats, chickens, etc., although I didn't know how he kept them from fighting each other, or the dogs and cats from eating the chickens, but things seemed to work out quite well in that respect between the animals.

This brings me to a very startling story which my father related to us one day about Mr Max and one of his pet animals, a story that I will never forget. It happened that Mr Max had a cat he called "Missy" which, for a long time, he had treated in a special way. She slept in the house in the master bed, she ate when he ate at the same table with him, and she enjoyed a position of privilege in the house. I don't know how cats think but I am sure this one thought that she was "it", the "princess", the "prima donna", the "mistress" of the household".

One day a lady friend came to spend the weekend with Mr Maximilian. That changed things quite a bit. When they sat down at the table to eat, the cat didn't do anything else but jump up on the table to declare her status, and to eat at her place with him as she always did. Well, Mr Max gave her a hell-of-a "box" knocked her off the table, and chased her away. Missy sulked and ran outside, and stayed away from the house 'till the guest was gone. Then Mr Max let her back into the house after the lady left. He thought the incident was over, but it wasn't to Missy. While he was sleeping that night the cat jumped on his face, nearly suffocating him! Luckily he awoke and managed to push her away; but she jumped on him again and grabbed his most private part and almost tore it off! Fortunately he had a gun nearby, which he grabbed and shot the poor jealous thing dead. But still, he had to go to the hospital for treatment. After Missy, he didn't keep another cat on his farm. You can understand why.

Mr Maximilian, who had neither children nor kin, had given up city life a long time ago to live by himself in the country. He loved his solitary life and he loved farming, raising animals and chickens, but being alone has its disadvantages. For instance, if he should suddenly take ill, there would be no one there to attend to him, or even call for emergency help. He didn't even have a telephone! It is true that it was his choice to live that way, but the worst possibility is exactly what happened to him one day. He became very ill, and by the time anyone went there to check on him it was too late! Perhaps it would not have saved his life in any case, if it was his time to go, and perhaps he left this world the way he wanted to; but there seems to be something very wrong, very sad about a person, anyone, passing on and there is nobody there to pray for them, or hold their hand, or comfort them. He must have thought of this possibility when he chose to live in the wilderness by himself, and I wonder if in his last moments he did not regret it. Nevertheless, I suppose some fatalist might say, "Why should he, since in nature life passes every day and new life takes its place, and who grieves for a fallen sparrow anyhow?" But I beg to differ, I think the angels do.

CALMETTO

The town of La Boca, C. Z. does not exist anymore. It was a little town on the Pacific Coast near the banks of the Panama Canal. It was one of many such towns along the "Canal Zone" that was built for "Silver" employees and their families. It was the town where I was born and spent my boyhood years. There, I went to Mrs St. Hilaire's dame school and to La Boca Elementary and Jr. High School which stood on the very edge of the bank overlooking the Pacific Ocean near the entrance to the Panama Canal. It was a great, long building two stories high, with a bell turret on top, 36 classrooms, 4 bathrooms, a library, a tailor shop, a carpentry training shop, a large home economics classroom, and the principal's office near the entrance on the 1st floor. The building had a total of approximately 190 windows, 5 or 6 per classroom, and from each classroom on the Oceanside was a picturesque view of the Pacific Ocean as far as the horizon. We had an excellent view of ships entering and leaving the Canal and we learned a lot about battleships, cruisers, and tankers by looking out during our breaks and spare time. Sometimes we would be allowed to view from the windows a spectacle like the U.S. fleet in single file entering the Canal from the Pacific Ocean.

In front of the school facing the town was a school playground where we played softball and soccer, and when there weren't any games we flew paper kites. During the butterfly migratory season, we caught butterflies in nets as thousands of them flew overhead.

Behind the school was a steep descent, past a second narrow ledge where railroad tracks were laid, down to the seashore to a place we called "Calmetto", which was our beach 'hideout' although it was not a formal beach and was usually not very safe. Many were the times when we played "hookie" from classes to hide out in Calmetto and ended up in the principal's office where we received a severe flogging for it!

Calmetto was the place where I learned to swim, believe it or not, by being tossed into the sea by older boys and given two choices, "sink or swim"! One might say that that wasn't the best method, but, for me and many others, it worked. Of course, there were a few boys my age who had to be rescued after they looked like they weren't going to make it and had gone under a couple of times. It was very unorthodox, to say the least, and maybe the reason why some of us developed unorthodox ways of swimming and making an awful big splash! I remember when John Beckles and his brother, Ivan, first arrived from Barbados and enrolled in La Boca elementary school.

73

They were so fresh from the island that their twang was very raw and heavy. I mean everybody from the West Indies had a slight accent but theirs would 'knock you down off your feet' when you heard them speak. John would boast: "Oi kyan swim bettah than all whoono. Oi swims so good oi doivs loik a peece o' led and oi floats loik a peece o' cork. And everybody would stop and take notice especially when he dived and made the biggest splash of all! As for me, I became very good at floating on my back and to this day, I'd rather float than swim!

Yet I was good enough at swimming, unorthodox or not, that one day, I remember, three of us took up the challenge to swim to the "danger cable" and back! It was high tide. and the sea was rough, but there was the danger cable daring us, and our peers calling us cowards if we didn't take up the challenge. Now, let me explain, the danger cable was a high-powered cable that ran on the bottom near the deeper part of the channel, but there was this four-post structure that stood in the water with a big sign on it that said, "Danger Cable". It stood approximately 900 yards from our starting point on the shore, and we were supposed to swim to that sign and back.

Melvin, Ashby and I started out for the danger cable posts. Since we knew that there was a strong southward current, we started out in a NW direction to compensate. At first, it seemed that our calculations were right, but we underestimated the current, and by the time we reached half the distance, we had drifted too far southward and were too far offline to reach the danger cable. In fact, we now had to swim directly against the current, which would have taken twice the strength we no longer had since we were already tired out, in order to reach our target. We were fighting against the current in dangerous waters and had to forget about the danger cable and think about survival! We knew we were not strong enough to swim back to shore either, but we could not stop swimming. We were about to panic!

As we struggled against the current, there was only one chance we had for survival. There was a pole sticking out of the water about 20 feet away south of our position, and, from the looks of things, we had a 50-50 chance of making it if we swam NW as hard as we could so that by the time we swam 30 feet the arc would bring us to the pole. Melvin, who was the strongest swimmer, grasped the significance of this and made the greatest effort until he finally reached the pole first. He held onto the pole with one hand and stretched out his other hand to grab us as we went by. If he hadn't done so, neither Ashby nor I would have survived. I grabbed his outstretched hand as I was nearest to him, and when Ashby came by struggling, I reached out and grabbed his outstretched hand, then we pulled each other to the pole that luckily held our combined weights and withstood the pressure of the current.

We held on to that pole for dear life and never moved for hours at least until the tide subsided low enough that we could swim back to shore. While we were out there, the other boys on the shore were frantic because they thought we were going to drown. Hours later, when the tide subsided and we regained our strength and courage and swam back to shore, we found out that word had gotten to our parents about our near disaster; but I didn't even mind the tanning I got for putting them through such a scare!

One day in the year 1985, after being away for almost 30 years, I revisited La Boca, but the house in which I was born, 1071 Gold Street and the house I later lived in, 1032 San Domingo Street that faced the school, as well as the church, St. Theresa Catholic Church, where I made my First Communion, the clubhouse where I frequented and saw many movies upstairs in its theatre when I was a boy, and the ballpark where I saw Vic Greenidge, Pat Scantlebury, Clyde Parrish, George Griffiths, etc. play ball, had all vanished! My brother had warned me, "You're not going to recognize the place, so don't be shocked!" And when I said, "Where's La Boca Elementary School and where's the Clubhouse?" He replied, "A lot of the buildings were sold to merchants and carted away or torn down. There's a place called La Boca Town in Rio Abajo, Panama where most of the buildings were transplanted, and where many retired Panama Canal workers and their families live."

I said, "I wonder where 1071 and 1032 are now, and who is living in our apartments?" My brother chuckled, "You're a funny one, I'd like to see you find that out! Anyway, as you can see, they have moved out all "silver" employees and their families and transformed La Boca, C.Z. It is now a plush residential town for U.S. Naval personnel and their families. Instead of tenements, they have private cottages, with private garages, and manicured lawns with sprinklers."

As we drove up to the embankment overlooking the sea, one thing hadn't changed, "Calmetto!" I asked him to wait fifteen minutes, and I climbed down the banks to have a closer look at my old beach "hideout". I went down the rugged path and came to the rocky shore and looked out at the sea. I didn't see the 'danger cable' sign or the pole that saved my life, but I saw buoys and barges. As I relived the past, I had to take a few flat stones in my hand and fling them over the surface of the water to watch them skip. Yes, this was Calmetto, the place where I learned to "float like a piece of cork and dive like a piece of lead."

Yes, Calmetto brought back memories. As I stood looking out at the sea, I could remember the time when Glen Isaacs swam from the east bank across the full width of the Canal to the other side, daring current, debris, passing ships and sharks! He was the only person ever to do that. I remembered admiring Matthew Prescott who could swim the "Australian crawl" faster than anyone in those days. I always thought he would have swum the Canal like Glen, but he never did. I could remember, too, the day that Jasper Cox drowned in Calmetto, when he and some companions were fishing on an oil barge and someone threw a lighted cigarette in the water that set fire to the oil slick. In a panic, they dove into the water under the blazing oil to swim away, but Jasper couldn't clear the flaming inferno and he drowned. It was a sad day in La Boca as divers went down but couldn't find the body that the current had carried away. It was said that the divers then sent for "Mother Lee", the tie-head lady who went out in a little "panga" with a candle in a "calabash". She let the boat drift quietly until the candlelight blew out; then she pointed to the place and that's where the divers found him. Yes, Calmetto brought back memories!

I returned to the car, and as we drove on what used to be called Martinique Street past where the commissary used to be, I marveled at how the place was transformed—even the trees were different, for there used to be many mango trees and coconut palm trees there in my youth! We drove onto La Boca Road to exit the town, and as we passed by the old ferry road, even that had vanished, for the ferry, too, had vanished, the ferry where my father had once worked as a seaman directing traffic and packing them like sardines so their total weights would be evenly balanced on both sides, yes, the ferry that had connected the east and west banks of the Panama Canal for years until it vanished; but of course, that was due to progress when a bridge, the Thatcher Bridge was built to take its place connecting the east and west shores some time ago, making the ferry obsolete.

Gradually, it seemed to me, that all the traces of life, the towns and the people who lived in the silver towns along the Canal were erased from the face of the earth. La Boca was not the only one, nor the first, nor the last. The proof of their existence, though, is in the minds and hearts of many who, like me, still carry their own special memories of those long-vanished places.

DREAMS AND ILLUSIONS

THE MAN WHO HAD EVERYTHING

On the door, the sign read, "Spiritual Reader/Fortune Teller." A restless temptation and a nagging curiosity had driven him to this place. His fortunes hadn't been going too well of late and he wanted to know if they would take a turn for the better.

He knocked on the door and a teenage girl opened it.

"You come to see Madam Saadi for a reading?"

"Yes, something like that," he replied.

"She is waiting for you, come with me, please!"

She led him to a backroom and told him to enter. As he entered the dimly lit room with all kinds of occult symbols on the walls, zodiac signs hanging from the ceiling, and incense pervading the air, he was struck by a table in the center of the room with a purple satin tablecloth whose edges were golden threads like tassels. It was rectangular and arranged so that the corners hung down from the four sides of the table. On the tabletop, at the center, was a crystal ball, large like a basketball, clear, transparent, sitting on a tripod stand. A little lady dressed like a gypsy, with a kind of turban on her head, spoke to him:

"Welcome, Mr Giles, please have a seat and we will begin."

They had dispensed with formalities which were taken care of by prior arrangement. He had learned about Madam Saadi's mystical powers from a friend whom she had given a reading and told that he would be rich and would win a lot of money. That same day his friend won a big jackpot in Atlantic City!

"So, you want me to tell you your future...if you will be lucky, maybe rich someday?" she said to him. "Anything is possible! I can tell you one thing already; you are a man who likes to gamble very much and take risks. I want you to know that there are no guarantees. I can promise you nothing! Maybe you do not want to know the future, no?"

"Madam, please dispense with the editorial comments, and let's proceed before I change my mind," he replied.

"Very well then, look into the crystal ball, please! Look deeply…very deeply…with all your mind and soul!"

Then she said some strange incantation in a foreign language while moving her hands in a circular motion over and around the crystal.

Suddenly the room darkened and the only light came from the crystal ball itself, which grew enormously in size until it filled the room, until it seemed to encompass all of space and time. In a scene that unfolded, the skies were blue and the evening sun beamed its light obliquely toward the earth. Below, people moved about in great relief that the earlier dark clouds had dissipated. It was about 4 o'clock in the afternoon and in a certain part of town, a man was seen standing in front of a building calling out from the street level.

"Hey, Jim", he shouted, "It's me, Arthur! Something's happening! Come, you have to see this!!"

It seems that there was a commotion in the street around the corner where some poor soul had apparently gone berserk!

"Come, Jim," repeated Arthur, "you have to come and see this; it will blow your mind!"

Jim, who lived in the second-floor apartment, stuck his head out of the window and replied to his friend.

"What's up, Arthur? What are you talking about?"

"Trust me, Jim, and come on down quick, you're not going to believe what you see!" Arthur heeded.

Jim Jones hurried and came downstairs to join his best friend, Arthur Grant, and warned him:

"This had better be good, or I'll break your neck for making me leave what I was doing!"

Then he and Arthur went around the corner where people were still gathered and police were keeping them a safe distance away. What Jim saw shocked his senses until he couldn't believe his eyes! His first reaction was disbelief.

"No! It's impossible…it can't be!"

In the street there were six policemen surrounding a man and trying to calm him down as he raved like a madman out of control, gnashing his teeth, screaming horribly, rolling over on the ground and banging his head against the concrete. He was no danger to anyone else; nevertheless, they couldn't allow him to seriously hurt himself in that deranged state of mind.

Again Jim turned to Arthur and exclaimed,

"Why, he looks like…No, it can't be!!"

The man was unkempt, his hair was standing straight up, half of it pulled out, his clothes were disheveled, and his appearance unclean like he hadn't bathed for months!

"How could this be?" repeated Jim.

He tried to reason against what he saw in disbelief, but, after he looked again and again he was sure there was no mistake. The officers were now trying to restrain the man from further harming himself while the emergency medical van was on its way. It was obvious that he was going to need psychiatric as well as medical attention.

Jim Jones and Arthur Grant started to converse between themselves about the wretched person they saw who, despite his present disfigurement, bore a striking resemblance to someone they both knew well in the past. Could that poor creature in the street really be their friend of a few years back? The person they knew was married and was a very successful businessman.

"He was everything that we all wished we could be," said Jim, "a rising corporate executive with a lovely wife and two children, a beautiful home in Long Island, two cars in the garage, and money in the bank. It seemed like he was very successful to me when I last saw him…"

"Remember, Jim," interrupted Arthur, "when he had that lawn party to celebrate his success and promotion as a junior executive? "

"Yes, he was very popular! He even got his picture in the papers once as the Executive of the Year. To anyone who knew him, he certainly looked like he had everything. What in the world happened to him?"

As Jim and Arthur were walking away from the scene, someone called out to them. It was Carlos.

"Hello, Jim! Arthur! I haven't seen you fellows in quite a while! What are you up to?"

"Right now, nothing!" said Jim. "By the way, Carlos, did you just see what happened back there? I still can't believe it!"

"Yes", said Carlos. "Isn't it sad?"

He said the very words that expressed how Jim and Arthur were feeling. Then Carlos made a suggestion to both of them.

"Look, fellows, if you're not in a hurry, why don't we stop and have a drink over at the Four-Star Club? It's not far from here. In the Four Star, you can find out all you want to know about anything."

The three of them went over to the Four-Star Club where Carlos was right at home. They sat down at a table for four and Carlos called the waitress over. While they were waiting, he began the conversation.

"Fellows, about what happened back there, you and I both know that that wasn't the same person we knew."

"You got that right," said Jim, "What happened to him? We don't have the slightest idea. We hadn't seen him in about four years, since that lawn party at his house in Long Island."

"Yes," chipped in Arthur, "if you know anything, tell us, Carlos."

"Well," said Carlos, "I don't know the whole story, but I heard that about three years ago his marriage broke up and his wife left him. I also heard he went bankrupt and lost his job and everything."

"How do you know all this?" asked Jim.

"Yeah, tell us more," injected Arthur.

"His wife is my cousin," said Carlos, "she told me they had some problems"

"What kind of problems?" They asked in unison.

"About 4 years ago things started happening in his life that at first no one suspected, least of all his wife. He was staying late in the city, claiming he had to work overtime, that things were piling up at the office, etc. You know what a nice wife he had; she went along with whatever he said. At that time he could do nothing wrong."

"But that wasn't unreasonable if he lived so far out on the island!" said Jim.

"Yeah, maybe," said Carlos, "but let me continue. As I said, he was coming home later and later, and staying over in the city, then on the weekends he would sometimes leave the house on Saturday and didn't come home until late Sunday evening. The first time it happened his wife didn't complain, but after that, their marriage started to go downhill. Not only that, the bank account was being depleted, the bills started to pile up, mortgage payments were falling behind, things around the house were falling apart from disrepair, and the children were complaining, a lot of strange phone calls started coming to the house, some threatening, and they all had to do with people who said her husband owed them money and what they were going to do to him, etcetera, etcetera. Even strange women were calling for him and insulting his wife. Things got so bad at one point that the company called the house to find out why he wasn't coming to work and why he was neglecting the job. His wife made up some excuses and apologies for him but she knew something had gone drastically wrong and, finally, she confronted him about it. They had a bitter quarrel and afterwards, they quarreled more and more as time went by, and more frequently, but he kept on and never changed, and things got worse. She had no choice then and after several ultimatums were ignored, she finally filed for divorce. It was not long after that he lost his job and was out on the street, and sank lower and lower. What you saw out there just now was only a mere shell of the man you used to know."

"But, Carlos," said Arthur, "what made him do those things? You haven't told us what caused him to change like that!"

"That's just the point," said Carlos, "I don't know, but let me call someone over here who I'm sure could shed some light on our friend for us."

Turning aside, Carlos called a woman named "Vie" over to the table.

"Violet", he said, "I want to introduce you to two of my friends. This is Jim, and this here is Arthur. Guys, meet Vie. You can ask her anything you wish."

"Hi," said Vie, "what are you two nice-looking fellows doing? Are you unattached?"

They laughed and kidded a bit. Just then the drinks came and they invited Vie to join them and also ordered a drink for her. Vie is one of those persons they used to call a "barfly". She would hang around bars for free drinks and whatever, and you'd see her there almost all the time. But Vie had her eyes and ears open all the time and knew a lot about almost everything, every piece of gossip that there was.

"Well", said Vie, "what did you fellows want to know about? Would you like me to tell you your fortune?"

"No, no", said Jim, "nothing like that. It's just that we'd like to know about this friend of ours."

"Well, you all came to the right place, Vie knows everything! What's your friend's name, honey?"

"Edward Giles," said Jim.

"Edward Giles!" retorted Vie, "That bum! That lousy bum! Ruined his whole life and his beautiful family, and for what? A lot of people would have given anything to have had the life he had before he threw it all away, the worthless bum!"

"But wait a minute Vie don't be calling our friend that! He was a decent, good, respectable man, at least when I knew him."

"Maybe he was. I'm sorry if he is your friend, but he was cursed with the gambler's curse and it destroyed him, you hear me, it destroyed him!"

"What do you mean?" said Jim and Arthur, "please explain."

"He got involved with gamblers," Vie continued, "fast women, cocaine and big-time operators. He would be hanging out in places in the city where he had no business hanging out. And in the casinos! Atlantic City, Las Vegas, you name it! I'm sorry but he lost sight of all the things that he should have valued most; he had everything and he lost it all. …and for what?"

As she was speaking, Jim could still hear in his mind Edward screaming in the street and ranting and raving like a madman, and he just now felt sorry for him, for the man who, in his opinion, had everything.

"So that's what happened," said Arthur. "I know one thing: that could never happen to me. No, Sir!"

- - - - - - - - - - - - --

Suddenly the scenes and characters started to get smaller and smaller and then faded into the shadows as the ominous dark clouds reappeared and filled the crystal dome which slowly shrank back to its normal size. The room, which was dark, was now dimly lit again. You could see again the occult symbols on the walls, the zodiac signs and fetishes hanging from the ceiling, and the smell of incense once more pervaded the air. In the center of the room lay the table with the purple satin tablecloth bordered with golden threads or fringes, with its rectangular edges arranged so that the corners hung down from the four sides of the table. The crystal ball was again the size of a basketball, perched on a little tripod stand.

On one side of the table sat the little gypsy lady, Madam Saadi, with a kind of turban around her head. On the other side of the table sitting directly across from her was the man who came to have his fortune told, whose eyes were transfixed, and who was now wet with perspiration from his head to his feet. He looked pale like a ghost!

"Now you have seen your future, Mr Edward Giles," said the gypsy, "I hope you are satisfied?"

In his heart he wished he had never seen her; he wished he had never listened to his friend who had told him about this Madam Saadi who had mystical powers, who could reveal the future with her magic.

He got up, slowly at first, weak and frightened, placed the money he had agreed to pay her on the table, then ran out of the room and out of that house in a great hurry. As he ran, he could hear Madam Saadi's diabolical laugh fill the room, the house, and the street behind him. "Ha ha ha ha ha ha…hee hee hee hee!!" The fear that gripped him made him jump into his car like a madman and drive away as fast as he could, muttering to himself all the way to Deer Park.

"No, it can't be true! It can't be true! It can't be…"

When he reached home that night he ran to his wife and hugged and kissed her, and hugged and kissed her repeatedly until she thought he had gone mad (though she didn't mind it!); but he hadn't gone mad, he had only come to his senses and realized how lucky he was. He had seen a vision of the future, his future if he did not stop in time, a vision that frightened him to his soul. He saw how precious the things were that he already had, and there was no way that he, Edward Giles, the man who really had everything, was ever going to risk losing it again as long as he lived.

SATAN'S PALACE

They had been driving for hours on the Garden State Parkway south when Jim Forbes saw the sign, "Exit 38 to Atlantic City." The excitement surged in the pit of his stomach and his brain began to fantasize about the large sums of money he was going to win. As the car drove off the highway leading into the city, he could see the tall, beautiful structures like palaces against the sky! There was Caesar's Palace, Trump's Castle, Trop World, Harrah's, Claridge, Bally's, etc.

The first palatial building they came to said, "Satan's Palace, free parking", so they drove right up the ramp to the 3rd level, pleased that they didn't have to look for parking on the street. Eager and full of confidence, Jim walked into the main building across the bridge, down the escalator and into the grand casino with all its glittering, noisy machines, multicolored flashing lights, baccarat, blackjack tables, roulette wheels, etc., and more people packed per square foot than on the busiest day in Time Square or on 5th Avenue in New York City. These people crowded about the gambling tables, roulette wheels, and slot machines like single-minded, programmed humanoids with unnaturally calm exteriors that belied their fragile, fearful, on-the-verge-of-cracking interiors as most of them saw their hard-earned money slowly disappear right before their very eyes. Some of them were even walking around in a 'dazed' state or some kind of trance. There were little old men and women, there were middle-aged people, and there were young people, of all ages gripped by this strange fever that brought them to this common converging point, all for the same apparent reason, to get rich!

As for the slot machine fanatics, you never saw so many possessed and zombie-like beings, for it seemed that the machines possessed their souls as they stood or sat in front of them feeding them frantically, steadily until all their money ran out. How they believed that they could outwit these programmed monsters, God only knows! Jim felt a deep repulsion for slot machines which are built for the sole purpose of swallowing up money while making funny faces, teasing, taunting, enticing you, and laughing at you with cold diabolical sneers. To him they seemed impassive as they fed ravenously on your hard-earned cash with music, too, singing, whistling and tooting you to your inevitable destruction!

Well, Jim Forbes wasn't a slot machine fanatic. Thank goodness! He wasn't going to be caught on one of those machines; his game was Blackjack! That's where he was going to make his fortune. He knew how to work at Blackjack. Like the time in San Juan when he took the casino for more than $5,000 in the space of 2 hours while killing time before going to the airport; and there was the time in the Bahamas when he cleaned up, or in San Jose when he won $2,000, and in Panama City when he won $3,000.

Yes, his game was blackjack alright! Here he was, though, in the casino of Satan's Palace and every Blackjack table was filled, not one vacant seat, and besides, there were people standing around ahead of him waiting to get in the game. There was no way he was going to get a seat. All he wanted was a chance to sit in a game! It was at this point, as he was roaming around the great hall, that he spied a door off in the corner with a sign above it that said, "VIP Room! Blackjack, Poker!" Some funny, unintelligible, small letters were written beneath those words which he didn't bother to read. All he saw in big letters was the word, "BLACKJACK"! And he didn't care how high the stakes were, he was game. Two well-dressed persons, a man and a woman were standing at the entrance beckoning him to enter, informing him that he was welcome to come in, and that there was plenty of space for him. He accepted and entered the VIP room and took an empty seat that was waiting for him on the Blackjack table. He was the sixth player on the table. The minimum bet was $100 and he started off with a small winning streak, 4 straight wins, $400! He felt good! He knew he was going to do well, he thought.

After the 4th game, one of the other players seemed to be having some difficulty and Jim heard the dealer say something to him.

"I'm afraid you've used up all your credit; you know the rules. You have to go to the Boss's office and settle your account."

Then the dealer called two big bruisers to come and escort him off. Well, the game continued for a while during which time Jim started to lose back some of his winnings. He also overheard the dealer say something to another player who had just signed an IOU or some kind of voucher for some credit from the house.

"This is your last, Mack unless you start winning soon! Wish you luck, plenty of luck, Mack."

The game continued. The first player who had left was replaced by another and Jim tried to settle down and concentrate. For a brief moment, he thought about that player who was escorted to the "Boss's" office and never returned. And he thought about what the dealer said to the 2nd player, "This is your last, Mack...etc." He thought about this but only briefly because he knew that in the casinos they often extend credit to many of the regular customers, so there couldn't be anything wrong.

The game continued. Jim began to lose his own money, but he wasn't worried yet. It happened that, at that same time, the 2nd player, the one who had signed the voucher, had just lost all of his cash and couldn't get any more credit! But worse than that, he started to act really weird! He was trembling and perspiring.

"Sorry, Mack, but that's it!" The dealer said to him.

This fellow, Mack, got up and started to run, but he didn't get very far! The bouncers grabbed him and escorted him to see the "Boss"! He, too, was replaced at the table, and the game continued. By now Jim had lost all his money, and one of the floor managers walked over, whispered something to the dealer and then spoke to Jim, offering him a credit voucher to sign for a huge amount of credit, or for whatever amount Jim wanted. Jim was tempted.

"The Boss would love to give you all the credit you need, all you have to do is sign this voucher!" The floor manager said to him.

"But you don't even know anything about me, or whether I can repay you," said Jim.

"Oh, don't worry about that, Jim, we know who you are. We know everything about you!" said the manager.

"I'll be right back," Jim wisely said, "I'm going to get some real money!"

He went outside to the MAC machine and withdrew some cash, over $500, and returned to the gambling table and resumed playing. The game continued for another 30-45 minutes without incident when the player next to Jim lost a big bet and was getting nervous. Just at that moment a female floor manager walked over to the dealer and whispered something in his ear.

"He seems like he is almost ready. What do you think?"

"Any moment now!" said the dealer.

"What the hell is going on here?" Jim wondered to himself.

They must have read his thoughts as one came over to Jim.

"You don't have anything to worry about, you are doing just fine!"

Jim wondered how fine that could be when he was losing his money! And it got much worse, he was down to his last $100 bet and was really worried because he had used up all of his credit card accounts. Then the worst possible thing happened, he had 20 points, and the dealer had 21! He was flat broke! Almost as if they were waiting for that to happen, they dangled

87

that voucher in his face like candy. What in the world possessed him to sign it, he didn't know; but he did! He didn't even take the time to read the damn piece of paper! Anyway, they advanced him $5,000 worth of chips and he went to work. Two, three, four hours went by and he was playing the hands and using every black Jack skill that he possessed. In the meantime, player after player was going into the Boss's office to settle their accounts, and none of them was coming back out! Jim wondered what was going on inside there, and who this Boss might be who was so generous with credit. It was about 12 midnight and in spite of his mastery of cards he lost the whole $5,000 and he knew he was in a deep, deep hole. But to his amazement, the floor manager came over and handed him another $5,000 voucher which he signed gladly just to have another chance to play and recoup his losses. The game continued. Two, three hours later his watch said, 3 a.m.! Then he asked them what time they closed.

"This place never closes," they said to him. "This game goes on day and night, night and day forever. We never get tired, and the Boss never runs out of credit."

Jim wondered about those people and their Boss, about how he had gotten into this mess in the first place, how he was going to get himself out of it, and how he could continue playing without falling asleep. He decided to bet heavier, like a thousand dollars or more a hand, win big or lose big! What he didn't seem to realize until a little later, however, was that there weren't any winners on that table! And as good as he was, eventually the dealer always got the upper hand.

About that time he saw a very well-dressed gentleman come out of the "Boss's" office and walk over toward his table. Jim turned to the dealer and asked him a question.

"Is that the Boss?"

"No," said the dealer, "that's the Boss's assistant. He came over to see how you were doing."

Jim got a good glimpse of the assistant. In spite of his clean-cut appearance, there was something sinister about his blood-shot eyes and long fingers and fingernails. If they thought they were going to get him, Jim Forbes, into that boss's office they had another guess coming! Besides, he still had a few thousand dollars left. But he couldn't help becoming curious as only now he began to wonder what was written on that so-called voucher he had signed. He had three thousand dollars left and he bet the entire three thousand on the next hand and waited as the cards were dealt. He called the floor manager over and asked to see the marker.

"What's the matter," she said, "you don't like the terms of the contract? It's a little too late for that now! Read it if you like."

Jim read the fine print which said:

"This contract is solely between the undersigned and the "Boss" and for $10,000 credit his (Jim's) immortal soul is being offered by the undersigned (Jim) as collateral for the loan, payable any time after the game concludes, or whenever the Boss decides!"

"Didn't you see the sign on the door as you came in?" added the floor manager. "It said, VIP Room and underneath it, "ysiyc".

"Yeah," said Jim, "but what the hell does ysiyc mean?"

"It means, you fool, 'your soul is your collateral'!" and she gave a grotesque laugh that pierced Jim's eardrum.

Just then the dealer asked him if he wanted a card. He had 17 points, and the dealer was showing an Ace face up. He couldn't chance to stay at 17, no, so with perspiration running down his face and neck, Jim flipped his finger indicating to the dealer to 'hit him'. Lo and behold, the dealer dealt him four, twenty-one points! Jim felt much better because he was then confident he would win the hand.

If he won, he was planning to bet the whole six thousand on the next hand and give these ghouls back their $10,000 and get the hell out of there. But all that was wishful thinking as the dealer turned over his face-down card and revealed a 10, Blackjack! Jim lost everything, including his composure. He thought about the bouncers and how they had escorted losers to the Boss; he thought about the player who tried to run away and didn't get far; about the players who entered the office but never came out again; about the dealer's cold, calculated remarks; about the floor manager's weird, diabolical laugh; about the assistant manager's bloodshot eyes and long fingernails, and now as the terror gripped him he had the urge to run.

Just then he felt a hand grab him by the shoulder from behind and mortal fear and stark insanity overtook him! What are they going to do to him? What is going to happen next? Is he going to disappear like the others? He turned ready to fight to the death, if necessary, as the hands grabbed him tighter! He heard a voice urgently calling him over and over.

"Jim, wake up! Jim, wake up! We are almost there! Look, you can see the Trump Castle from here, and Harrah's, and Caesar's Palace! This is a very impressive sight, don't you think?"

It appears that Jim was a passenger in a car with some friends going to Atlantic City, and he must have fallen asleep and slept all the way. He rubbed his eyes, confused but relieved, as he looked out the window happy and relieved that it was all a dream.

"Yeah," he said, "it is the most spectacular sight I have ever seen; it's really beautiful."

He was still trying to collect himself as he realized where he was. And as the car drove through the main street and his friends were debating which casino they would visit first, Jim was still looking out in disbelief as he beheld the bright, glittering lights of Atlantic City!

MY FATHER'S DREAM IN ARRAIJAN

Scorched by the tropic sun in the daytime, cooled by the trade winds during the night, the town of La Boca, Canal Zone was nestled on the southeast banks of the Isthmus of Panama, near the mouth of the Panama Canal looking out at the Pacific Ocean. Sometimes in the early morning, you could see the sunrise breaking over the horizon where the sea and sky seem to meet in the distance as the sunlight comes creeping across the ocean and all around us. Our town was the only world I knew when I was a boy, except for an occasional trip to the cities of Panama and Colon and to a place called "down the line" with my parents to visit with relatives. Like every boy my age, I found La Boca the most exciting place on earth, for a day never went by that did not bring its share of adventures -- from the moment I awoke in the morning to curfew at seven in the evening, later nine when I reached the age of fourteen. My youthful eyes and ears and heart were drunk with the fullness of life and the excitement that our little town provided.

Playing ball in the yard between the houses, or on the school playground, going on mango walks, climbing trees, even the tallest coconut palm trees, playing "platillo" and hopscotch on the sidewalks, roller skating on the streets and sidewalks, flying kites on windy days, and, when it rained, playing marbles under the "cellar" (the space beneath the houses that were raised high above the ground), not to mention the times when my companions and I raided somebody's vegetable garden or hunted wild animals in the bushes, or went swimming or fishing in the Pacific Ocean. These were some of the itineraries of our daily lives; but aside from such adventures, just observing festive events like the Salvation Army band marching down San Domingo Street with Ms Agard in the lead playing her triangle and tambourine, or the Labor Day parades with union workers with banners and posters, and, at times, when the parades were over, the beer fests in the ballpark. At other times there were amateur baseball games, cricket games, soccer games and track and field meets on the ball ground. A seven, ten or twelve-year-old in La Boca town could never find life dull. And that was not all, for the frailties and fallibilities, the trials and tribulations, the comedies and dramas of daily life brought their share of tension and levity on many occasions as well.

I remember when I was nine years old my family had moved from 1071 Trinidad Street to house #1032 San Domingo Street, facing the La Boca

Elementary/Junior High School. We lived in a second-floor apartment in a two-story frame building that was supposed to house 12 families, each apartment with one bedroom in the middle, a tiny kitchen and bathroom in the back, and a living room in the front. We were a family of seven. In those days in the silver towns, apartment buildings were built for twelve to forty-eight families ranging from two to twelve in a family. The apartment I just described was a later constructed model in a way of speaking, since the earlier ones were of a design that did not even have bathrooms inside the buildings, but had washhouses, toilets and bathhouses outside, separate from the living quarters, and people had to go outdoors to use the bathrooms (except at nights they kept a "po" (chamber) inside the apartment which they used and emptied it outside in the morning).

As a slight improvement over the first design, the C.Z. Housing Division started adding a community bathroom inside the apartment buildings so you wouldn't have to go outside to use the bathroom, although it was down the hallway outside the apartments like the one we previously lived in, house #1071, on Trinidad Street. (You still had to leave the apartment with an escort at night if you had to go, or else you used the po.) Then, finally, as if to outdo themselves, in the latest model buildings they built the bathrooms inside the apartments themselves like those on San Domingo Street where we had moved in 1937. Anyway, no matter how many improvements they made, the silver quarters for West Indians, by comparison to the gold quarters for whites in the white communities, were like slave quarters compared to the luxurious homes of the slave masters in the old plantation days.

I remember when I was 9 years old my father owned an old used Model T Ford pick-up truck that his boss had sold to him when it was too old and worth what my father could afford to pay for it. Though it was about ten years old at the time, miraculously it could still run. My father rebuilt it with passenger seats and a roof in the rear and repainted the whole thing. It still looked a little crude but it accommodated our family of seven: my two sisters, my two brothers and I seated in the rear, and my mother and father seated in the front. Dad used to park it in the open space between houses 1032 and 1031 which had a driveway between them that you could enter from San Domingo Street. Anyway, one Saturday morning in 1937, my father decided to drive us in his rebuilt pick-up truck to his piece of land in Arraijan across the ferry --- land in the interior in those days was so cheap it was almost free when Arraijan was mostly undeveloped wilderness. In the early days, there were no roads connecting Panama City to the interior. In fact, they had to travel by boat and steamship to get from the interior to the city and vice versa.

It wasn't until the presidency of Belisario Porras (1912-1924) that an attempt was made to build a national highway between Panama City and David. A road was completed in the year 1931 and this first road to the interior by land was very crude and rough and remained so for a number of years. So when my father took us to Arraijan the roads were still rough and poorly paved, if at all. Therefore, our celebrated family excursion to Arraijan in 1937, a distance of approximately 12 miles west from the ferry, I will never forget.

I think my father, who was in his forties at the time, was a dreamer in those days. He was already thinking about the future and the time that would come when he would be "disabled" — I can't call it retired because "Silver" workers in those days weren't given retirement, they were forced to stop working around the age of 65, given a "disability" dispensation (somewhere between $0 - $45 per month based on a number of factors which I won't go into here), and were forced to move out of their quarters and off the canal zone. On the other hand, white people were paid at least five times the silver workers' pay, lived rent-free and received handsome retirement packages. Anyway, getting back to my father, he was a dreamer who wanted his own land, his own little kingdom on earth for his family, even though his means of obtaining it were limited, as were the means of most West Indians ("Silvermen") who lived and worked in the Panama Canal Zone. To a man, though, West Indians always had a love for the land and for working it with their strong backs and hands, even though they had very little wealth. Sometimes I could see in my father's eyes both the hope and despair that dreaming beyond his limited means brought him. I didn't think of his limitations though, I only knew that he meant to do his very best for his family. He never gave up trying, though, and that is why we were on our way to see his piece of land, his dream in Arraijan.

On the day of the trip to the "interior," we were up early in the morning packing necessities like food that my mother cooked the night before, and other vittles and sandwiches we would consume on the way and while we were in the wilderness. Besides drinking water, we also carried a couple of extra gallons of it for the car engine (I'll explain later). We wore very comfortable clothing that was fitting for the country, and, of course, I was more excited about the trip than my older brothers and sisters who had been a little inconvenienced since they had to postpone their social commitments and other plans for that day. In those days the family business, meaning our parent's decisions, always came first. In 1937 my elder sister was eighteen, my next sister was 16, my eldest brother was 15, my next brother was 11, and I was 9, the little fledgling in the family.

The sun came up with a glint and promise of a bright and sunny day as we boarded our passenger pick-up truck to start our journey. My oldest brother, the crank operator in chief, had to crank the engine up with an L-shaped crank that fits into the crankshaft slot in the front of the engine. My father, who was sitting at the wheel, called out instructions to my brother.

"Ready now, son! Crank her up!"

And my brother cranked 2, 3, 4 times with hefty rotary motions to get the engine started. Once the engine was started, my father kept it going by feeding it gas with a foot pedal. When that was done, and everyone was seated, we were ready for our great adventure.

Off we went that bright Saturday morning, on my father's day off, heading for the ferry to cross over the canal to the west bank on the road to Arraijan. Not too many people were up that early Saturday morning when we drove through town, down St. Thomas Street to Main Street (La Boca Road) then turned left towards the ferry road, then left onto the ferry ramp to stop and wait in line for the docking of the ferry on the east bank, then board her when our turn came like the many cars waiting in line. I did not envy my brother, crank operator in chief, for if the engine should shut off while we were waiting, you know who had to get out and use some elbow grease. Anyway, we boarded the ferry; and it was amazing to see how neatly they packed every kind of vehicle, car, truck, busses, etc., in that limited space on both sides of the ferry deck so that the ferry would remain balanced and wouldn't tilt on either side while crossing the canal. Incidentally, my father knew all about that danger since he was a seaman who worked on the same Thatcher ferry and the ferry workers recognized him as soon as we boarded.

"Hey, Dick, how's it going?" They said to him. "Taking the family for a ride in the country?"

"Yes," replied my father. "We're going to Arraijan."

Even the ferry captain, his boss, waved to him from the captain's post above deck.

"Have a nice trip," he called out.

And this made me feel a little bit of pride that my father commanded the respect of his co-workers as well as his boss.

After the ferry was full to capacity, the crossing took about fifteen to twenty minutes, and we disembarked on the west bank from which only about twelve miles stood between us and my father's dream in Arraijan. We chugged along at a pace of approximately 10 miles or less per hour, my father not in any particular hurry even if the car had the capacity to go faster. On the way as we passed an entrance off to the left my eldest brother explained:

"That's the entrance to Far Fan Beach where white people go to swim. Remember when we came off the ferry, we had passed a hill on the left, that's the hill you must climb to get to the other side to go to Hide Away beach where non-white people like us are allowed to swim."

As we drove past another entrance on the right-hand side our self-appointed travel guide continued.

"That entrance leads to a U.S. installation or supply depot. I think they are planning to build a great big naval station there soon."

(Of course, that would one day become the famous Rodman Naval Station.)

Again, on the left-hand side, as we passed another entrance, my eldest brother did not hesitate to explain to us.

"That exit on the left leads to Palo Seco where there's a leper colony for people who are sick with leprosy."

I couldn't help interrupting him then with a question.

"What is leprosy?"

And he explained to me.

"Leprosy is a fatal disease that causes skin sores, lumps and bumps on the arms, legs, face and body. It destroys the nerves in the fingers and toes, the nose and eyes until they drop off; and it disfigures anyone who has it. There is no cure for it and if you come in contact with a leper, you can catch it. That's why they keep them in a separate colony where they live out the rest of their lives away from civilization. I am sure you read about lepers in the Bible."

"Yes, we were taught in Bible class how Jesus healed the lepers of their sores and so on;" but I felt very sad after he answered my question, and I didn't want to hear any more about leprosy.

As we passed the next entrance on the left-hand side my brother was happy to change the topic.

"That's the entrance to Fort Bruja (Fort Kobbe) a U.S. army fort. The U.S. has all kinds of military installations around the Panama Canal to protect it."

Anyway, after that we didn't pass any more of them as we went further west away from the canal.

Thus, our brief tour ended.

We were lucky so far that there were no mechanical breakdowns but after what seemed like an hour or so, we had our first emergency. The engine overheated and we had to stop. It was a good thing, too, for it was our first snack break as well, and I loved those bologna and cheese sandwiches my mother made for us, as well as sorrel to wash it down.

"Anyone who wants to take a toilet break had better do so now while you can," said my mother. "Just go in the bush over there and do what you have to do quickly before we leave you behind." And she was very emphatic.

After about twenty minutes to half an hour when our break was over, the crank operator in chief poured water into the engine radiator which was a little cooler by then, cranked the engine up, and we were ready to continue on our journey. No sooner than we had gone a few more miles from where we stopped, a wild animal ran from the bushes and crossed the road in front of our path.

"O my God, you going to kill us all, Dick!" My mother said to my father.

Thank heavens he was only doing about 8 mph because when he put his foot on the brakes if he was going any faster, I am sure we would have had an accident. Still, we had a scare and the engine must have been scared, too, because it shut right off on us. Crank operator in chief to the rescue. Out my brother jumped.

"That damn so-and-so deer!" He swore at the deer or whatever animal it was.

Then he went to work cranking up our rebuilt 1925 Ford pick-up. We didn't run into any more animals crossing the road, but we did see a snake or two and I believe we may have run over one of them, to my mother's alarm and trepidation.

"O my God, Dick! Maybe we should turn around and go back home. I can't take this!" She cried out.

This was the moment I believe that my mother started wondering what kind of country it was we were getting ourselves into. I heard her say something else to my father, but I couldn't tell what it was since she spoke to him in Patoit, a language I never mastered. Anyway, we resumed our trip although I started to have suspicions that there had better not be any more surprises and scares –– as far as my mother's demeanor indicated to me. By then we must have been about two hours into the trip, a distance of about 10 miles from home (9 miles from the ferry) when we made our third stop and had our second snack break – and how I loved that! We ate our sandwiches and all who needed to take their second toilet break while the engine cooled down. While we were parked on the side of the road we could hear several animals in the bushes and I knew right then that my mother did not care too much for the wilderness of the "interior." When we resumed our journey again, --which took about another twenty minutes -- my father slowed down (if he could go any slower).

"We are almost there! We will be there in a minute," he said.

And he made a left turn off the main road into what looked like bushes. My mother looked out, trying her best to contain herself, as my father drove a little way from the main road into the bushes, following a narrow dirt road until he came to a stop. We looked around and all we could see was bush, a makeshift fence, and a few hundred yards in the bush a small window-less shack that he must have built on a previous trip and more and more bush. He pointed to the left and spoke to my mother.

"This is the land my dear, our future home!"

Maybe he shouldn't have said those words, because he was seeing a vision that I think only he could see. It was a good size lot, indeed, but it needed so much work to clear and bulldoze and build on; and who was going to do all that work? And how much was it going to cost?

We got off the truck and he gave us a couple of machetes to help him cut the tall grass, but it seemed impossible! As soon as we cut that grass, it wouldn't take long before it would grow back again, as we could see where he had cut on a previous trip the grass had fully grown back already. There were a couple of banana trees and mango trees that he had planted, but that was not enough. He tried to explain to my mother that he knew there was a lot of work needed to be done but if she only visualized the possibilities when he got it all cleaned up, and built an 8-bedroom mansion on it, a paved cement road, a landscaped lawn, a large garden, and a beautiful gazebo, and fruit trees, etc. I am sorry! He believed in his dream, but, after Mrs Evans got out of the truck and felt the prickly bushes, and saw a few iguanas running by, and I believe snakes, too, my mother could never swallow that vision that my father, the dreamer, tried to sell to her in that wild jungle of a place, so far away besides. She said some harsh words to him in Patoit (that to this day I don't know what they meant), and then she got right back into that

97

truck and from the look on her face, I knew that was the end of my father's dream in Arraijan. I am afraid we were never going to live in Arraijan, Panama.

By then my father's head was slumped down, and he knew what he had to do. He told his helpers, my brothers and me, to pack the machetes away and all get back into the truck. It was a sad moment for him, I am sure, and one day maybe his dream in Arraijan will come true for somebody else when that country is built up, and near his dreamland a modern city rises up and beautiful houses are built; but I am afraid that won't be happening in his lifetime. This was 1937 and he would have to find another dream somewhere else closer to civilization that would make my mother happy.

We got back into our pick-up truck and made our way back out of the bushes onto the rugged highway, and, after a few emergency stops, back to the ferry and back home to La Boca, C.Z. All the way back my father and mother never spoke a word to each other, but I knew the feelings were deep. We got home safely, and, somehow they made peace with each other, my mother also knew that my father's feelings were hurt, but she consoled him by suggesting that he should not give up, but he should try to find another dream somewhere else for our family.

Things didn't work out too badly in the years to come, for that was how a place called Parque Lefevre in the suburbs of Panama City came to replace the jungle of Arraijan, and eventually, my father built our home there (with the help of friends and neighbors) and my mother had her little garden and her chickens, and she was close to her friends and family, and did not see any snakes, iguanas, or wild deer, and she was happy during the remaining years of her life.

THE OLD SAILOR

There he sat in the doctor's office waiting to hear the result of the examination. The examination was completed but the doctor was conferring with two other specialists about his findings, so as to be sure. They must have come to a final decision as he came into the office and sat down behind his desk across from his patient, Cornelius Richard Irons. Cornelius, otherwise known as "Dick," looked at the doctor.

"Well, Doc, what is the verdict? Give it to me straight, and don't pull any punches. It looks bad, doesn't it?"

Dr Curtis looked at him almost as if he didn't want to say the words, but he knew he had to tell his patient the result of the tests.

"Mr Irons, I am afraid I have to tell you that it looks very bad! You have an advanced case of cancer, and there is nothing that can be done to cure it at this stage."

"Yes, doc, but cut the long speech and tell me how much time I got left!"

"Maybe three months, maybe less. It could happen in two or three weeks from now.

"I see," said Mr Irons in a reflective tone.

"At your age," continued the doctor, "this type of cancer is not unusual; I am sorry, Mr Irons!"

"Oh, that's alright, doc, I knew I had to go sometime. It's not so bad, I am 75 and I've lived long enough already. But listen, doc, there's one favor I want to ask of you."

"Yes, what is it?"

"Please don't tell my daughter anything about this, do you hear? I want to handle it in my own way. If she asks, just tell her it's rheumatism or some old-age sickness. Okay, doc?"

"Only if you promise to tell your children yourself," said Dr. Curtis.

"Yes, yes, I'll do that, don't you worry, Doc."

He left the doctor's office almost as if a heavy burden had been lifted from him. At least, now he knew how much time he had left and the guessing was over. How many people are walking around in this world and are going to die within days, weeks, months or a year and they don't even know it yet? So many of them will just drop dead, or have an accident and never even think it is going to happen to them. At least he knew the most he had was 3 months and he wasn't going to feel sorry for himself. He decided he wasn't going to go straight home, he was going to take a cab, get off down by the seaside and take a walk and look at the ocean.

He always did like the sea. He remembered when he was a little boy he wanted to go to sea. He wanted to be a sailor so bad he used to watch the ships coming and going through the Panama Canal and wishing he was on one of them. There was a retired old sailor who used to come from the city to visit relatives in La Boca and Dick remembered how he would talk about far-away places like Japan, China, India, Australia and countries in South America. He would describe the Pacific Islands and the Far East 'till "Dick" could see those far-away places with his eyes closed, and the old sailor would tell seamen's jokes and thrilling adventure stories as well. He used to love to hear him sing and recite verses about the sea:

In the fairest of weather or in hurricanes

I sailed with the meanest, the bravest and best,

with the wind in my hair and the salt in my veins

and the rhythm of the sea throbbing in my breast.

From Alaska to the Cape to the Florida Keys,

from the China Sea to the shores of Dakar,

from Japan to Australia to the Southern Seas,

from Shanghai to Borneo to Zanzibar!

So here's to my youth, to adventure and fun,

to the life that was Heaven to me.

Lord knows I'd give a barrel of rum

If I could return to the sea!"

As a boy, he just knew he was going to be a sailor when he grew up! He used to read books about the sea, like Moby Dick, Captains Courageous, Robinson Crusoe, Captain Hook, Blackbeard, Treasure Island, and as many pirate stories as he could get his hands on.

When he was a young man, he almost joined the merchant marines. He couldn't join the U.S. Navy then, because he wasn't an American citizen, but he could join the merchant marines. Yes, he came close to joining, in the same way that Carl, Wesley, Jake and many of his boyhood friends had done; but he never did! He never did because in life the roads we take are not always the ones we want to take, but circumstances sometimes dictate our choices and cause us to make different ones than the ones we would like. He is not bitter about what happened, no, sir, because he would probably make the same choice again given the same circumstances. He was the younger one of two children. His father had died several years back, and his brother had left for the United States, so he was the only one remaining to take care of his mother who was an invalid. He couldn't abandon her even if it meant giving up his dream. So he postponed it hoping that maybe one day, if things changed, he could still pursue his ambition. But again fate stepped in and he met the girl of his dreams and got married. They lived in his mother's home and together they both cared for her until she passed away several years later. In the meantime, they raised a family of five children of their own, and as far as his dream was concerned, well, that was the end of that, even though, from time to time, he kept it alive in his heart. It would never really die.

Now, as he glanced at the waves and the ships on the ocean he remembered his boyhood friends who went to sea. "They are probably all dead by now, anyway," he said to himself. He knew that the old sailor had long passed away; bless his soul for enriching his boyhood with his stories! China, Japan, Hong Kong, Borneo, Africa, the names still stuck in his head. Maybe, thanks to that old sailor, he did go to sea after all, and sailed the seven seas, at least in his imagination! It would have been nice, though, to have gone to those places in real life.

He lived out his mature years in Panama raising his family, and after many years he retired from the Panama Canal Company. All of his children had grown up by then and had left Panama; and when his wife, Emilia, died, he, too, came to the U.S. to live with his youngest daughter, Adriana, who lived in the Fort Green section of Brooklyn, N.Y. It was there that he went after returning from his walk along the seashore. His daughter, who looked after him, was worried that he took so long to come home from the doctor. He told her he stopped by a friend to visit for a while.

"And what about the examination?" she asked, "What did the doctor say?"

"Oh, nothing, just a little rheumatism; you know how it is when you're getting up in age."

"Don't scare me like that again, Daddy, you know I don't want anything to happen to you!"

And he went off to his room without another word.

Three weeks later, he complained of back pain and he knew it must be time. His daughter rushed him to the hospital where he was admitted without delay. There was no way now that he could keep her from finding out the truth. She chided him a little, but he told her he didn't want to worry her, that he was hoping he could sail on a ship far away and die somewhere at sea, so nobody could see him suffer. She chided him again for talking about such things that frightened her.

He was laid up in the hospital for two more weeks before the end came. When it did, all his children who had traveled from far away were at his bedside. He was delirious and began hallucinating.

"I am glad you all could come to see me off! You're going to have to go ashore soon, though, because my ship is getting ready to sail. We are going to Hong Kong and the Far East, and then I am going to see the sands of Borneo, Java, and Hawaii, and we're going to Taiwan and Japan! Isn't it wonderful! I am going to sea. I am going to sea at last! Do you hear the captain calling? Yes, it's time to go now. Oh, the water's so lovely! And the sky…Goodbye…"

And with those words, the old sailor finally went to sea after all.

RICHARD GRAVES

He was sitting at the bar sipping a shot of brandy trying hard to forget, if that were possible, when he overheard a conversation between two men sitting next to him. It was the usual bar talk, mostly idle talk, that drinking men engage in. This time the topic was "Old-Man-Young-Girl Relationships."

"An older man in his fifties and a young woman in her early twenties is a doomed relationship right from the start!" said one man.

"Why do you say that? That isn't necessarily true," replied the other man.

"Oh, but it is, my friend. What can a young woman do for you, except run you ragged, burn you out, and eventually leave you for a younger man? Besides, she is not going to spend her time taking care of you. Believe me, such a relationship is doomed!"

"Maybe it is doomed as you say, but what percentage of so-called normal relationships -- I mean with partners the same age -- aren't? Do you think we live in a perfect world where the perfect man meets the perfect woman, they fall in perfect love and live happily ever after like in the fairy tales? Wake up, man, there's no such thing, and age has nothing to do with it at all!"

"I admit that a lot of marriages fail with so-called normal couples, and there are a lot of unhappy people who are yoked, and that the divorce rate is too high, but at least there's a chance that it might work if they are closer in age."

"You think so? I've seen a lot of old immature people and young mature ones; it isn't chronological age alone that makes maturity, you know."

"Yes, but in the majority of cases it does."

"Since you think that age makes such a difference, which would you rather have: an unpredictable marriage with a partner your age, given the odds that such a marriage has of succeeding in today's society, or a short but sweet relationship with a young woman with no strings or chains attached? In other words, would you rather have bitters and some honey or just all honey alone?"

"I don't know who is talking fairy tales now because every relationship has some problem You think an old-man-young-woman affair doesn't have any?"

"Yeah, but it's different; at least you don't have to put up with it!"

As he listened to these two argue he wondered, "What do these two idiots know about anything anyway? I bet neither one of them was talking from personal experience. They are probably two middle-aged, hen-pecked husbands who escaped from the coop tonight and are wishing their wings weren't clipped, just talking for the sake of talking. He took a big sip of brandy and, as the fire went down his esophagus, it did nothing for the pain he was feeling -- not physical pain, a sort of hollowness inside that wouldn't go away. Instead of drowning it, the brandy only made it worse. It would be good if he could stop his brain from thinking, but he might as well acquiesce and not fight the thoughts. They say that that's half the battle won, when you learn to live with your pain, and breaking up always brings a little pain. It was not more than an hour ago, just before he came to La Detente to get a drink, when he sat in his car watching her walk away from him, knowing that he would never see her again. He always knew that it would end this way but he tried to believe otherwise. He realized now that he was only fooling himself, that he had been just an amusement to her, a convenience, a temporary fling, one that perhaps had lasted too long already, almost three years. She was biding her time with him, it seemed, that was all it was! Yes, it was bound to happen and she made no bones about flirting with other men, dating as she pleased, flaunting them in his face; maybe, as he liked to think now, to make him jealous. Perhaps, though, it was to make him leave her, or maybe she just liked to treat him that way because she felt it gave her a feeling of independence or power over him.

He, on the other hand, loved her despite everything, loved her body, her touch, her laughter, her lively company, her youthful vitality, and her self-assuredness. Her energy filled the room around her; her passion-infused life into his mature body; her impulses sparked and motivated him. He was filled with ecstasy whenever they were alone being intimate, and he was thrilled by the vigorous way his older body responded. He wasn't sure if it was she or him that was the source of his own energy, but he only knew he became vibrantly alive with her. So in spite of everything he loved her still, and although his manhood made him angry with her for her flirtations, and made him even threaten (though not seriously) to leave her several times, when she called him a few days or weeks later he would come running back ready to forgive and forget. He knew he had to give her space, so he accepted her freedom and independence, even her flirtations, hoping each time that they would never last and would quickly fizzle away. But he also knew that it was a game of Russian roulette and that it was only a matter of time. So, when he sat in his car watching her walk away, watching her hurry to be in the arms of another, younger man, he knew then that the games were over, and even if she called him this time there would be no running back, there would be no forgiving, not this time. Perhaps it was because he had a sense that this latest flirtation was more than just a flirtation, or perhaps it was because he had grown tired of the game, of playing Russian roulette with his emotions. Whichever it was, for in his heart he knew at last it was over, he was glad! He thought about a lot of things as he remembered her nervously hurried gait when she disappeared into the co-op building in Forest Hills, Queens, the building where on many occasions he had accompanied her, where he had once had a key to her apartment when the romance was hot and new.

He reminisced about their first meeting three summers ago, in the month of June. He remembered that he had walked into the club around 6 p.m. and sat at the bar.

"Ola, Fritz, comment sa va?" he had said to the bartender, Fritz.

"Sa va bien, et vous?"

"Peu fatigue, mais pas mal."

He liked to speak in French to the bartender, who was Haitian because it gave him a chance to practice the little French he knew.

"Vous bouviez?" asked Fritz.

"Oui!"

"Comme d'habitud?"

"Oui, comme d'habitud," he responded.

The bartender poured him his usual drink, B & B straight up. Soon his French was exhausted and he switched over to English or kept quiet for a while. He was sitting on a swivel chair at the end of the bar close to the section with tables facing the bandstand and dance floor. There was some chatter off in the corner by the tables. He looked sideways in that direction and saw three ladies and one gentleman having drinks and laughing. He recognized one of the ladies and got up and went over.

"Hello, Jeannie, how have you been?"

"Hello, Mr Richards, I'm fine, thank you!"

There was a little birthday cake on the table with a candle in the middle so he said,

"Are you celebrating your birthday today?"

"No, it's Doreen's farewell, she's moving to Atlanta. Let me introduce you, these are my friends from the office, we stopped by to have a drink with Doreen. Meet..."

As she started to introduce him to her girlfriend across from her, his eyes met Sylvia's for the first time and the fire lit up inside him. A second or two seemed like ten minutes or more during which time his glance was glued, and he drank in her face and her body even in that dimly lit room, and swore he felt her vibrations, too!

"Meet Sylvia," Jeannie continued, "and this here is Doreen, the guest of honor, and this gentleman is Bill."

"Hi, everybody," he said still holding Sylvia's hand that he had clasped.

Then, as if suddenly self-conscious, he let go and said to Doreen, "I know you will love Atlanta. I hear it is a beautiful city!"

"Yes, I am looking forward to it."

He pulled up his chair between Doreen and Sylvia and blended into the little party, making friendly conversation at every opportunity with Sylvia to whom he was attracted. She, likewise, must have felt the electricity between them as the evening progressed, for when it was time to go she did not refuse his offer to drive her home; and, at her doorstep after a kiss on the cheek, she gave him her phone number before they parted.

He wasted no time and the next day he called her, eager to continue the acquaintance. He discovered that she was just as eager when she agreed to go out with him to dinner and later to a movie, where they held hands and got closer and closer till the electricity built up its momentum. It was not until the third date, however, that it really took off! They went for a drive, a drive that took them through the Holland Tunnel, into New Jersey, near Newark Airport. She must have known when they pulled into the Marriott Courtyard and walked up to the front desk what he had in mind, but she was well prepared for it and went willingly. That was how their love affair began three years ago, and, from that moment, that wintry night in the Marriott, a romantic adventure began that would take them to the deep South, to the Caribbean Islands, to the European continent, to Mexico, and the mountains of Pennsylvania. They let the new love that was born between them have its way, and it swept them across the land, sea and sky in a great adventure of the heart. There's something about new love when an older man finds it with a young woman, that lights all the old fires, rings all the rusty bells, breaks all the barriers, and leaps all the heights (short-lived or not) that you could ever imagine! In Jamaica he was the love of her life; in Paris, she was his eternal love; in New Orleans, they would never part; in Mexico, it was amour and more amour; but as blissful as it was, it was like a train that was traveling without a known destination, or with a destination that they chose not to think of, for the journey was too wonderful to hasten its end. Each time when they returned from one place it was, "Where shall we go next? Let's go here, let's go there!" How many hotels they stayed in, how many cities they visited, how many beaches, how many clubs, how many exotic places! Yet of all the places, he loved Paris best. In fact, they were supposed to return there, though they never did. He loved standing on the top of the Eiffel Tower looking out over all of Paris, the harbors, the bridges, the river Seine, the rooftops, the left bank, the right bank, the whole panorama. He loved visiting the Louvre, the cathedrals, the gardens, the Champs Elysees, the Arc de Triomphe, Napoleon's tomb, walking along the Seine, such a romantic city! They dined in Paris at night, strolled through the French Quarter, and even got lost on the left bank. It was on one of these evenings when they overdid it and stayed too late in the French Quarter, strolling who knows where, that they tried to take the metro to go home but the metros were closed at 12 a.m. and it was hard finding a cab there. They were walking, which I suppose was better than standing still when they saw a cab parked in front of a building. Rushing towards it, they soon discovered that the cab driver was waiting for a passenger in the apartment building who had called for the cab by phone. Three young people came out.

"Pardonez mois, s'il vous plais, mais nous sommes perdu, et nous avon besoin d'un taxi," said Richard in the best French he knew.

One of the two young men who were helping their female friend into the taxi spoke in English.

"This taxi is taken, but perhaps we can help you. Come with us and I'll call one for you."

It was after midnight and it started to rain; they were lost and his offer sounded too good to pass up, so they went upstairs with them. In a large loft apartment, eight young people were gathered sitting on pillows and partying and having fun. After introducing themselves, the two lovers told them where they were staying and of their misadventure, which everybody understood and reassured them that everything would be alright. One of the young people was from England, and the others Scotland, Germany, America, Paris, etc. They were an international group studying at the Sorbonne. They were all children of wealthy families. They talked freely about their backgrounds and travels and were friendly and hospitable to Richard and Sylvia who joined them in telling jokes, laughing and partying with total strangers whom they might never see again, but who at that moment were a godsend and were the most important people in their lives, for they were their rescuers in a foreign city. The taxi eventually came and after exchanging goodbyes, Richard and Sylvia left for their hotel on the right bank of Paris.

O Paris, it was such a romantic place, he recalled, and, of course, he could not forget how they made love every night and morning to French music. The French have the loveliest music! And in the mornings how he loved to look out the window of their bedroom overlooking the Rue de Constantinople to watch people walking in the streets with their 8- and 9-foot French bread under their arms, and up the street he could see at a glance part of the street market where everything from fresh vegetables to boar's meat was sold! Yes, he would never forget Paris, the ride in the metro that didn't take tokens, only tickets; the visit to the Louvre with the large glass pyramid in the plaza, the Tuileries, the Moulin Rouge, the little tourist train that took them through the narrow streets of Mont Martre on tour, the Catedral de Notre Dame, the Basilica de Sacre Cour, the painters in the street, the strolls at night. Yes, Paris was truly lovely!

Next to Paris, Jamaica was the place they loved best. From the moment they landed there they loved the "twang" of the island, "Be 'appy, don't worry, no problem, man!" They stayed in Montego Bay at the Montego Bay Club overlooking the bay, across the street from the beach. It was paradise! The lovemaking every day was divine! The food, the people, and, of course, the reggae were great. They frequented the Strip at nights, "reggaeing" the night away in Sir Winston, in the #1 Club, the Holiday Inn, etc. They danced their booties off.

"I love Jamaica," Sylvia said.

"I love Jamaica, too," he agreed.

And do you think either of them was thinking then about the end of their relationship? At that point, in fact, it seemed it would never end! In such relationships, the end is never worth coming to or worth remembering. It could well have been that at the beginning it was already a doomed relationship, but that fact was never thought of; it was pushed aside, for, that was reality, and reality is seldom associated with happiness. So there he was, three summers later, sitting on a bar stool in La Detente trying to forget about the last three years, about an affair with a young woman half his age. What do those two jive turkeys know about it anyway, they never lived it, tasted it, felt it like he did. How he would like to tell them to shut up and stop reminding him! How he would like to close his ears to what they were saying!

"Fritz, another drink, please, and make it a double this time!"

That ought to do it. And if that doesn't fix it, then there'll be another and another still. As he was about to put down his third double B & B, the two middle-aged men suddenly stopped their chatter and looked off toward the entrance, gaping at the person who just walked in, a beautiful young woman in her twenties with all the trimmings and attributes a woman could possess. She walked over toward the bar counter and approached Richard Graves. As he slowly turned around to see who had touched him on his shoulder, he realized that it was Sylvia.

ICEMAN AND RUBY

They called him "Iceman!" He was normal in every way; in fact, he was more than normal, he was handsome, tall, dark and well-spoken, neat in attire with his fancy rings and gold necklaces, except for one thing, in matters of the heart he was cold as ice! He could charm ladies just with his looks alone; but soon they would discover to their dismay that all they tried, they just could not thaw the ice around his heart in spite of their voluptuousness and inspired flirtatiousness. Many times they would deliberately pass close to him and rub against him, try to tantalize and arouse him, whisper naughty little things in his ear, wink at him, stare at him, and do everything they could think of, offer him anything, anything he desired; still, he never melted and was cold as ice! He was a challenge for the hottest 'femme fatale' around, all, that is, except for sweet, sweet Ruby. Sweet Ruby had a reputation for melting the coldest iceberg. She was torrid heat from a volcano, and she focused her heat wherever she wanted it to be focused. Men were known to faint when she entered a room, and babble as if speaking in tongues. Fully clothed, even with a heavy fur coat on, she made the coat bounce off her hot body as she walked, and when she eased it off her, her slithery form shot bolts of lightning and waves of heat in all directions. Ruby, nobody could resist Ruby.

One Thursday evening at the club when the place was moderately filled, folks were sitting around at the bar and at tables chatting and carrying on, and the band was taking a break while drinks were pouring when someone said, "Here comes Iceman, watch out let Iceman through!" Iceman was cool as he walked into the club without saying too much. He looked sharp and suave and the ladies who didn't know him were eyeing him and swooning as Iceman sat in his usual place at the bar.

"The usual, Iceman?" asked Fritz the bartender.

"Yea, the usual!" replied Iceman.

His usual was a Long Island iced tea, of which he had several, and which didn't seem to do anything for him, it didn't even warm him up.

The fellows in the bar started to talk:

"That Iceman is something else! He got all those pretty women throwing themselves at him and he doesn't even bat an eyelash; he acts as if he doesn't even see them and pays them no mind. We, fellows, can't even get one of them foxes, and he can have them all, only he doesn't warm up to any of them. Iceman is cold, I tell you!"

Somewhere in another part of town, in a luxurious apartment in an expensive brownstone, Ruby was polishing her toenails, or having her maid do it for her.

"I wonder what there is to do in this town on a Thursday night," she said, "I feel like going out tonight!"

"But Ruby, isn't Big Eddie coming by tonight? You know he's your favorite," said Sissy her maid.

"Big Eddie, I'm tired of Big Eddie! I'm tired of all these simple men, they're all the same. I just flip my little finger and they all fall apart. I want to meet a real man, you hear me, Sissy, a real man! Now, where can I find some excitement in this town?"

"Ruby, you know I heard my brother-in-law mention this new club…"

"Yeah, what club is that?" interrupted Ruby.

"It's out in LaGuardia someplace. It's got a French name, something like 'The Tent' or something."

"The Tent -- what kind of a French name is that?"

"Well, I'm not sure. Let me call Charlie and find out."

"If it's not too much trouble, go ahead!" said Ruby.

Sissy went over to the telephone and dialed. A voice on the other end answered.

"Hello!"

"Hello, Charlie, this is your brother's wife, Sissy!"

"Hi, Sissy, what's on your mind?"

"Remember that club you were talking about the other day, what's the name again?"

"You mean the new Haitian club in Queens?

"Yeah, that's the one."

"The name is La Détente, it's the best! It's got a cocktail lounge, a restaurant with great food, great live music and entertainment, especially from

Thursday night through the weekend. Why do you ask, are you thinking about going there?"

"Ruby wants to go there. She's itching to go out tonight."

"Sissy, what a coincidence, Diane and I are going there tonight to hear Frank Bell and his band play. She can come with us if she likes. Let me talk to Ruby."

"Hold on, Charlie!"

Sissy gave the phone to Ruby who told Charlie she wouldn't mind going out with him and his wife and she was looking forward to a fine evening.

Charlie and Diane picked Ruby up at around 10:30 p.m. and they arrived at the club around 11:00 p.m., just when the band was taking a break and getting ready to start the next set. When they walked into the club and they peeled off their coats to give to the checkroom attendant, the light in the vestibule seemed to glow as it settled on Ruby in her low-cut red dress that clung to her body like it was her skin.

"Chile," said Diane, "you goin' cause some trouble here tonight!"

"Well, honey," said Ruby, "who can't stand the heat better move aside, 'cause here I come!"

And as she walked into the club — she never seemed to walk straight, she seemed always to walk zigzag or with a swagger or a wavy motion from side to side — whatever conversations were in progress, and every action except Ruby's, stopped suddenly and all eyes focused on sweet Ruby. You could hear the sighs and feel the thoughts of every man in the place as she swaggered past them. The 'bouncer,' Roy, led Ruby, Diane and Charlie to a table across from the bar and near the bandstand.

While she was glancing around the room her eyes fell on Iceman who was looking straight at her. Ruby was aware of his glance which wasn't the only one, and when Charlie asked her how she liked the club she answered:

"I like it, it has a little class; but tell me, who is that tall nigger with the gold necklace who can't keep his eyes off me?"

"Oh, you mean Iceman. Well, let me tell you, Ruby, you see all these women in this place they're just dying to get next to Iceman. All he has to do is flip his little finger," responded Charlie.

"That's so! Well, Ruby don't go for that jive! I bet you he's just another hot-in-the-pants nigger that ain't worth shit! I know the type. I bet you I'll have him kissing my ass in no time!"

"I don't think so, Ruby. Not Iceman!"

"O yeah," said Ruby, "you get the nigger over here and I'll show you."

"This I got to see," said Charlie, and he walked over to where Iceman was sitting. They seemed to know each other because Iceman called him by his first name.

"Hey, Charlie, how's everything with you?"

"Everything's okay, Iceman…ah…ah…"

"What's on your mind, bro', tell Iceman what you got!"

"Iceman, will you do me a favor, please?"

"What's the favor bro?"

"I'd like to introduce you to someone, then if you don't like the scene you can always walk away. What do you say?"

The Iceman knew well he was talking about Ruby and he had to admit to himself that even he was a little curious, if not interested.

"Sure, bro, sure, anything for you, lead me to the chic," he said.

They both walked over toward Ruby and Diane. Iceman seemed to know Diane for he called her by her first name.

"Hi, Diane, is Charlie taking good care of you?"

"The finest," said Diane.

Then Charlie started to introduce Iceman to Ruby.

"This is a friend of ours..."

Iceman stopped him before he finished and turning to Ruby said,

"Hi, babe, you know who I am?"

"Yeah," said Ruby, "somebody said your name is Iceman. You don't look icy!"

"And what do you call you?"

"They call me Sweet Ruby as in honey, molasses, sugar - pick your choice!"

And Iceman, whose real name was Charlie Smith and whose other alias was "Pretty Boy" sat down beside Ruby. They ordered drinks and chatted for a while until the music started playing when the four of them got up to dance. Naturally, all eyes in the club were on them, the men swooning over Ruby's curves, the women looking on jealously, filled with envy of her.

It seemed like Ruby and Iceman were hitting it off because she was sizzling so much it caused some of his ice to melt. During their conversation, he found out that Ruby owned a beauty parlor somewhere in Queens, and he had in mind to get to know her better, so he could use her shop as a drop for his "business"—he was involved in numbers, dope, you name it. Ruby, on the other hand, saw him only as a new challenge and she wanted to prove that she could have him eating out of her hand – not to mention that she, too, had a fencing operation for stolen jewelry in which she could use him.

Well, before the night was over they were like old friends already, if not bordering on intimacy. They both had plans for each other. Ruby was going to find out what made him tick and also use him with her jewelry business, so she cooked up a plan to get him up to her apartment to look at some jewelry she wanted him to fence for her.

The following Wednesday, sure enough, he came. Her place was exotic as expected, with plush white carpeting, the latest in modern furniture, and the rooms mysteriously and dimly lit in warm colors. That night she gave Sissy off, so they would be all alone. She led him into the living room. Of course, she was wearing fine black lingerie which was very suggestive.

"Make yourself at home, Iceman! I'll be right back with the merchandise." And she went into the bedroom and brought out the jewelry to show Iceman. "What you think, Iceman?" she asked as she showed him the merchandise.

"Well, babe, I don't see a problem as long as we can work something out."

"Of course," said Ruby, "I'll give you 10%."

"Well," said Iceman, "that's not all I want!"

"What more do you want?" asked Ruby who was thinking, if it's sex he wants he doesn't waste any time.

"The money is alright," Iceman said, "but I, too, would like you to do a little favor for me."

"Tell sweetie what it is," said Ruby.

114

"I have some merchandise I'd like to leave at your store from time to time to be picked up. That would go along with our arrangement fine."

"Wait a minute," said Ruby, "if you want me to take risks for you, how do you expect me to pay you 10%? Man, that's a wash in my books, you scratch mine and I scratch yours!"

"Ok, ok," said Iceman, "it's a deal."

Then Ruby said, "Enough of this business talk, let's have a drink and change the subject if you know what I mean."

Iceman knew exactly what Ruby had in mind, and it seemed like there was no way he was going to get out of it. She took off the house coat, brought out the drinks, and they sat on the sofa cozy and cuddly-like, with Ruby making innuendos:

"Tell me, Iceman, how you like your women, rare or well done, sizzling or lukewarm?"

"Look, baby," said Iceman, "I know what you got in mind and all that, but don't you think…"

Ruby cut him off, "You not thinking of turning this fine, sizzling piece of ass down, are you?"

"Well, not exactly, Ruby, but I…"

"What you trying to tell me, pretty boy, who got all the ladies crazy, don't you want the best ass in town? You not trying to chicken out are you?"

"No, Ruby, it's not that; you look fine and all, but…"

"What? What are you trying to say, Iceman, what the hell's the matter with you, anyway?"

"Now don't get all mad with me, Ruby, I'm just trying to explain…"

"Explain what? That something's wrong with me? That I'm not good enough for you?"

"No, Ruby, no…it's not that; it's just that…"

"Then tell me what it is then!" said Ruby.

In the meantime, they didn't realize that while they were up there, the police who had staked out Ruby's apartment on suspicion she was involved in some kind of jewelry theft, were moving in. At the very moment when she and

115

Iceman were heating up, suddenly there was a loud banging on her door and the cops called out,

"This is the police, open up or we're going to break the door down!"

Ruby didn't know what to do.

"Damn it," she said, "the police! What am I going to do?"

Luckily Iceman grabbed the jewelry and dashed through the window, down the fire escape, and got away, saving not only Ruby but his own skin as well since he didn't have to prove his manhood that night after all, which he couldn't do anyway, for he had lost his virility and could no longer perform – and that was what he couldn't divulge!

In fact, since it happened to him a few months ago he went to his doctor who told him he didn't have the power any longer, probably from too much abuse and an overactive sex life, and he might never get it back, or eventually he might with treatment, who knows? Does this mean he would have to give up sex? Iceman would die first before that happened, so he played Russian Roulette with it, hoping that he would never have to pull the trigger, and continued getting by bluffing to keep up appearances, as long as no one knew or suspected his secret while he was buying time and taking treatment. Yes, this time he was lucky, but it is certain he will not be able to go on living on his reputation and getting by with the "Iceman" persona much longer without having to prove his manhood unless he gets lucky again the next time sweet Ruby has him in her clutches. Will Iceman recover in time? Will he survive? Who knows?

MARIA'S DREAM

"It was a great hall, the walls of which were painted in the most gorgeous sceneries of Madonnas and cherubims against a light bluish-white background, and the floors were polished marble adorned with colorful floral designs. From the ceiling hung the most magnificent crystal chandeliers decorated with gold and sparkling gems, and from their streaming lamps, shone a beautifully golden-white light that flooded the room. On the right wing of the hall, there was a door flanked with the finest drapes of burgundy velvet that stood like sentinels about to witness, or announce, a crowning spectacle. Then into the room, with fairy-like footsteps, came a maiden dressed in a white evening gown and white gloves, who bore the smile of an angel, with eyes of a clear, amber hue. She walked over to the marble floor and stopped in the center of the hall. She was like a work of art, her figure sheer perfection and she stood with the grace of a goddess!

Suddenly, the sound of music started to fill the room, very softly at first, then a little mezzo forte! It was a waltz to which the maiden started to dance. She danced gracefully, moving in an ever-widening circle around the room, her gown swirling with circular movements. From another entrance at the back of the room, another figure stood, following her movements. It was the figure of a man dressed in black, with a black cape and a black mask over his eyes. He moved toward the maiden to the rhythm of the music. As he approached her, he reached out his hand and clasped hers, and they joined in the dance, turning and swirling around and around. Her eyes were fixed on him but she could not see his face. Suddenly he held her closer, then closer still. They moved toward the center of the room. The music started to die down as he slid his hands around her waist, then over her shoulders as she kept looking at him, then up to her neck, and, as the music stopped completely both his hands fastened about her neck! Then a frightful look came over her face, a look of terror that transformed her sweet, angelic face, and then there was a scream that pierced the hall and echoed throughout the corridors...

"It was at that instant when I awoke screaming with a dreadful fright, my hands and body trembling, tears flowing down my face, and perspiration down my brow and neck." These were the words Maria said as she sat in the doctor's office trying to explain her dream to him.

It was the same dream she had been having for the past 6 months, and it kept happening 2 and 3 times a week. The trouble was, whenever she had the dream she woke up screaming at the same point in the dream, and could not go back to sleep. It was causing her health and her mind to be affected, that's why she went to see Dr Schaffer, a psychologist, to try to get help.

"Dreams are only an expression of our anxieties and fears which we repress in our state of consciousness," said Dr Schaffer, "but when our conscious mind shuts down during sleep, these fears are manifested. Have you been having any anxieties lately, either about yourself or a close relative?"

"No, doctor, I haven't. Unless…"

"Yes, what is it?" asked the doctor.

"I used to have a fear of choking and I sometimes have shortness of breath, but I can't see that is anything."

"You never know," said Dr Shaffer, "the mind has a way of playing tricks on us. In the dream, did you identify with any of the characters?"

"In a way, yes, with the lady in white, but she is too perfect to be me!"

"Not necessarily; you see, we tend to idealize ourselves in dreams sometimes. In any case, the male character in your dream may represent your fascination with and/or fear of the opposite sex. The screaming may be an expression of your fear of the consequences of surrendering to the male ego. Repeating the dream over and over may be a sort of death wish to invite the very thing you feared. I believe the dream will go away once you understand the nature of it and the causes. Perhaps, too, a successful male-female relationship in your life would help remove your fears. I suggest you take some time to think about what I have said, see if the dream recurs, and with what frequency, then come back and see me about a month from now."

Maria felt much better after hearing what the doctor said, she thanked him and left the office with a better outlook towards the solution of her problem. As a matter of fact, the dream did not recur as several months went by and it was almost forgotten. Maria went on with her life and even fell in love with Carlos, whom she thought the world of. If there was fear of the opposite sex before, it had disappeared completely when she met Carlos. The only kind of dreams she had now were dreams of marital bliss.

A year later, before a host of relatives and friends, they took their marital vows. It was on a Sunday afternoon in the summer. They were married in the Cathedral with the wedding reception taking place afterwards at a sumptuous and elegant place called "The Celestial Hall". It was truly a magnificent hall, with all the guests commenting on the charm and beauty of the place. In the reception hall, the walls were painted in the most gorgeous sceneries of Madonna and cherubim against a bluish-white background, and the floors were polished marble adorned with colorful floral designs. From the ceiling hung the most magnificent crystal chandeliers decorated with gold and sparkling gems, and a golden-white light streamed from their lamps that flooded the room. The guests were all seated and awaiting the arrival of the bride and groom who were still at the photographer taking pictures.

When the bridal party arrived, they marched into the hall most regally, the maids in pink and their partners in grey tuxedos, the bride dressed in a most gorgeous and voluptuous white wedding gown with white gloves on her hands. She truly looked like an angel, like a goddess! As for the groom, he was most handsomely dressed in a black tuxedo with tails, a black cummerbund, and a black bow tie! They marched to regal music as they were announced and took their places afterwards at the dais. The room was alive with happy chatter as dinner was being served. They looked so lovely, the bride and groom, 'till every unmarried person in the room must have wished they could trade places with them.

The Master of Ceremonies made his speech, the toasts were given, well wishes were expressed, and everyone was waiting for the bridal couple to have the first dance alone, the Anniversary Waltz, to open the evening's terpsichorean festivity. She came to the center of the hall and Carlos joined her, as the music started to play. He reached out his hands and clasped hers, and they started to dance to the rhythm of the music, moving gracefully, in an ever-widening circle around the room, her gown swirling with the circular movements. Her eyes were fixed on his as he held her closer, then closer still. They moved toward the center as the music started to die down. He slid his hands around her waist, then over her shoulders as she kept looking at him, then suddenly, without warning...a single shot rang out! a shot that shattered the beauty of the evening...a fatal shot as Carlos slumped in her arms Maria screamed a scream of horror that could be heard in all the corridors of Heaven above, as well as in the nether world! A few seconds passed before the audience, gripped with shock, fully grasped what had happened! A woman, someone in Carlos's past, apparently fired the shot. It was only then that the pieces came together, that the dream Maria had had two years ago made any sense and could be explained, not by any Freudian theories either. What a terrible way for a dream to have come true!

THE FOUNTAIN PEN

This is a story that you may find hard to believe. But I am sure it wouldn't be the first time you have heard about something or some event that you thought was impossible or improbable. There are many things that are beyond our comprehension or that seem incredible, nevertheless, they happen to be true. If you have any doubts just consult Robert Ripley's collection of rare and hard-to-believe facts, artifacts, and stories. The mind should always be kept open to every possibility.

I was visiting a museum in the city one day in the summer of 2007 when my attention was drawn to an item in a round glass case set on a five-foot pedestal. There were other curious artifacts, to be sure, such as ancient pottery, weird masks, strange sculptures, mummies, unusual artwork and fashions, relics, and items uncovered from ancient history all over the world; but in a glass case among ancient jewelry and relics was a fountain pen that seemed out of place. It was about 70 or 80 years old but it was not as ancient and odd-looking as the other items in the exhibit. I wondered what its story could be. I was standing there looking at it for quite a while when a strange-looking gray-haired gentleman who seemed to have been observing me came up to me and spoke to me.

"I have been observing you standing there for quite some time staring at that one item, sir. Do you know the history of that fountain pen and why it is encased there?"

"No," I said to him.

"Would you like to hear the story of how it came to be there?"

"Yes, if you could enlighten me please, it would certainly help me to understand."

He looked at his watch and said to me he was about to take a short break and would be glad to continue the conversation if I didn't mind joining him in the coffee shop down the hallway and having a cup of coffee with him. I accompanied him and he ordered coffee and Danish for both of us as we sat at a little table and he started to relate to me the history of the fountain pen.

"That pen," he said to me, "was added to the collection about 30 years ago, not only because it is approximately 75 years old but because it has special properties that no one can explain. By the way, are you familiar with the county of Queens, N.Y.?" he asked.

"Yes, I live in Queens, N.Y.," I reassured him. Then he continued to tell the following story.

"A schoolteacher by the name of Alan Ferguson, in his mid-thirties at the time, lived in the Midland Gardens apartment building near the intersection of Wexford Terrace and Midland Parkway, Jamaica, Queens, N. Y. He chose to live there for its proximity to Hillside Avenue and the 179th Street 7th Avenue Subway station (less than a half block away). One day he was walking along Hillside Avenue looking up at all the names and signs on the store displays. Then he saw the sign, "Ruth and Naomi's Stationery-Antiques-Gifts-Greeting Cards." He entered to purchase some extra cards that he was sure he would need to complete his Christmas mailing. Inside the store, he couldn't help noticing how unorganized and dusty, how ancient in décor was the interior. In fact, it looked like an antique shop with old antiquarian dolls, clocks, books, costume jewelry, and of course, greeting cards that had faded so badly they looked like they had been entombed for thousands of years! Even the writing was old script writing. Everything in the store looked like it was from another age, another century, with books and artifacts lying all over the floor and shelves haphazardly arranged. You had to be careful not to step on things or trip as you walked by.

The lady at the cash register -- an ancient-looking, grey-haired old woman with ancient spectacles -- said, "Good morning, sir! May I be of help to you?"

Almost half-wanting to turn around and exit the store, he reluctantly answered, "Why...I don't know exactly..."

"Maybe I can help you," she said. "Was it a gift you were looking for?"

"Actually," he replied, "I was looking for a greeting card, but I see..."

He was about to say he didn't think they had what he wanted when she interrupted, "But of course, we have a great assortment of Christmas cards right over here. Just a moment, I'll call my sister to help you." Then she called out to the back of the store, "Naomi, we have a customer! Can you help him, please??"

Another very old lady with a slight hump and somewhat unsteady walk approached and feebly answered, "I'm coming, Ruthie!"

She came forward and seeing him standing there, approached Alan Ferguson and was almost in his face as she looked over her thick lenses into his eyes.

"So you want a gift, eh, sonny, for your lady friend I suppose?"

"No, ma'am, but I'd like to see some greeting cards," said Al.

"Well alright then, just the same I think you might like to look at some of our nice gifts in our collection."

Then pointing to a crooked-like stand, she said to him, "There are the cards, sonny. Remember, when you are finished with that, I have something else to show you."

Alan somehow regretted that he had entered the store and felt he was at the mercy of these two strange old women, one of whom had apparently decided that he was not going to leave until they had sold him something he hadn't even wanted, whether he liked it or not.

After selecting a card, he tried to sneak past Naomi, but he could not escape her hawkish eyes. If he thought he was getting away he could forget it. Besides, he would have to get by "Ruthie" at the cash register anyway, and neither one was going to let him go without another purchase.

Naomi walked up to him, held him by his arm and said, "Come over here, sonny, I've got the very thing that is right for you!"

Letting her take advantage of his good nature, for he was reluctant to offend these two cranky but harmless old ladies, he obliged her and went along.

Among her antiques, she picked up a small box, opened it and showed him an ancient fountain pen. It was one of those old-type pens with a nib point and a tube inside it to hold ink. It was a well-preserved turquoise color with a thin lever on the main stem for squeezing the tube inside by lifting it with your fingernail. That way the suction would draw the ink into the tube and you'd always have a supply to keep the ink flowing into the nib as you write.

She said, "Such a nice young man like you! I know you are a schoolteacher and you certainly can use a nice pen like this one, even though it may be an older model, but excellent nonetheless. And it's only $5.00. Quite a bargain, in fact, a very good bargain I would say!"

Alan looked at the pen and thought, "It does look cute." It was his favorite color besides, and if it was the price he had to pay for his escape from their clutches, he could afford to pay it.

He said, "I will take the pen, but that is all; I really am late and must be leaving."

He took the pen from her and was going toward the cashier to pay but she stopped him, "Hold on, sonny, you forgot the ink! Here, the pen will not write without it, you know." And she gave him a small, cube-shaped bottle of ink; then she added urgently, "One more thing, whenever this bottle of ink is finished, you must destroy the pen, or return it!"

He hesitated for a second when he heard that but she quickly added, "Oh, don't worry, the ink will last a very long time, and then you **must destroy the pen --- or return it to this store. You cannot keep it after that!"**

He thought that that was strange; but the two ladies, as well as the store, already seemed strange to him. At least, he thought, they only got $5.25 out of him, even if it turns out that the pen can't write, or doesn't last a very long time.

He took the subway and rushed off to work in Manhattan where he taught English in one of the High schools. That day at school was uneventful except for the fact that he had a lot of work to take home and a paper to write for a graduate class he attended at Columbia University.

When he came home that night he was feeling a little tired and lazy and was reluctant to stay up late to do any work; however, he forced himself to sit at his desk and make the effort. He started to correct the English compositions he had brought home when his ballpoint pen quit on him; it apparently had seen the end of its days. The turquoise fountain pen, however, lay on the desk in front of him and he decided to try it out. When he touched it to the paper it wrote so smoothly and felt so comfortable in his hand that he thought, "Hey, this old pen is alright!" It was more than alright, it was amazing, for in his hand it seemed to give him adeptness, amazing skill and speed, so much so that he was able to finish correcting all the papers, write his graduate paper in no time flat, and still felt like writing some more.

At first, he thought it was his own spark of energy that he, himself, had induced through sheer willpower, but he noticed that when he put the pen down, the spark wasn't there any longer! He thought that that was strange but dismissed it and went to bed.

The next day he left the pen at home inadvertently. He had several pens at work anyway, besides he didn't want to chance losing it. When he came home that night he decided to write his brother a letter that he had been putting off for some time. He picked up the pen and started to write, and page after page flowed from the pen. He found he had a whole lot to write, which surprised him since in the past he never wrote his brother more than a few lines! But even more amazing, his striking new energy made him write a dozen more letters to other relatives and friends who had never received a letter from him before. He was in a writing frenzy and couldn't stop! With the pen in his hand, he felt a surge of energy, a strange power that flowed through his mind, his fingers, his hand, and through his entire body. It was exhilarating! He had never felt anything like it before in his life.

After that, he started to write every chance he got, and it all came so easy, so amazingly easy. Not only was the content he wrote extraordinary, but the penmanship was fabulous! He even fell in love with his own penmanship for the first time! He could take notes, too, in a long hand very rapidly, so much so that he could copy important information quickly from talk shows and TV and the radio etc. He was never short of what to write and manuscripts and notes were piling up in his handwriting. Short stories were pouring forth, essays, etc.

But all this excitement came to a halt one day because the bottle of ink ran out! He was in the middle of an essay when the pen went dry. He squeezed the tube, he could not make it write. He started to panic for it had not occurred to him to check the ink and conserve it before this happened. "Well," he thought, "I'll just go and get me another bottle of ink from those two old ladies!"

It was a Saturday morning when he left his apartment to go out to "Ruth & Naomi's". When he got to where the stationery store was supposed to be, he saw that the name Ruth & Naomi was no longer there. In fact, it wasn't even a stationery store anymore; it was a candy store! But he couldn't be mistaken! It was the same address, the very same location. He went inside and inquired and the East Indian man who ran the candy store told him he was mistaken, that he had owned the store and had been selling candy there for the last eight years, and he didn't know any two old ladies named Ruth and Naomi.

"You can go next door", he said, "and ask the grocer, Mr Harper; he's been here much longer than I, maybe he knows."

Mr Harper told him, "I have been here about twenty-five years now and, yes, I do remember one time there was a stationery store next door, yes. The man who owned it had told me that the previous owners who were there before his grandparents acquired the store were two old ladies. He remembered because he had said his grandfather told him they were eccentric (weird). He later sold the store and the new owner made it into a candy store, then that owner sold it to the present East Indian people who run it. But as far as the two old ladies are concerned, they must be dead by now, that was so long ago!"

Alan Ferguson did not know what to make of this and started to doubt his sanity for he could not explain these developments. He had to stop thinking about it, though, for even if some miraculous transposition or warp in time had taken place the day he was walking by and caused the past and present to come together in Ruth & Naomi's stationery, it would not do him any good to worry about that now. All he wanted was to obtain some ink for the pen. So, he got on the subway, went into Manhattan and checked a number of stationery stores until he found one that sold ink for old fountain pens.

He returned home and tried to finish his essay, but he discovered now that writing was a painful process once more. He was using the same fountain pen, yet his handwriting started to slow down and it wasn't as fancy and neat as before; in fact, it got worse and worse until it looked like awful scribbling. Even more disturbing, he began to lose energy and power in his fingers, hand, arm, mind and body. The energy was draining from him until he started to get weak and pale. He could not understand it.

After a couple more weeks it had gotten so bad he went to see a doctor who could find nothing wrong with him, yet his condition continued to worsen. He was sitting at home one Friday evening when he began to recall exactly the details of the events of the day when he had bought the pen from the mysterious old ladies. **"Remember, whenever this bottle of ink is finished, you must destroy the pen – or return it to the store,"** he now remembered one of them saying that to him. He realized then that he had not done as she had said, for he had kept the fountain pen and used a different bottle of ink instead! That must be the reason he was experiencing his weakened condition. It must have something to do with that pen! Yes, that had to be it! It seemed like the pen was taking back what it had given. It was now draining energy from the user instead of giving energy.

This time he was determined to follow the old lady's instructions and destroy the fountain pen. He had liked its cute, antiquated look; but after all, he had gotten more than $5.00 worth out of it. He wouldn't want to let it fall into anyone else's hands and they try to write with it; that would be tragic. So he took a hammer and tried to smash it on the concrete sidewalk, but could not even make a dent or scratch on it. He put it in the street so cars and trucks could run over it; but still no use, the pen remained undamaged. He put it in a vice and applied maximum pressure that would crush any metal except kryptonite, and the vice almost broke, but not the pen. He tried to melt it in a furnace, but it could not melt. He saw that it was no use trying to destroy the fountain pen, and then he remembered the other words the old lady said, **"...or return it to the store!"** Now, he couldn't destroy it; but how could he return it if the two old ladies had disappeared and the stationery store was no longer there? Somehow, he had to find those two old ladies.

He thought for a very long time and then decided that if this entire adventure from the beginning was some kind of cosmic distortion or time-space inversion, maybe by recreating the same identical physical conditions as before, who knows, the same event might occur again. He set about to recreate every condition exactly as before that he had any control over. He put on the same clothes he had worn; he fixed the furniture the exact same way; he spilled some milk on the kitchen table just like before. He remembered on that day the wall clock was telling the wrong time, 1 o'clock p.m. when it was 11 a.m., so he advanced it to 1 o'clock. He also remembered that the wall pictures were hanging crooked, so he changed them back so they hung crooked again. The last thing he remembered, he had left the lights on, so he made sure they were on when he left the apartment. He also remembered that when he was leaving the building that day, he had stopped to re-tie his shoe lace that was loose, and, as he bent down, his hat fell off; so he did the same thing again just as before, and then he was ready. He walked toward Hillside Avenue, crossed the street at 179 St. and walked east on Hillside Avenue.

It was 11:15 a.m. on a Saturday morning and the skies were overcast, just as it was before. As a matter of fact, it was almost the identical time, he remembered, a year ago, several weeks before Christmas. So, if the cosmic universe were to repeat the same phenomenon, what better time than when the date, atmosphere and circumstances were exactly the same? He kept walking east on Hillside Avenue looking at the stores and signs, hoping to see that same ancient-looking store with worn-out items in the display window. Then he looked up and saw the sign and couldn't believe his eyes, NAOMI and RUTH's Stationery-Gifts-Greeting Cards! The names were not in the same order, but it did say the same names of the two eccentric sisters, nevertheless. He entered through the squeaking doors as if he was afraid the store would disappear while he was inside; but there, to greet him at the entrance was Naomi, the elder sister herself.

"Come in, come in, and don't be afraid! I won't eat you! I know you came to return the merchandise. It is a good thing you did, too, because we could not wait any longer. The pen is a source of good and evil and the good was all used up with the bottle of ink I gave you. If you did not return it today; you would never be able to do so – at least for another 100 years! Give me the pen; it will stay with us until the next time."

He hardly heard that last remark when suddenly he was distracted by a loud crash and a commotion that had taken place outside in the street. It seems that there was an accident right in front of the stationery store and he rushed outside out of curiosity to see what had happened and if anyone was hurt. In

126

his haste, he had not handed the pen back to Naomi and it was still clutched in his hand. He must have stayed outside for at least half an hour with all the curious spectators who had gathered. By the time the police and the ambulance came and the injured were taken away, he suddenly realized that he had not returned the pen and it was still in his possession. He turned to re-enter the store but the door was locked and there was no sight of the owners; they must have closed the store and left while the commotion was going on. He felt disappointed and decided that he would return the next day to accomplish his purpose. But the next day Naomi and Ruth had vanished like before, the stationery store had disappeared again, and he was permanently stuck with the fountain pen. That was when another idea came into his head.

Two days later he approached the museum in Manhattan and showed them the fountain pen. He offered to sell it to them for their collection of strange and unusual iteMs They almost laughed at him but he seemed like an intelligent and educated person so they asked him why they should want to include an ordinary old-fashioned fountain pen in their collection.

"If you would try to destroy it in every way possible," he told them, "then you would know the first of two reasons why it is no ordinary pen. By the way, this is a challenge I put to you, and I take full responsibility if you should succeed in making a single dent in this pen."

The museum director called a worker over and handed him the pen.

"Take this pen down to the basement immediately," he said, "and with a sledgehammer or any tool you can find, smash it into pieces and bring me back what is left."

The worker, or custodian, hesitated for a moment but he saw that the director was serious, so he left with the intention of doing what he was told to do. Meanwhile, Mr Ferguson was asked to wait a few minutes and he would have his answer.

They waited a half-hour, forty-five minutes, then one hour later the worker returned with the pen, or what was left of it. He handed it to the director with a look of incredulity and frustration. There wasn't a single dent, not even a scratch of any kind on the pen.

"Didn't you do what I told you to do?" asked the supervisor, a little annoyed.

"Yes, Sir, I tried to smash it with a sledgehammer, then I put it in a heavy-duty vice and applied thousands of pounds of pressure which nothing I know of could withstand; and the damn pen almost broke the vice. It can't be done, sir!" he replied.

The manager took the pen from him and looked at it and seeing that there wasn't even a scratch on the turquoise surface, he turned to Alan Ferguson again.

"Where did you say you got this fountain pen?" he asked.

"Now that the pen has gotten your attention," said Alan, "will you purchase it for your collection?"

The manager looked at the pen again much closer this time. On the nib were the initials N&R which made him ask the question.

"What's N&R? What do those initials mean?"

"Naomi and Ruth," responded Alan. "They were the original owners of the pen."

"Who are they?"

"They are two eccentric sisters, two old ladies, who used to own a stationery and antique store in Queens, N. Y. They closed the store and mysteriously disappeared. No one knows where they came from or where they went."

"Hmm… This is a mystery all the way around! And what was that second reason you had for the pen being so extraordinary?"

"I don't know how to explain this. The pen seems to have some occult power about it. One thing you must never do is try to write with it. It takes away your energy and weakens you physically and mentally. There's more to it but that's all you need to know."

Of course, Mr Shipley, the director, insisted on knowing more about this second quality and insisted on learning more about the pen. So he invited him into his office and Mr Ferguson then proceeded to tell the director the whole story from the beginning.

The museum was so convinced after that that they paid Alan what he wanted for the pen, $500, and offered him a part-time job besides, as an attendant at the museum."

We had just about finished our coffee and Danish.

"Now you know the entire story of the mysterious fountain pen. The museum is very proud of that pen, that's why it's hermetically sealed in an unbreakable case made of plexiglass with a wired alarm system attached to it. Well, I've got to get back to my station now. I hope you've enjoyed the story," he calmly said to me.

Then he shook my hand and told me to enjoy the rest of my visit and that he hopes to see me again soon.

Alan Ferguson, by the way, happens to be his name. It is no coincidence that it happens to be the name of the same gray-haired gentleman who approached me when I stood gazing at the fountain pen in the glass case, and this is his story, as hard as it may seem to believe. I have been back to the museum several times and he never fails to greet me with a smile whenever I pass him by. If I believe his story, and I do, then maybe 100 years from now, if this museum is still standing, the two sisters will return to reclaim their fountain pen. What will the museum do then? Anyway, I am sure neither Alan Ferguson nor I will be around at that time to see the outcome.

THE MISSING SEVEN HOURS

Suddenly a flashing red light appeared in his rearview mirror. Soon it was alongside his car and the officer in the pursuing vehicle signaled him to pull over to the roadside. He drove his car over to the side of the road and waited for the officer to approach. It was certainly not the friendly encounter he was anticipating as he anxiously wondered what went wrong. What had he done? Was he speeding? Did he violate some law? His adrenaline started to flow. He must have been driving on the L.I.E. for a long time, he figured, but he was not aware of how long. He wasn't even aware -- until he saw the flashing red lights -- that he was on the L.I.E. in the first place. He couldn't even remember leaving New York City, crossing the Triborough Bridge, or how many miles he had been travelling. It was as if he had suddenly been transported, unaware, mysteriously to where he now found himself between exits 50 and 51 on the Long Island expressway being stopped by a traffic cop. What happened between the time he had gotten into his car in the garage at work and the time he was stopped, how he had put 350 miles on his speedometer when he only lived 50 miles away, and how he got to where he was, were a total mystery to him. The last thing he recalled was having some refreshments in the office in celebration of a staff member's birthday that evening just before leaving the office, and nothing else.

John Bascombe, 48, married schoolteacher, lived in Deer Park, L.I., worked in New York City and commuted via the L.I.E. every day to work. He could account for everything in his life, every second of every day, every moment certainly every trip he took and every time he drove his car even to go a block away; but in this instance, he could not remember anything that had happened from 5 p.m. that evening when he left work until 12 p.m., the moment when he first saw the flashing red lights, some 7 hours later. He left the office at about 4:55 p.m. that Wednesday evening, went to the garage of the State Office Building where he worked and got into his car. That was as much as he could remember.

By now the officer was standing over him on the driver's side.

"Let me have your license and registration. Do you know you could have been killed?" he said as he pointed his flashlight into John Bascombe's face.

John had no idea what the officer meant and he very apologetically responded.

"Officer, was I speeding?" He asked.

"No, but you were driving in three lanes at the same time, swerving your car from left to right and even going off the road a couple of times, that's all!"

John, realizing that he couldn't remember anything and trying to extricate himself as best as he could, attempted to play on the officer's sympathy and compassion.

"Officer, I worked at the homeless center 'till very late tonight after teaching a full day; I was so drained and tired I didn't realize how tired I was. I live in Deer Park and this is my exit, 51, just up ahead."

He looked so pitiful, holding up in his hand the Bible that he keeps in the front of his car that the officer had no alternative since he was a compassionate man, but to let him go with a warning in response to his pleas and his explanation.

"Well, you obviously need some rest, but if you don't keep your eyes open you're never going to get home tonight. I am going to let you go this time, but you'd better exit off the expressway and be very careful so you don't have an accident!"

"Yes, sir, thank you, and God bless you, sir!"

He said to the officer as his adrenaline came back down to normal so that he felt relieved as he watched the officer walk back to his car. He was lucky this time, he thought, but he also knew that this close encounter with the "law" was the least of his worries.

As he drove home he tried to piece things together, but he could not remember a thing! Did he stop somewhere on the way home in some social club (which he had done several times before) and have a few drinks? Did he stop to visit some friend (which he had also done before) and lose track of the time? Did he take someone home and spent most of the evening with them? He just couldn't understand this sudden amnesia. Maybe, he said to himself as he drove into his driveway, it was his brain's way of telling him he was too tired to think, and, after a good night's sleep he would remember everything. Fortunately for him, his wife had been away visiting her sister who was ill, in Miami, Florida and he was spared the difficult task of explaining to her why he was late coming home in the first place and why he did not even call. Somehow, he didn't think she would have bought the story he gave the highway patrol officer, nor even the truth, for that matter, that he couldn't remember what he did, or where he was, for the last 7 hours. No one in this world would have believed that! So, as it turned out, he was

131

spared an unpleasant domestic fight, and, as tired as he was, he got ready for bed with the mystery still on his mind. After trying to deal with it for a while, he managed to fall asleep for which his conscious mind was most grateful.

As soon as he drifted off into a deep sleep his subconscious mind took over and he found himself back on the highway --- only this time *he is climbing up the West Side Highway ramp, heading...heading... towards...the...George Washington Bridge. It is about 5:15 p.m. and traffic is very heavy. He makes his way onto the upper bridge way, crosses into New Jersey onto Route 80 and continues west by some seemingly pre-charted course, exits at exit 62, gets on the Garden State Parkway at exit 159 and continues south for approximately 50 miles. He then takes an exit he has never taken before, turns down a seemingly deserted road that he has never seen before and comes upon a scene that shocks his senses. On the side of the road, in a ditch, there is a Buick lying almost completely turned over. He hadn't even seen it at first but something made him stop. Perhaps it was the headlights or the faint glimmer of its dome light, or perhaps it was something else that made him stop and realize that something was wrong. Whatever it was, he pulls over and parks carefully on the opposite side of the road, since there is hardly any shoulder on the other side, only a dangerous drop into a ditch where the crashed car is lodged. He crawls down to the nearly over-turned vehicle, looks inside and sees a young woman trapped in the driver's seat. Gas fumes are everywhere and it doesn't look good. She was not moving at first and he tries to determine if she is alive.*

"Help me," the young lady feebly whispers.

His heart starts to pound as he sees the gravity of the situation--her life is in grave danger! Although the car is anchored in the ditch, just beyond is an even steeper drop down a ravine and there is no telling in the moonlight just how dangerous the situation really is. He manages to pry a door open and speaks to her and asks if she can move any part of her body to see if anything is broken. She complains about her leg and her back, so he knows she has suffered some damage, possibly a broken leg and/or an injured back. He doesn't know what to do. Should he leave her there and try to find help or should he try to remove her himself? If she stayed in the car the gas fumes would overcome her, and any moment now the car could go up in flames! This is an abandoned road with hardly any traffic, and where is he going to get help around here, or how long would it take him if he chose that option? Something needed to be done immediately! He decided what he must do. He tells her she will be alright and that if she can help him, he is going to pull her out and with a little help carry her to safety and drive her in his car to a place where she can receive proper medical attention. Somehow, with her help, he manages to extricate her, carry her to his car, and make her as comfortable as he can. He drives back to the main road with his injured passenger and continues north until they come to the first gas station. From there he calls police emergency and obtains directions to the nearest hospital.

She was conscious all the time, although in great pain, while they were driving to the hospital in Bloomfield and she managed to tell him her name, Norma Jones and thanked him and told him that it was God who had sent him to find her and rescue her, otherwise, she would still be lying there and might be dead by morning. It was the answer to her prayers while she lay there injured and trapped on that abandoned road. He just listened silently as she spoke with tears in her eyes and he wondered to himself if all of this was real or if he was just imagining it. Finally, they arrived at the hospital and she is admitted as an emergency patient. A complete report of the accident is written up. He is satisfied that she is receiving the best care andthere was nothing more that he could do. He gives the police and the hospital a statement, as well as his name and address, takes care of all the details and is assured that her next of kin will be notified and they will get in touch with him if they need any more information from him. Norma Jones, still conscious, thanks him one last time and hands him a card which he places in his wallet. With that done, he is on his way again. He is now back on the Garden State Parkway ... traveling north...north...north...north.

Suddenly he awoke as if from a startling nightmare...It must have been about 2 a.m. He felt very strange and he got out of bed, went to the kitchen and poured himself a drink of water, half awake and pondering the dream he just had. What did it mean? What tricks was his mind playing on him? Still puzzled, he returned to bed and went back to sleep.

When he awoke that morning, he started the day off in the usual manner. He showered, dressed, ate breakfast by himself and got into his car to drive to work in the city. Just before he drove off, he reached into his wallet to check to see if his funds were alright and he saw a business card that made him curious. He took it out, looked at it and saw written the name, Norma Jones, Jason Realty Co. etc. Of course, it could have been a card that some real estate agent had given him when he was trying to purchase or rent a piece of property in New Jersey. A few weeks ago he remembered making some inquiries as he was considering moving to New Jersey in the future. But he couldn't recall any agent named Norma Jones. He didn't remember how he got that card and why he put it in his wallet. He would have known as he looked at the card again and it seemed to be a weird coincidence that the name on the card was the same as the woman in his dream! He pulled over to the curb and checked the back seat. Lying on the floor there was a woman's pendant that he had never seen before, although several women passengers had driven in his car before and any of them could have dropped it there. Was it a coincidence or something else? He had found earrings and hair pins before and that didn't seem unusual to him; however, in this case, the dream he had the previous night seemed to indicate something more sinister, and the puzzle that was locked within his brain cried for a solution. The card and/or the pendant had to have something to do with the answer. When he got to work the first thing he did was call to see if the hospital in New Jersey in his dream where he took Ms Jones was real. The hospital, Bloomfield Hospital, was real alright, very real; but when he spoke to the admitting desk and asked if there was a Ms Jones who was a patient treated there the night before, the clerk said they had no patient by that name in the hospital, that no emergency like that was admitted the previous night, and that he must be mistaken.

"Are you sure?" He asked.

"Yes, I certainly would know; our records don't show anything."

He decided then to call the Jason Realty Co....he will get to the bottom of this because he had this business card with that name and its number. The telephone rang!

"Hello, is this the Jason Realty Co.?" he asked.

"The what Co.?" the person on the other end replied.

"Is this the Jason Realty Co.? Please!" he said pleadingly.

"No, Sir! You must have the wrong number, there's no Jason Realty Co. here!" The voice responded.

And they hung up on him a little bit annoyed. There went the first two keys of his puzzle regarding the hospital and the Jason Realty Co. He was completely confused now and was questioning his own sanity. Then he looked at the back of the card and saw another telephone number with an address: 16 Spencer Drive, Morristown, N. J. 07860, and he thought that this time he would surely get to the bottom of this mystery. He dialed and waited as the phone rang a few times, but no one answered. He let the phone ring again and again for several minutes and still, there was no answer. He couldn't stay on the phone all day so he decided to call again later. Around 4:30 p.m. he called again and not getting anyone, he decided to do the unthinkable thing since he was basing his decision on his dream the night before. He planned to leave work a few minutes early and drive out to Morristown, N.J. to the address written on the back of the card to prove to himself that he was not going insane!

He left the office early, drove over the George Washington Bridge into New Jersey onto I-78W to I-287W/Springfield-Morristown to I-287S right, onto Morris St/County Hwy-510 onto Kahdena Rd left, onto Spencer Drive. It would be worth the trip if only he could find the answer to the mystery of the previous evening.

He arrived at the front door and knocked and was pleasantly surprised that there was indeed someone at home. A young lady with a pleasant voice came to the door and spoke to him.

"Hello, can I help you, sir?"

"Good evening, Ma'am," he said, "I am sorry to disturb you, but I had called several times earlier and since no one answered, and since the hospital couldn't give me any information, I decided to come in person to speak to Norma Jones or to a relative to find out how she was doing after the accident."

She looked at him completely puzzled and mystified and thought he had a mental problem although he looked like a sane young man. Still, she felt sorry for him.

"I am afraid it would be impossible for you to speak to her. What did you say your name was? But please come in anyway and I'll try to explain the answer to your question."

He came in and she offered him a seat and asked him to excuse her for a minute as she went into another room and returned very shortly with a family album. When she returned, he followed up her last remark by asking her the following question.

"Why did you say it was impossible to speak to Norma Jones? I do not understand, Miss..."

"Mary...Mary Jones." She completed his sentence for him since they had somehow neglected to properly introduce each other.

"I am sorry, too, for my bad manners," he said apologetically, "my name is John Bascombe."

"Take a look at this album, please," she said to him.

And she showed him pictures of Norma Jones who used to live there when she was a young lady almost seventy-five years ago.

"You couldn't have known Norma Jones unless you are over 100 years old! And you don't look a day over 30!" she added.

As he looked at a couple more pages in the album he noticed that there was a page showing Norma Jones walking with crutches and a bandaged leg, and the picture was dated July 14, 1939. The most startling thing about it was that the person in the picture looked like the same young lady whom he had pulled from the wreck in his dream. But that was impossible! Mary saw that he was taken aback by the photographs and she explained.

"That picture of my grandmother was taken when she came out of the hospital after a car accident in 1939. For a long time, she could not stop talking about a miracle that God had sent to save her life; and the angel (that's what she called him) disappeared right after he took her to the hospital. No one ever saw him again! That is the story we have heard many, many times through the years from her, but she is gone now. She was 90 years old when she died in 2004. Norma Jones was my grandmother who raised me from a little girl."

"What did your grandmother mean when she said she was saved by a miracle? Did she mention the name of the person who took her to the hospital?"

"No, she didn't mention his name, only that he was an angel. Perhaps she forgot to mention it. She did say, however, from what was told to her, that after he pulled her from the wreck not long afterwards the car burst into flames and burned to ashes in the ravine, and no one knows how anybody could have gotten out of it alive! What a remarkable story, don't you think so, Mr Bascombe?"

"O yes, very remarkable," he said.

He had heard enough by then. He knew he would sound crazy if he said anything about his dream for he did not believe the events in the dream could have happened, not by all the laws of physics. So when she asked him why it was so important that he wanted to speak to her grandmother who had been dead for so many years, he had only one explanation he could give.

"You see," he said, "I am doing some research on spiritual phenomena and miracles that happened in people's lives which no one can explain and which we hardly ever hear about. Someone had mentioned your grandmother's name to me and I wanted to know more about her experience. I am glad that you were able to help me for I find it a very fascinating story."

136

She brought him some refreshments and they continued to talk a while longer about herself and her grandmother and about all the strange things that happened in people's lives that they knew or had heard about, all of which helped John in his pseudo research but left him, nevertheless, without the rational answer that he had sought. Perhaps there was none!

It appeared that he would either have to become a believer in miracles or else he was never going to find out the answer to his dilemma, which was even more compounded now, and would remain a mystery for the rest of his natural life.

THE REUNION

Five college seniors were out one night drinking at a popular local club. They realized that this was the last time they would be together as college chums since they were graduating three days later. They were more or less best friends all through high school and college. They played on the same football teams, softball teams, varsity, etc. This time together, therefore, was a parting of ways, as each was going in a different direction after graduation. One was going into the Navy, one into the Marine Corp., one into the Air Force, one to medical school, and the 5th to law school. In the height of the evening, full of emotion, they made a pledge, a sort of brotherhood pledge that no matter what happened or where they were or what circumstances befell them, they would have a reunion on the 25th anniversary of this evening, June 5, 1940, in the same club where they sat drinking. They took a twenty dollar bill and tore it into 5 parts whereas each one of them was to preserve his part which would be reunited when the five of them met again in 1965.

June 5, 1965, was an unseasonably mild day with temperatures in the 70's. In fact, the evening was a very pleasant one. It was about 9 o'clock at night and two men sat at a table in the corner of the club conversing.

"What time have you got, Bill? They should have been here by now, don't you think?"

"Aw, take it easy Tom, what's the hurry? They'll be here alright, just give them a few more minutes!"

Just then a tall, serious young man in uniform entered and, behind him, entered another. They greeted Bill and Tom who acknowledged them.

"Hi, Sal; hi Norm, gee it's good to see you guys!"

Sal and Norm sat at the same table after shaking the hands of their buddies. They looked at each other in a strange kind of way, though they never said what it was that was strange, although everyone felt it.

At this point, Tom spoke.

"I guess we are all accounted for, aren't we?"

"No, we're not!" said Bill, "Gene is missing! We are not complete without him. I say we wait a little while longer, and if I know Gene he'll be walking through the door any minute now, late as usual!"

"Yeah, with some tall story behind it," said Norm chuckling.

Just then as if on cue by that last remark, in popped Gene!

"Hi, fellas, don't tell me I am holding up the party! Is that Sal over there and Tom? That's you, Norm? Is that Bill? Geez it's sure good to see all you guys together, I thought I was never going to see you ever again!"

After greeting and shaking hands they all sat around the table taking turns as they talked about their lives since the last time they were together. Sal, who was wearing a Medal of Honor pinned to his uniform stood up and started to speak.

"You know, fellows, after I left you guys in '40 a few weeks later I enlisted in the Navy; I always wanted to be a Navy brass. Well, I made lieutenant and shipped out on the Arizona in '41. I was in Pearl Harbor when the attack came. We were in the harbor refueling when the sky full of Japanese dive bombers and fighter planes flew overhead. They started bombing and strafing everything in sight. I was standing on deck when the first wave came in, no one was expecting it. We quickly ran to battle stations and took up the fight as best we could when one of those damn kamikazes hit the magazine and everything went blank...I can't...seem to remember anything after that..."

His speech waned a little and he seemed slightly bewildered as he excused himself and slowly sat down. Then Tom spoke.

"Remember what it was like back in '42? We marines had to go in and take back those damn Pacific islands from those damn Nipponese after the Pearl treachery. General Mac had given a very inspirational speech just a few days ago and we were stirred up and determined to route the enemy from every piece of real estate. We were fighting on Guadalcanal and it wasn't easy taking back jungle after jungle, being sniped at and booby-trapped. I guess I didn't see…one of those danged things…the day I ...the day I..."

And he, too, started to blur and slur as he looked around and apologized, then sat down without completing his statement.

Bill got up next and spoke.

"Guys, you know how badly I wanted to go to medical school. Well, I was in my first year when "D" day occurred, but I couldn't sit still while all that action was taking place in the Pacific and in Europe; besides, I knew I was going to be drafted anyhow so I signed up in the medical corp. and asked to be shipped overseas to active duty. That's when I joined the front line as a medic in France. We were giving them hell! The will of the German army seemed to be crumbling as they turned in swift retreat all across France into Belgium; but we knew that the Jerries weren't through yet, that sooner or later they would make a stand and then we would be really tested. It happened in Belgium in the famous 'Battle of the Bulge'. They dug in and put up the fiercest resistance in a desperate attempt to stop the Allied advance. I remember during that battle I had to go in and out of the line of fire to help the wounded. It was on the third day of battle I was crossing a creek to get to a wounded G.I. and saw a blinding flash...a blinding flash..."

At this point Bill seemed to have lost his concentration and stared blankly for a few minutes... then he shook his head slightly and gave the floor to Gene.

"As for me," said Gene, "you know how I felt about the Air Force, not that I had anything against the other branches but I just had to fly! You don't know what it's like up there in the clouds! It's so beautiful and peaceful like you're among the angels, that is when you're not looking for Messerschmitt 109s or you're not flying some dangerous mission over enemy territory. The German flyers were good but they were no match for our guys. I remember when we were sent on a mission to provide escort protection for our B-52s on a bombing mission over Berlin, a German fighter squadron came out of nowhere from 8 o'clock high and swooped down on the bombers. I was covering my squadron leader's wing in formation when we spotted the Luftwaffe fighters and we turned to intercept them. It was a real dogfight! A Jerry was on my commander's tail, and I maneuvered behind him and caught him in my line of sight. I scored a hit... but... at the same time... I didn't see another Jerry on my tail and all I tried I still couldn't shake him loose. I remember seeing smoke issuing from my fuselage... and I was going down... but I must have parachuted...sure I did...or did I? I can't seem to remember..." He sat down not quite sure of what did happen and continued with the question in his mind.

Norm, the only one not in uniform, had been sitting quietly throughout. He got up finally and confessed that he, unlike all the others, never served in the Armed Forces... not that he didn't want to, but because of his classification-- he had a bad heart.

"While you guys were risking your lives for your country," he said, "I was back home doing what I could to support the war effort. I tried to get in but they didn't want me; you see, they said it because of medical reasons or something. I got my law degree but it didn't stop me from organizing fund-raising drives to help the sale of war bonds, serving in the civilian volunteer corp., and giving my service wherever I could. I remember I was driving to Washington, D.C., to attend a special program for the war effort. I was on the highway just outside of Baltimore, Md. I guess I was less than a half hour from the capital. Somehow, though, I don't remember ever getting there. That's strange! I guess I must have turned around...unless...do you think..."

At that point, before he could ask or answer his own question, Tom interrupted him.

"Why are we all looking and acting so seriously? Is this a reunion or a wake? Come on, guys, we haven't seen each other for a very long time, remember? Let's tell some jokes or sing some songs or something."

They all agreed, and they carried on all night into the morning, singing and telling jokes, trying to make up for lost years, renewing their old camaraderie as if the events of the past 25 years had never happened, as if it was still June 5, 1940. Just before they left, each one of them took out his torn part of the twenty-dollar bill and they mapped them together like the parts of a jigsaw puzzle on the table.

Gene addressed the group.

"I guess we kept our pledge, didn't we, fellows?"

"Yeah, we all did!" they said in unison.

Then they all huddled around the table arms extended, hugging each other in a circle.

The next day, June 6, 1965, some kids were playing in the area which seemed to be deserted and run down. They were throwing stones and using the building for target practice. They would have broken all the windows, but somebody had beaten them to it. Besides, the windows that weren't broken were boarded up anyway. One of the boys in the group said something about the building.

"This old building would make a good hideout for us kids! Nobody uses it anymore. As far as I can remember it was always boarded up. What they boarded it up for anyway?"

"This used to be a nightclub before they closed it down," said another boy, "I heard my father talk about it".

"Look, there's a loose board, let's go inside!" said a third boy.

Inside they roamed around. It was a little dark but some daylight shone through the narrow openings sufficient enough to see that there was a counter and empty shelves behind it, a few tables and chairs, some broken. The whole place was dusty and clammy.

One boy made the following observation.

"I guess grown-ups used to come in here and drink up and party a lot at one time. This must have been some hangout!"

While they were exploring another boy noticed something on the floor. He picked it up and saw that it was an old brass button like the kind on soldiers' uniforms. Then he glanced on one of the tables and saw what looked like a twenty-dollar bill! He called his two pals and they, too, confirmed it.

One of the three boys remarked:

"What's a twenty dollar bill doing on the table?"

As he reached for it he saw that it was torn into five pieces as if someone had set the parts together on the table to try to reconnect them.

"This is very strange! Who would want to do that? You think we will be able to spend it?" he posed the question.

"Sure! We'll just tape it back together and it'll be just like new!" said another boy.

As they walked away from the abandoned building the boy who first discovered the twenty-dollar bill spoke again.

"We really are lucky. Twenty dollars! I'm sure glad you talked me into going into that abandoned building. We'll split the twenty-three ways, okay?"

Arms wrapped around each other's shoulders, and they walked away like it was just another event on an otherwise normal day, except that they were each a few dollars richer.

JAMES BAKER

He looked into the window directly facing him and saw a ghostly image. "It cannot be!" he said to himself in a state of denial. He tried to read a newspaper that was left on the seat beside him, but the pages were full of words and symbols that had no meaning, for he could not concentrate. He looked again at the image in the window and the imposter cynically smiled at him.

"It cannot be! It cannot be!" he repeated to himself over and over as he sat in the subway car heading to Manhattan.

Soon he closed his eyes and his mind started to drift. He was in "knickers" again, on a Sunday afternoon, sitting at the dinner table, his two older brothers facing him, his father seated at the head of the table and his mother next to him.

"Well, now," said his father, "have you boys given any thought about your future? What do you want to be when you grow up? Let's start with you Samuel, tell us what you would like to be and the reason for your choice."

"I want to be an electrician," said his eldest brother, Samuel, "so I can fix people's appliances and they would always have electricity to run things."

"I would like to open my own bank one day," said his second brother, Bill, "I want to be a banker so I can safeguard people's hard-earned savings and show them how to use their money wisely and invest in the future."

Then it was his turn.

"I want to be a minister," said James, the youngest, "so I can teach people about God, and how to love each other, and care for each other so there'd be no hate and greed and cruelty in the world."

His father was very pleased and praised all three of them for their choices.

He, James Baker, was so proud of himself! He remembered how he used to take seriously his duties as an altar boy at the St. Theresa Church on Sunday mornings, and, after mass how he would attend Sunday school classes. Reverend Peters, the pastor, and Sister St. Claire, his Bible teacher, used to say nice things to his parents about him and they were very proud of him. For reciting his catechism so well he would receive picture cards of saints and certificates of merits.

He so emulated Reverend Peters that he would often pretend to be like him, reciting after him some of the prayers that he memorized. He even learned to walk like him and talk calmly and politely the way he did. At home, he would ask to say the prayers over dinner and the grace after meals. How he looked forward to Sunday mornings, to wearing the acolyte's vesture and serving at mass, and going to Bible classes! It was the only world he knew then, a simple, ordered world as it seemed through the eyes of a ten-year-old. It was a sheltered world, indeed, and his role models were the first two persons who had influenced his life the most at that time, his father and the Reverend Peters.

For several years he continued on that path until just after his sixteenth birthday. He was not certain of the exact date; nevertheless, he began to skip mass and Sunday school, occasionally at first, and then more regularly until he stopped going altogether. As he approached adulthood, he became absorbed in other things, in other pursuits and pleasures. The days of serving as an altar boy on Sunday mornings were gradually left behind. It was just after his twentieth birthday, he remembered, that he set out on his own and left home. He went away to a big city in a big country where he found work and where he even obtained a college degree and pursued several career options. It didn't take him long to become totally immersed in the hectic, fast-moving pace of life in that big city and the years simply sped by. He learned how to survive and how to flow with the rhythms and realities of a fast-paced world, where Time is an ever-changing state of being, where experience is a cruel teacher, fate a fool's absolver, and flesh a manifestation of life reduced by the passage of time to a ghostly image in a mirror along the way in a subway train. To him, after many, many years had mysteriously passed by his physical transformation was hard to accept.

In his mind, the past seemed like a fairy tale from long ago. So long ago! What happened, he wondered, to the altar boy? The one who loved to recite his catechism every day and make his parents proud? He could not answer; it was now like a forgotten dream. Yet his conscience was real and found its voice at last. No longer pushed aside, no longer quieted by the dominant voices and forces in his life that for too long had ruled his will, his subconscious mind emerged from the quiet background at last and asserted itself. Now he was bound to listen, now with creeping senility overtaking him, now too late to reconcile the past, his weary flesh cringed in the grips of 'This-cannot-be' and 'what-might-have-been' and was forced to listen to his surging sub-conscious mind that now was no longer intimidated and spoke out loud and clear to him:

"Don't you remember?" said his weaker conscience. "Don't you remember what happened to the little boy, how he changed and how you let him get lost back there in a world of phantoms and phantom chasers? How else can you explain away the years that vanished so fast with nothing now to show for them? Phantom chaser indeed, don't you recall the many times when you entered through the glittering gates of temptation pursuing worldly pleasures and you were soon delighted and quickly deceived, like the foolish moth lured by the flame until consumed? How many times did you find yourself chasing on the wheels of chance the phantom Wealth? What arrogance men have who claw, cheat, kill to own her, only to know at last the final truth that they own nothing except what they brought naked into the world and will take with them after their brief sojourn? And Power, too, that most deceptive phantom of all phantoms! Did you not grasp at it in your feeble way, or wish that you could touch its mantle, or envy those who did, and curse the fate that made you powerless? Did you not do these things, James Baker? You should have listened to the prophets and not wasted your time, for those who seek power, blinded by it, only hide their human weaknesses behind its scepter, not knowing that the greater the power they seem to have, the greater the fall in the end, for mere mortals cannot shape a star, or breathe life into clay, or conquer death, and, such as do believe that they possess real Power only possess the key to self-destruction. Such claim to Power is nothing, for mankind cannot destroy that which it cannot create, nor create from nothing that which never existed, nor breach the ends of the universe, nor, with a thought, change water into wine! How many times, I ask you, did you not strut blinded by Vanity? Vanity, ah, yes, the parent of all phantoms that makes one see oneself falsely, that makes one wear a mask (one's real identity obscured), build monuments, pretend to be what one is not, and posture to the world of creatures like oneself, and act as if one could impress the sea, sun, universe, and, top it off, wage wars against one's own kind, from individuals to nations, whenever one's respective posture, or monuments, or masks are threatened by another? Vanity, therefore, what good is it, when all has turned to dust?

Be it, then, chasing after lust, Wealth, Power, Vanity, or whatever phantom, caught between the long ago, the yesterdays and tomorrows, skilled in all the reasons and excuses, all the good and bad times have passed, having vanished, 'midst all the fallen heaps, midst all the unrealized ambitions and dreams unfulfilled, what have you to say for yourself now, James Baker? I could gloat and say to you, yes, didn't I tell you so many times what would happen to you and you never listened? But what good would that do now?"

And so his sub-conscience admonished him very harshly till all that he could do was listen like a beaten rag doll or try his best to stop from thinking. Finally, he did, for he grew weary and all his thoughts faded, and he dozed off into a deep, deep sleep as the train sped on its way through Queens into Manhattan. It was somewhere in Manhattan when he thought he heard the conductor's voice over the loudspeaker:

"Next stop 116th Street!"

Instinctively he must have joined the crowd of people getting off the train. He was still drowsy and yet he seemed to make his way up the stairs to the street level. The air seemed so refreshing and clean! He felt an exhilarating vitality surge through his veins. He looked around and felt strange, however. The whole place was immaculate; he had never seen the streets so clean! There was no graffiti anywhere, no boarded up and gutted houses, no junkyards, dirty lawns, no beggars, panhandlers, hustlers, drug addicts, pushers, prostitutes anywhere. The whole neighborhood had changed; the houses and yards vied with each other in attractiveness. There was a sense of serenity, security, a sense of peace and harmony and love. People passing by were beaming with contentment and love as they were going and coming with a purpose and a friendly smile. Just then he felt a tap on his shoulder.

"Reverend James Baker, I've been waiting ever so long for you. What took you so long?"

A little startled, he turned to greet his welcoming committee, "Uh, oh ... Thank you! ... Who...?"

"I am Deacon Frye, I came to meet you! I was worried! We've got to hurry; they're waiting at the church."

"Waiting at the church?" he thought to himself, "maybe I had been dreaming all along, and just now woke up! Yes, it all made sense!"

Deacon Frye and Reverend Baker started to walk towards the church which was only a couple blocks away. "Deacon," said Rev. Baker, "will you do something for me?"

"Yes, reverend."

"Pinch me hard, please, Deacon Frye. Don't think I'm crazy, just pinch me hard!"

He wanted to make sure that this was really real! Poor deacon was confused, but he did what was asked of him.

"Thanks," said the Rev., "and tell me one more thing, deacon," he continued, "how long have you known me?"

"Why, why, Rev. ever since you had been our pastor these past fifty years! I was a little boy when you first came to our church and you taught me a great deal, don't you remember, Rev.?"

"Yes, yes, deacon, I was just wondering how time has flown, that's all!"

"Yes, it certainly has," said Deacon Frye.

After walking about ten minutes they arrived at the church where to his surprise a crowd of people were gathered, apparently waiting for his arrival. Inside the church was packed; it was not a regular service, but a special program in his honor. He had preached his last sermon only a few weeks ago; now the entire community came out to honor him on his retirement. This would be his last official day as their pastor. When he and Deacon Frye entered the hall there was a rousing applause by the whole congregation who were on their feet. Reverend Baker was moved to tears as the applause lasted several minutes. During the applause his mind flashed back to the time when he was a little boy and he had made a promise to his father, also to his early years when he had served as an altar boy. He had kept his pledge.

If only his father could see him now! He sat in the seat of honor as the ceremony proceeded and the singing, speeches and different items on the program were rendered. They highlighted all the good works he had done to teach and lead his congregation, all the changes that came about because of him, how the lives of the people had changed, how the community had changed, and they were so proud and happy! Even though they were rejoicing on this day, however, they were sad that it had come, for it meant that he would be leaving them. It was such a beautiful program. He was particularly moved when a group of small children gave a rendition and one after another thanked him for everything he had done to make their lives better and their future brighter; and they sang for him after reciting speeches.

At the height of the children's rendition, the imposter in the mirror reappeared, only this time there was a golden crown on his head, his face was bright, and there was no look of cynicism, but a warm smile and a look of admiration and sublime satisfaction. The wrinkles were gone, and the gray was turned to gold as if blending with the crown on his head. This time he did not mind, he did not chase the image away, he did not reject what he saw, he was more than overjoyed.

While the children were still singing, and his mind was still joyfully meandering, it appears he was so moved by the experience that he started swaying and clapping like the rest of the congregation, with the rhythm, when he felt a gentle force at his side and he heard a soft and sublime voice in his ear.

"It is time to go home, James Baker! It is time to go home!"

Then all at once everything was quiet and peaceful, as the singing ceased, and the soft voice gradually faded away…; but, almost at that same instant James Baker could not know that someone else was shouting with all his might, yes, in a loud, inhumane voice that, fortunately, no matter how loud the shouting, it would never be able to shatter his ear drums as the conductor came closer, repeating:

"Wake up! Wake up, mister! This train is heading to the yard!!..."

The conductor reached out his hand to nudge him; then he suddenly realized that the gray-haired, old gentleman could no more hear him even if he shouted 'till kingdom come, as, falling forward from his seat, James Baker had indeed gone home! Good night, James Baker!

THE BUS

A group of passengers were traveling in a bus on a highway through a barren, desolate countryside late in the evening, after dark; and, as they seemingly sped along at the speed permitted in that region, for a very long while no one said a word or made a sound. They were all sitting quietly, sleeping, or thinking, or gazing out into the darkness. The bus must have been traveling for hours and hours until, finally, one man spoke. He had been sitting quietly, wide awake, for a very long time, but now he could hold it in no longer.

"What are we doing here?" he asked. "Will someone please tell me what we are doing here and why, for God's sake, are we on this bus?"

He paused, with his eyes wide open, mouth gaping as if expecting an answer; but everyone just looked at him in a rather strange way.

He continued, "What madness is this? Doesn't anybody know why we are here?"

Then he turned to one of the other passengers, an old man, and said,

"You, sir, would you tell me what you are doing on this bus?"

"Why…why…I…I…" replied the old man.

"See what I mean, he doesn't know why he is here! Can't somebody give me a sensible answer?" Turning to a younger man he said, "You, young man with the earphone stuck in your ears, what are you doing on this bus?"

"What you say? You talking to me…you talking to me, man?"

"Yes, I'm talking to you! I said, why are you on this bus, and where are you going?"

"Well, now, the fact that I am here and not some place else, must mean that's the reason, man, and as for the second question, I got to be going someplace 'cause we ain't standing still, are we?"

"There is another example! All doubletalk but he doesn't know from A to Z what he is doing here. I doubt that he even knows who he is, or where he is, much less why he is here!"

Suddenly another passenger, a young lady, spoke up, "Why are you asking us these questions anyway? Why don't you ask yourself why you are here? Tell us why you are here!"

"Why would I be asking a question if I knew the answer?" he said to her.

"What? Didn't you know when you first got on the bus what you were getting on the bus for, and where you were going?"

"You think you're smart don't you!" he replied, "Well then tell me, did you see me get on this bus? Did you see anybody else, for that matter, get on this bus? Can you tell me where you got on this bus? I bet you can't even tell me that?

"What a silly thing to say! Why sure I can! I..., I..., I..." and without finishing her sentence she sat down and didn't say another word.

At that moment a man who said he was a retired lawyer made the following remark, "Why is it important to know why we are here? Would it make any difference? Would it change anything?"

"Why is it important? Of course, it is important," said the first man. "If we don't know why any of us is here, then we might as well not exist because you, me, none of us would have any meaning or purpose!"

"That's just the point," said the lawyer, "maybe we don't! For all we know, we don't even exist. Maybe we are just a weird dream in somebody's head and aren't even real! As soon as the dreamer awakens, poof, all our troubles will be over!"

"I wish it were as simple as that, really, I do. But if that were true, we would have no past or future, nor substance. Yet I know I have a past! I am somebody! I can feel! I can think!"

"Alright, you are somebody and you have a past, then what was the last thing you were doing before you found yourself on this bus, or even yesterday, or the day before for that matter? Just where were you? And what were you doing? That is your past, isn't it? So tell us what you remember!"

"That's easy... let me think... Let me think. I remember I...I remember I was... I was...What the hell's happening to me? I can't even remember where I was or what I was doing before I got on this bus."

At this point an elderly lady said to him, "Young man, why do you torture yourself like that? Why don't you take it easy and stop thinking so much? Sooner or later it all has to come to an end. It's no use to worry! Sit down and enjoy the ride!"

Then a white goateed, bespectacled man, a professor who was sitting at the back of the bus listening to everything called out and said, "Wait a minute, maybe I can solve this mystery! I have a theory as to why we are here. Have you ever heard of mass hypnosis? The reason you can't remember anything, or anybody else can't for that matter, is because we have been hypnotized, all of us! It must be the air that we breathed when we entered the bus, or something in the air condition that caused it. Look outside, even though it is dark, all you can see is the shadows of trees and open land. I believe we are being taken somewhere against our will for what purpose I don't know!"

What the professor said disturbed everyone and almost started a pandemonium until the first man calmed them down, "What are you trying to do, cause a panic? Are you trying to get us all killed? Calm down! I think we should ask the bus driver where we are going before we all get excited!"

Just then someone said, "Quiet everybody! … Quiet! Listen to what the driver is saying over the CB. They talk to each other all the time, you know, these bus drivers!" then everybody was quiet as they listened.

"Hey, Mac! How's it on your end, buddy!" said one chauffeur.

"Everything is fine! Road's wide open, ain't nothing moving as far as the eyes can see. What's your cargo tonight, Billy Boy! What you got?"

"Oh I got about 40 or so, not a bad load at that; but they're acting a bit restless right now. How about you? What you got, Mac?"

"'Bout the same as you, Billy Boy! Looking forward to some hot coffee and chow! Ten-four, Billy Boy!"

"Ten-four Mac! See you later!"

"See what I told you," said the first man, "the driver knows where we are going!"

"Yeah, ask him, ask him," they all said in unison!

The first man approached the driver, "Billy Boy, where you taking us? We all would like to know where you're taking us?"

"What you mean, where I'm taking you? Every one of you bought a ticket that says where you're going. Look on your ticket receipts and don't be bugging me before you make me wreck this bus!"

They all looked for their ticket receipts, searching in their pockets, their wallets, their pocketbooks, but nobody could find a receipt. That was strange! Very strange, they thought!

So the first man went back to the driver and said, "Look, Bill Boy, something strange is going on here, nobody can't seem to find their receipt!"

"Well, I ain't got nothing to do with that, all I know is I didn't let nobody on my bus unless they had a ticket!"

"Yeah," said the first man, "well if that's the case, then you've got all the tickets or stubs. Where are the tickets you collected? Show them to us!"

"Where are the what? Where are the what? What tickets? What stubs? What are you talking about?" Then he paused and said, "Come to think of it...you're right, I should, .. but I don't! I mean...I mean...Maybe you...better sit down...When you get to...terminal...ask all the questions... you like...don't know...don't know...I...I..."

So the first man went back and told the people, "The bus driver is crazy! He doesn't know any more than we do! We got one of two choices, we can wreck the bus (cause he's not stopping no matter what we say), or we can wait until we reach wherever we're going and speak to the management. Somebody will have to give us an explanation one way or the other!"

Most of them thought that that was a good idea, but one woman said, "Wait a minute now! That means that you think the professor is right. But what if he is wrong and we are not hypnotized as he said. After all, I never heard of air in a bus or air condition hypnotizing people. That's not how people are hypnotized at all! And I don't buy the other theory about being in somebody's dream, either!"

"Then what is your theory? Do you have one?" asked the first man.

"Well," she said, "look at it this way. We are all on the bus and we don't know why we are here or where we are going. We don't know how we got on the bus. People are not apt to forget such things. This is not real!...although some people would say, how do we know anything is real, and that we have been walking around in a dream all our lives anyway, making up things and calling it real, or they might say, its just as well we don't remember what never existed; but I'm not into metaphysics!"

"Yeah, well get to the point! What is your theory?" they demanded of her.

"Alright, this is what I think. I think we are all dead! In another dimension, in limbo, somewhere, and we've lost all past consciousness! I think it wouldn't matter if we jumped off this bus, or ran it off a cliff, or put a bullet in our heads, we can't die because we're already dead! We are 40 lost souls in purgatory!"

"Well," said the first man, "That's a fine theory, but nobody's going to test it, 'cause I am sure not going to jump off this bus or shoot myself to find out. You, Ms Smarty, you jump off and anybody else with you! Anyone else has any more theories or bright ideas?"

No one answered, and they all started to look at him again in a rather strange way, as, one by one they resumed sitting quietly, sleeping, or thinking or gazing out into the darkness as the bus seemed to speed on its journey on a lonely highway in a lonely countryside. The first man, too, finally became weary, and he, too, at last sat down quietly, wide awake, staring into nowhere!

Before you knew it, it was daybreak and daylight shone through every window of the house. A little boy yawned and rubbed his eyes as he awoke from an alarming dream that he had during the night. He had to go and see if everything was alright. First, he rushed to the bathroom and freshened up and dressed. Then in a little while you heard the sounds of happy greetings and voices coming from very close by. It was the sound of the little boy and that of an older person, his father, who said to him, to the boy's delight, "Alright, son, you have permission! You can go ahead but remember breakfast will soon be ready!" And the boy burst into the room where there was a huge model of a country landscape and highways and hills, and little toy greyhound buses with toy people inside. It was a model he and his father had put together several days ago. There was one toy bus that seemed to have fallen into a ravine and capsized. The boy carefully picked it up and set it on the highway again pointing north, and he carefully picked up the first man, the professor, the young woman, the retired lawyer, the old man, etc., each little toy person, and carefully set them in their seats again in their imaginary and unreal world, but a world nevertheless that in the mind of a little boy was real and brought him so much joy and happiness!

MOST UNFORGETTABLE CHARACTERS

CARUSO

When I was twelve years old the little town of La Boca, C.Z. was the most exciting place on earth to me. A day never went by without some adventure from the moment I awoke in the morning until curfew at seven in the evening. My youthful eyes and ears and heart were drunk with the fullness of life and activities that this little town afforded.

Playing ball in the yard between the houses or on the school playground, going on mango walks, climbing trees, even the tallest coconut palm trees, playing "platillos" on the sidewalks, roller skating in the streets, flying kites on windy days, and when it rained, playing marbles under the cellars, not to mention that raiding people's vegetable gardens, or hunting wild animals in the bushes, or swimming or fishing in the Pacific Ocean were enough to fill our itinerary. But aside from such adventures, there was also the treat of observing festive events like the Salvation Army Band marching on San Domingo Street on Sunday mornings with Ms Agard in the lead playing her triangle, cymbals and tambourine, or on Labor Day the Labor Day parades with union workers with banners and posters and, afterwards when the parades were over, the beer fests on the ball ground; and at other times there were the amateur baseball games, cricket and soccer games, and track and field meets in the ball park. No, a nine-, ten- or twelve-year old could never find life dull.

In 1939 my family moved to San Domingo Street, building 1032 that housed 12 families. We lived in a second-floor apartment in a two- story frame house. Next to our apartment on one side was the Codrington family, and on the other side the Braithwaites (a very kind and religious 7th Day Adventist couple); and next to the Braithwaites were the Bests and next to them the Youngs and next to the Youngs the Pickerings. Downstairs in the corner apartment beneath the Codringtons were the Collins, and beside them were the Joneses, then the Yearwoods, then the Lashleys and lastly, the Watleys who lived in the other corner apartment downstairs.

Across San Domingo Street facing our building was house #1030. Upstairs lived the Grants, the Hobbs, the Davises, and the Harrisons and downstairs were the Johns, the Bascombs, the Clarkes and the Husbands who lived in the corner apartment facing the intersection of St. Thomas Street and San Domingo Street in front of the corner streetlamp. Caruso lived in the Husbands' apartment and this story is about Caruso.

It had to be a rainy day when you saw dark clouds hovering in the sky all morning and when it rained in La Boca it really rained. Torrents came down all day, off and on, sometimes for days. I remember, as children we used to sit on the porch and sing, "Rain, rain, go away, come again some other day. Rain, rain, go away, come again some other day!" And as soon as it would let up we would run into the streets and sail our paper boats in the gutters that were flooded. Mostly, though, on rainy days we would play marbles under the cellar, or shooflao with soda bottle caps. Some of us would even run about in the rain which on humid days would cool us off quite a bit despite our being soaked to the bone.

One rainy day was special because of Caruso. Who was Caruso? Caruso was a parrot and John-John Husband's favorite pet that he was so proud of, that is, until they fell out. Let me go back to the beginning and start from where this parrot became a favorite pet. I believe John-John, or his brother, Shorty, caught him in the wild when he was young and brought him home. There are a lot of parrots in the wilds of Panama and Central America. Anyway, this one was a green parrot, a cockatoo I believe, I am not sure.

When Caruso first came to the civilized environment of 1030 San Domingo Street, La Boca, Canal Zone, he was a quiet parrot at first, perhaps because he was homesick or scared of these strange-looking people who had captured him and forced him into captivity to live in their strange kind of world (At least to a parrot). After a little while, though, he would screech and scream like parrots do in the wild; and as time passed and they continued to feed him well and to take good care of him, he became domesticated and employed his pipes a lot more. After he heard all that chatter going on in the apartment, he started mimicking what he heard. One morning he spoke for the first time.

"Good morning to you, aaaaaak! aaaaaak! aaaaaak! Good morning to you."

And everybody thought that that was amazing, so John-John started encouraging him to speak and taught him to say things.

"My name is Caruso, my name is Caruso. What is your name?"

Then John-John decided to teach him a song learned in school.

"Row, row, row your boat gently down the stream, merrily, merrily, merrily, merrily life is but a dream" over and over and over again.

Then he started whistling the tune and Caruso imitated him in harmony until he had it down so pat, he couldn't stop singing, living up to his famous name.

Then John-John started singing and whistling a favorite new tune in the morning.

"Somewhere over the rainbow, way up high,

There's a land that I heard of once in a lullaby.

Somewhere over the rainbow, skies are blue,

And the dreams that you dare to dream,

Really do come true."

And that's when they knew that Caruso had an exceptional ear for a parrot. Out of the clear blue he would sing the tune just as John-John did (only sweeter) and then he would whistle it afterwards. They were so amazed!

Sometimes while we boys and girls in the neighborhood were playing on the sidewalk and in the street, we would hear the parrot singing and we couldn't believe our ears. It was beautiful. And every time we heard Caruso sing, we would stop and listen in wonderment.

"Someday I'll wish upon a star,

And wake up where the clouds are far behind me.

Where troubles melt like lemon drops,

High above the chimney tops,

That's where you'll find me..."

But as Caruso grew older and learned more words and phrases, they also found out that they could not always control what Caruso would say. On several occasions in the morning, he would hear Mrs Husband reprimanding John-John and his brother. After that guess who took over?

"Get up, get up, you lazy bastards…Get up…You going to be late for school!! You're going to be late for work!!! …aaaaaak …aaaaaak ….aaaaaak." It was Caruso mimicking Mrs Husband.

Then another time you heard an unpleasant remonstrance from Edmund Husband to his wife and that, too, was added to his repertoire.

"Matilda…Matilda…where me damn socks? ... Where me damn socks? Me can't find nothing in this place….aaaaaak …aaaaaak ….aaaaaak." That was Caruso again mimicking.

And another time you heard a female voice.

"You blind bajan, yuh, it right in front yuh face. Even a bat can see bettah than you...aaaaaak...aaaaaak ...aaaaaak." Caruso again.

And when Mr Husband came home late one evening from gallivanting or whatever, as he had done a few times before, and he was trying not to attract attention, he heard a strange voice call out.

"Hey Mr big Nuts, Hey Mr Big Nuts so you come home at last, where yuh been? Where yuh been? ...aaaaaak...aaaaaak ...aaaaaak."

Then one day John-John and his older brother Shorty had a fight and Shorty was so mad he said a lot of things he regretted. John-John, too, had called his brother a short-ass numbskull. Later on when they were eating supper they heard a voice coming from the kitchen.

"You f.....g son-of-a-bitch....You f......g son-of-a-bitch...A going teach you a lesson...aaaaaak ...aaaaaak...aaaaaak."

And then you heard some sweet renditions following in succession.

"Row, row, row your boat....gently down a stream...

merrily, merrily, merrily, merrily,

Life is but a dream...." followed by:

"Somewhere over the rainbow, blue birds fly,

birds fly over the rainbow,

Why then, oh why can't I?

If happy little bluebirds fly beyond a rainbow

Why, oh why can't I?"

Now they were all beginning to have mixed emotions about Caruso, and they didn't know what to do, whether to love that bird or to kill him. Was this bird so smart that he was playing them like that? Or were they the ones to blame for being so careless about the things they said and did in front of a talking parrot? They should be a little more careful about such things.

The next morning when they woke up Caruso greeted them as he always did, except this time he changed some of the words in the greeting. To Mrs Husband he said,

"Good morning, Matilda my love!"

"Good morning Caruso!" replied Mrs Husband.

To Mr Husband he said:

"Good morning Mr Big Nuts!"

Mr Husband didn't answer.

To Shorty he said:

"Good morning short-ass numbskull."

And to John-John he said:

"Good morning yuh f…..g son-of-a-bitch."

Well, I am afraid Caruso was in the doghouse after that, but he made one more fatal misstep, his last one, that really cooked his goose. Mrs Husband had a practice of portioning out the meat at dinner time so that there was exactly the right amount for each person and so that the biggest portion was reserved for her husband, the master of the house. That evening when she was cooking dinner and was preparing some sumptuous lamb chops, just before Mr Husband came home John-John was snooping around in the kitchen when Mrs Husband had stepped out briefly. He couldn't wait for dinner. That lamb chops smelled so good! He sneaked into the kitchen and lifted up the pot cover and gingerly took a piece of meat, carefully dividing the biggest piece into two parts so the number of pieces would remain the same minus the piece he stole. Oh he enjoyed that lamb chops so much and when he was finished he sneaked back out of the kitchen.

Now it was almost time for dinner and Mrs Husband was about to serve it but when she looked into the pot, she couldn't find the big piece of meat that she had set aside for her husband. And then the misstep occurred. Caruso looking down from his perch in the kitchen cried out:

"Aaaaak….aaaaak….John-John   went   in   the   pot. Aaaaaak ….aaaaaak…John-John went in the pot and steal piece of the meat ….aaaaaak….aaaaaak. John-John ate the meat… John-John ate the meat."

Mrs Husband turned to the family seated at the table and said,

"Well, now, John-John, you won't be getting any meat today. You already ate your share." And she gave her husband the two pieces that John-John had divided.

After that evening it was very strange. We never heard any more bell canto singing coming from the Husbands apartment. Days, weeks, and months went by and we didn't hear Caruso the singing parrot again, and he was never seen ever again. Poor Caruso! I wonder what happened to him.

LAMB

In the early 1940's the Panama Canal Zone softball leagues were organized by the workers in the silver towns on both the Atlantic and Pacific sides of the Canal. Each labor division was represented by a team, such as the Commissary Division, the Electrical Division, the Mechanical Division, Supply Division, etc. and they played in the ball parks every day after work as well as on the weekends during the dry season or summer months (mid-December to mid-April). In La Boca, Canal Zone, for example, I remember when I was 12 years old my brother Hubert played for the Electrical Division team. He was a catcher and although he was not big and muscular, he protected home plate like any giant if anybody tried to run him down on a close play at the plate. He was not intimidating, neither was he ever intimidated. He could take a licking and could dish it out as well. Those young men in the prime of their youth played the game of softball hard and they liked to celebrate equally as hard after the game was over, especially if they won. One evening when my brother and his teammates were hanging out after a game, which they did a lot, with a good supply of Balboa beer on hand, they were joking and posed to each other the question: "What animal do you compare yourself with on the base paths during a game?"

"I am like a gazelle because I am fast!" said Clifford Nurse.

"I am like a lion because I am fierce and aggressive," said Willie Raveneu.

"I am like a bandit because I like to steal bases," said George Griffith.

And they chewed George out because a bandit is not an animal, but he said he didn't care; he was a bandit anyway. So they went on to the next person.

"I am like a bear because you'd better get out of my way or I'll run you over!" said Harry.

Then it was my brother Hubert's turn and with a sheepish grin he said:

"I am like a lamb!"

And they laughed and asked him why he chose a lamb.

"Because when I come to bat I am always asked to sacrifice to move runners over!" was his answer. And from that day they gave him the nickname "Lamb."

My oldest brother, Hubert Michael Evans, otherwise known as "Lamb," was not a great scholar, never earned any degrees, never went to college nor held

161

any high positions. He was not wealthy and famous and yet he was a very special human being. When I was a little boy I used to call him my "big brother." He was always there to protect and fight for me if I was ever in trouble. He had the bravest and the most courageous heart. He would fight the biggest bullies and would not back down from anyone. He took bullies on, win, loses or draws to defend his honor and his little brother. One evening after school, I recall, a certain bully named "Putty Knife," because he was angry for some reason or other or just because he was just plain ornery, hit me and knocked me down. As he was going to swing at me again, I don't know from where Lamb came from but he jumped onto Putty Knife, who was much bigger and more muscular and traded blows with him, tussling and rolling over on the ground. Rising to their feet Putty was getting the better of him and punched him several times; but Lamb didn't care, all he wanted was to get in one good punch which he was able to do finally and knocked Putty Knife squarely on his chin so hard that he caused him to buckle just before several grown men stepped in and stopped the fight. I heard my brother swearing with clenched fists as they separated the two pugilists:

"Don't ever put your hands on my brother again! I'll kill you!"

In truth, I don't think that in the end he could have beaten Putty Knife if they hadn't stopped the fight. But you couldn't tell that by his courage and indomitable spirit. He was never going to quit unless he stopped breathing. During the fight Putty Knife's jaw was broken from the punch that Lamb threw, but since Putty Knife's jaw was so hard Lamb's hand was fractured. When we got home and my father saw his face and hand he was very angry with him of course.

"Boy, who you fight with that you come home all bruised and battered like this? I hardly recognize you!"

And Lamb replied,

"Yes, pa, but if you think I look bad you should see the other fellow!"

And after he explained what happened and that he was only trying to protect his little brother as my father had told him to always do, my father softened up and told him to go and clean himself up and take care to soak his hand in Epsom salt and warm water.

There was another side to Lamb. Throughout his life he was the most down-to-earth, the most jovial, loveable, most friendly person I ever knew. Years later when I visited him in Siquirres, Costa Rica, where he lived with his second wife Maria for many years before moving back to Panama, he would take me around the town and introduce me to everyone on the street, in the marketplace, in the shops, in the restaurants, and in the homes. Whenever there was a housewarming or a birthday party in Siquirres he was invited. He knew everybody in that town and everyone knew and liked him. I thought of calling him the unofficial mayor of Siquirres at one time, the way he knew and got along so well with everybody.

His wife Maria was born in Costa Rica and attended college there and even got a teaching license. In 1975 she was spending time in Panama when she and Lamb met for the first time and fell in love they got married and he moved to Costa Rica with her. Maria being a native of Costa Rica and being fluent in Spanish made the adjustment very easy for him. She and Lamb lived in a small cottage near the outskirts of the town of Siquirres and within walking distance of the town where they went almost daily to shop and socialize. In their home, she would teach the local children English and typing (mecanografia). She was also an excellent cook.

"Hey, cunado," she would say to me, "I'm going to cook you something special while you are staying with us, 'arroz con pollo con habichuelo con Salza lizano (chicken and rice with black beans served with a special Costa Rican sauce named lizano.)"

And I could see why Lamb left Panama to go and live with Maria in Costa Rica. She took excellent care of him.

Lamb was such a gregarious person. He loved people and loved to make them laugh. He was always telling jokes. He made you see the humorous side of life. That was a special gift that he had. I remember I would call him on the telephone from New York City and he wouldn't stop telling me his latest jokes until I had to remind him that it was a long-distance call. He would make jokes about things that you and I wouldn't even think of. He could look at a cockroach crawling on the wall and make a joke about it. He could look at a clothesline and crack a joke, or a roll of toilet paper. I bet many of you never thought you could make jokes about such things. He could! I even suggested to him once that he should write his jokes down and mail them to me so that one day I could help him write a book of jokes and become famous. He got a kick out of that! I loved my brother. Around him, I forgot about my troubles and how hard life can be, and I learned not to take myself too seriously.

He came to New York to visit me once, in 1971, years before he moved to Costa Rica when he was living in Panama and I was living on St. Marks

Ave., Brooklyn, N.Y. I lived in a one-bedroom apartment with a kitchen, living room, bedroom, bathroom, and a little foyer at the entrance. He stayed with me for three weeks and during that time we hung out together when I came home from work and on the weekends. I remember one day I left for work and when I returned in the evening the apartment looked new and shiny! He had shellacked the floors of the whole apartment and did such a great job by himself that I was amazed and speechless. We didn't eat-in that evening; I took him out to dinner and we stayed out all night partying which helped the apartment to dry. It looked so fine that the following weekend I had a party in his honor and celebrated with him and a few friends whom I had invited. He got a kick out of that.

While he was staying with me, on several occasions I would accompany him to New York City to visit one of his girlfriends from Panama who lived in upper Manhattan. He was still more vigorous than back in the 70s. Sometimes I would leave him there overnight and the next day he would call me to come and pick him up. When he came home he would kid with me and ask me repeatedly the same question which he liked to ask.

"How are the girls treating you? When was the last time you got some?"

This was his way of ribbing me and teasing me in a jovial brotherly manner. He knew I didn't like to brag about such things, and I didn't want to 'show him up' so I just smiled. Even up to a couple of months before he died in the year 2003 when I spoke with him on the telephone, he would ask me the same question:

"By the way, did you get some lately?"

Of course, I knew what he meant and I always laughed! He could always make me laugh!

I had visited him twice in Costa Rica since he had moved there with his second wife, Maria, who was fluent in Spanish and English and who treated me royally whenever I visited. We corresponded often and we spoke a lot on the phone as the years went by. But in the year 2000 Maria suddenly took ill and died. Her passing may have had some effect on his health, we will never know, but his health began to deteriorate after that and he wasn't doing too well. He developed a heart condition and was hospitalized in the Limon hospital. When he was released from the hospital, he was too frail and was living alone, so my other brother in Panama, Kinkerd, and I decided that since he was still a Panamanian citizen one of us should go and bring him back to Panama to live where he could be taken care of. Kinkerd went across the border to Costa Rica and brought him back to Panama to live with him and his wife, Theresa, where his health began to improve. He was seeing a doctor regularly and was taking pills for his heart condition. But in spite of his condition, he never lost his sense of humor.

Another side of my brother was his love for dogs. He loved them and they loved him back by the way they seemed to gravitate towards him. There were several dogs in the house in Parque LeFevre and he called each one by a boy or girl name and they always seemed to understand every word he said to them. Whenever I called from New York to speak to him I could hear the sounds of dogs barking. I knew he loved dogs from back in Siquirres where he kept a couple of them that he was very fond of. So, as he was talking to me on the phone I heard him speaking to one of the dogs.

"Come and say hello to your uncle. Tell him to bow wow two times."

And the dog barked twice, "arf, arf" into the telephone. Then he said to me,

"That's Charlie! He said 'Hello.'"

Lamb spoke to dogs like they are people.

"Butch," he said to another one of them, "Go and keep watch by the gate!" And the dog would get up and go outside and go by the gate and squat there and never move unless someone was coming near the house then he would summon all the other dogs from wherever they were and they all came running toward the gate to join him, ready to defend the property.

Then there was Portia who was the mother of all of them. Lamb spoke to Portia.

"Go and get Charles and bring him here to me!"

Then she went outside and in a few minutes she came back and Charles was with her.

"Charles," said Lamb, "didn't I tell you not to poop inside the house? Don't ever do it again! Go outside the gate next time you want to poop. Now get in the corner over there and sit down and don't move till I tell you!"

Charles would bow his head and obediently creep to the corner and sit quietly in punishment.

And when they made sounds like 'woof' and 'arf' he knew what they meant. If the door was locked and they came and nudged him with their nose and then run to the door he knew they wanted to go outside and do something, so he let them out. The dogs had their hierarchy, too, and respected their mother, Portia, who would snarl and snap at them if they didn't behave when they were around her. They were like children and Lamb was like their grandparents. When he slept at night they all slept at the foot of his bed.

And the strangest thing: after Lamb passed away they all gathered in his room each night and lay there at the foot of his bed as if in mourning. Sometimes you heard slight moaning and whimpering sounds coming from the room as if they were calling to him as if they were saying how much they missed him.

I recall during the last few months he was alive, when he spoke to me on the telephone from Panama, he seemed a little anxious.

"When are you coming to Panama to see me? When are you coming?" he asked me.

Of course, I said soon; but I kept putting it off until finally, I went down in the year 2003 for the "Centenario" celebration of Panama's Independence from Columbia. I got to see him and my other brother, Kinkerd, and the three of us spent some quality time together again as three brothers. We travelled to various scenic sights, including Ancon Hill; we visited friends in Panama City, Rio Abajo, and Gamboa; we dined out a few times, and one day we visited our parent's gravesite together and placed some flowers there. And when I looked at him, and he leaned on me to keep from falling at the gravesite, I felt a loathsome foreboding.

Thinking about it now, I am very happy that I made that trip to Panama when I did, not for the celebration, but for the wonderful time we had, which was the last time we spent together. When I returned to New York, it wasn't two weeks before I received a phone call telling me that he had died of a heart attack. I was so hoping that I could return again to see him alive once more, but that was not meant to be. I shall miss my "Big Brother Lamb."

J. C.

When I first came from Panama to New York City, I took a lot of odd jobs while attending Brooklyn College at night. First, I worked in the garment district as a garment worker pushing garment racks through the streets of Manhattan, believe it or not. This job didn't pay anything, but it was a temporary job to satisfy a commitment my brother-in-law had made for me to get my visa when he sponsored me to come to the U.S.A. It wasn't long before I left there to go to work for a German Import-Export Company, Karl A. Neize, in Woodside, N. Y., where I worked as an office assistant taking orders over the phone and typing invoices, etc. The pay was a little better than the first job, and the title was an improvement.

Then I saw an ad in the papers for an office clerk to work in a screw, cylinder, valve, and rotary table manufacturing company out in Mineola, L. I., that required not only filing and typing but the ability to handle correspondence and respond to product inquiries, etc. The pay was much better than both of the previous jobs, and since I already had two years of college studies and felt secure with my spelling, grammar, and writing ability, I went and applied for the job. To make a long story short, I was hired by the Chief Engineer, J. C., to work as his Office Assistant (Correspondence Secretary, as it later turned out).

J.C.'s actual name was Jacque Claude Kelly, but they called him J.C., which he somehow didn't mind from people he tolerated; people he despised had to call him Mr. Kelly. I came to learn from many of the other workers that he was not a well-liked person in the company. They talked about him all the time behind his back.

"That S.O.B.," they would say, or "that f----ng white bastard," and they would swear, "Man, if I didn't need this job so bad, I'd...," and they didn't have to finish the sentence, you knew exactly what they meant.

Like the time when a shop supervisor messed up and machined a whole batch of screws to the wrong tolerance, you knew it wasn't going to go well for him because such a thing was never going to pass J. C.'s inspection. After he checked a few random samples and found the error, he almost threw the whole batch of screws at the supervisor's head and cursed him so badly in French, broken English, and four-letter words that the supervisor almost quit. If it wasn't for the owner, Mr. Albert, who talked him out of it, he would have done so. Anyway, J. C. had them do the whole job over again and work late that evening to get it done right. And that was what he did to a supervisor!

If he did that to a supervisor, imagine the contemptuous way he would have treated a lower rank employee.

Yes, J. C. was mean, hard, selfish, arrogant, insulting, and incapable of handling people with civility, and the meaning of kindness and compassion was not his understanding. Some people would not hesitate to tell you that if they were to meet him in a dark alley, they would send him back to Hades, where he came from. Those who had to meet him by choice other than their own were polite when they addressed him -- hiding a certain fear and contempt for him at the same time. They took his abuse, moreover, when their human fallibilities caused them to err, and they showed signs of weakness -- but, oh, they held back the wrath they felt! Countless were the curses sworn on his head (behind his back), and by what charm, they wondered, did he still exist, unchanged, cold, arrogant, abusive, intensely disliked as a human being? The gods must love him, they added, to have protected him so long from bodily harm!

All who knew J. C., though they may have disliked him, had to admit one truth, however: he was unusually intelligent. He was more. He was seething with energy; he was ambitious and extremely productive. In the C. K. Albert Manufacturing Co., he held the positions of Sales Manager, Chief Engineer, Chief Designer, and Chief Inspector. The company, an air cylinder, valve, screw, and hydraulic equipment manufacturing company, largely owed to him the fact that it did a volume of business ten times greater than it did four years before. There were over eighty people working in the plant alone, and the company had a long list of over a thousand distributors throughout the country who sold its products far and wide.

From the Sales Department all the sales campaigns were planned by the same man and a mass of correspondence was answered daily. All the new designs of new products were created on his table, and endless calls were answered by him daily. Besides, he often traveled to other cities on visits to distributors. I was often amazed at the amount of energy and ability he possessed!

J.C., the man disliked by so many, and understood by so few, stood about six feet tall; was very skinny; did not weigh more than a hundred and thirty pounds; had brown, somewhat dried hair, and, unlike the might and power of his raving voice (he was mostly shouting, especially when the question of who was at fault arose), his stature and appearance were frail, he was susceptible to mortal pains and colds, especially in the wintertime. He was of mixed Irish, French, and American stock but proud most of all of his French background — his mother was born in France, and his father was

Irish. His English was barely passable, and, in fact, he always abused the rules of spelling and good grammar. He did not deny it, though; in fact, he covered it up with: "My forte is French, not English"! He was right about that statement. I ought to know because ever since I was hired as his Office Assistant — and he found out that I could write almost flawless English and my grammar and spelling were superior -- he made me handle all his correspondence and type all his letters until I became an expert at translating his crab toe and scribblings into decent and respectable English.

O how he loved to write (I mean scribble) and pass it on to his translator-in-chief, who made him look like a scholarly writer — he was so elated with the final drafts I put before him for his signature that he almost forgot that it was I who was his grammarian and ghostwriter. I didn't mind, though, because there was a kind of tacit understanding between us that he would not attempt to abuse me the way he did the other employees. (I was his silent master, in a kind of way, and he knew it!)

In every other respect, though, apart from his character defects and his poor English, J.C. was the most brilliant, multitalented, workaholic, and productive person you could ever find. He often boasted of how he had to learn the hard way in France under the old apprentice-type set-up where his boss was a dictator, how he had to walk miles and miles to work, and it stung his gall to see how soft people were and how easily they got by in America. In fact, he said, he disliked most of all people who were too sentimental and wimpy, and he was hardest on them. Was J.C. as hard as all that? Wasn't there any tenderness in him at all? I used to wonder. One day in the summer of 1959, however, I found out.

I remember we were working late that evening to complete some back-orders, and I was sitting at my desk in the office typing his correspondence as usual when J.C. received a certain phone call. I knew that it was no ordinary phone call because J.C. was not yelling and swearing and carrying on as usual, but he was calm and was listening quietly during most of the conversation with the person on the other end. I couldn't hear clearly what was being said, but I only knew that what I witnessed shocked me out of my senses! J.C. suddenly burst into tears, livid, real, uncontrollable, mortal eye-water tears as he listened to the caller. I was sitting there dumbfounded! Was this the same hard, mean, unsympathetic, cruel person that I and everyone else knew? Crying so pitifully? I didn't know what to do! I felt that I had to do something, however, and quickly walked over to the door of the office and closed it from the inside so that no one could suddenly enter the office and see J.C. in that condition. Can you imagine what would have happened? His reputation would have been ruined! Then I walked over and handed him my handkerchief as the least I could do then. He took the handkerchief and reached out, and held on to me for support while sobbing uncontrollably like a baby.

"Boo…hoo! Boo…boo! Bobby died! Bobby just died! My precious little Bobby died! Poor Bobby, poor Bobby!...Boo…hoo! **Boo…hoo!"**

I was sympathetic.

"How sad," I said as I tried to comfort him.

I knew what it was like to lose a close relative; I had just lost my father only a few months ago. J.C., still sobbing, continued:

"Poor Bobby, poor Bobby, he was such a beautiful dog. Such a beautiful dog. I am going to miss him so much! Boo…hoo!…Boo…hoo!"

"What??? Did he say dog???" I said to myself. "Bobby is a dog?"

Was this the same hard, mean, cruel J.C. who hated weak and squeamish people, whimpering and sobbing like a child over a dog? The man came apart emotionally! Then all that veneer was just a fake, a masquerade! This must be the real J.C. after all, I thought. He is a sentimentalist and a softy in secret. Nevertheless, I tried to cheer him up as best as I could, and after he had calmed down a bit, he thanked me for what I did and made me swear not to say a word to anyone about this! He didn't want them to get the wrong impression. Actually, he didn't want them to know he was a "softy" or a sentimentalist at heart, but at least I knew it. The next day he went back to being his old hard-nosed, mean, arrogant, insulting self once more, showing no sympathy for weaklings and "softies." If the rest of the company only knew what I knew!

I think he trusted me, though, although he didn't have much choice, and he showed his deep appreciation to me from then on, for he made sure I got a raise in pay ever so often without my even asking for it! I was also given a new desk and a new telephone, and as long as I worked for C.K.A. Manufacturing Co., I received special treatment. Thanks, J.C.!

COLONEL PITTS

"Hey, sonny, mind if I sit beside you? You look like a clean-cut fellow. I bet you're an attorney or something! You know, you should get a briefcase. You would look like a big-time executive. All those executives do is carry a briefcase in their hands. Do you know why?"

"No. Why?" Jeff Collins responded.

"It's because they are carrying bologna, cheese, salami, and bread in their fancy briefcases so when nobody is looking, they can fill their stomachs! Heh! Heh! Heh!...No offense to you, though, if you're an executive."

Jeff smiled and assured him that he wasn't, and the remark didn't offend him in the least. His unsolicited neighbor then took further license to continue a friendly conversation that, it seemed, he would have done anyway, with or without Jeff's approval.

"Sorry," he said, "by the way, my name is Pitts, Colonel Pitts to you. What's yours?"

"Jeff Collins," Jeff said softly, having no desire to offend the intruder of his solitude.

"That's a nice name; it has a certain ring to it. You take the bus often?"

"No, as a matter of fact, this is my first trip to Atlantic City. I guess you're a regular customer?"

"You bet you! You can find me on this here bus any Saturday in the year, except maybe next week Saturday."

"What's special about next week Saturday?" asked Jeff.

"That's Veterans Day! Are you a veteran?"

"No!"

"Well, I am! Yes, sir, I'm a retired colonel from the Army...served in the Korean War, you know! Got a scar right here on my hip to show for it; want to see it, sonny?"

"That won't be necessary, I believe you!" answered Jeff.

"You know something? I like you! I like all colored people. I was raised by a West Indian lady named Mrs Bynoe in the Bronx, N.Y. You ever been to the Bronx?"

"Yes, a few times," responded Jeff (thinking to himself how he could get this colonel, what's-his-name to shut up?)

Just then, two old ladies sitting across from the colonel looked over to him, and they both made signs to Jeff (which Pitts didn't see) by twirling their fingers about their heads and pointing to the colonel, indicating that he wasn't right in the head. The colonel meanwhile must have sensed it and turned towards them. Before he could say anything to them, they spoke first.

"Why don't you stop bothering that nice young man? Can't you see he doesn't want to be bothered!" and they said to Jeff, "Don't pay him any mind, he's 'whacko'!"

But the colonel, not being the type to be discouraged, only took that to be an invitation to entertain the two old ladies, which he did with relish for the rest of the trip and for which Jeff quietly thanked them to himself as he laid back and dozed off.

After about an hour or so, Jeff felt someone nudge him on the shoulder.

"Wake up, sonny, we're in Atlantic City! Let's go and make a bundle!"

It was the colonel, all eager and still talkative. They got off the bus and briskly invaded the Trump Taj Mahal casino. Jeff then lost sight of the colonel as he and the ladies headed for the slot machines while Jeff went to play Blackjack.

Six hours later, at approximately 5:40 p.m. Jeff rushed back to the departure stalls out of breath because the bus was leaving in 5 minutes, 5:45 p.m. sharp! When he got there, the majority of people were already boarded, and it seemed that the Funaway bus was warming up to leave. He got to his seat, and someone was sitting in it. It was a rule, printed on the bus that each person must take the same seat he/she came in, so Jeff told the middle eastern looking man who was in his seat that he had to move. The man was reluctant at first, but he must have decided that Jeff was too big to tangle with, so he got up and went and sat in someone else's seat. Apparently, his seat was in the back of the bus, but he decided he wasn't going to sit there. The last few passengers soon got on the bus so that all were accounted for. Suddenly, just before it took off, there was a discussion behind Jeff. It seems that a lady was asking the middle eastern man to get up from her seat, and he refused! He should have known better than to mess with an old Jewish lady who knows her rights. She promptly called the bus driver to come and get the arrogant and presumptuous squatter out of her seat. It seemed to Jeff that there was going to be another Israeli-Arab war right there on the bus because the middle eastern man decided he wasn't giving his seat up to the Jewish lady no matter who told him to! Well, for 15 minutes, the bus stood there. The chauffeur sent for security to physically handle the matter because he wasn't driving off until the man got up and let the lady have her seat. By the time security police got there, the man wisely decided that he wasn't going to win this war and got up and returned to the back of the bus. The matter was resolved, and they finally took off from Atlantic City around 6:05 p.m.

Don't you know it that no sooner the excitement died down and they were on their way, Colonel Pitts started talking again. He was teasing the ladies and telling everybody he hoped they hadn't lost their rent money in the casino, that he knew a man once who not only lost his whole paycheck, his rent money, and his savings but he also lost his mind in Atlantic City.

"As for me," he said, "I lost a bundle, but I wouldn't lose my mind over that. It's only money!"

The ladies couldn't stand to hear him talk, and they embarrassed him.

"How in the world could you lose a bundle if you were only playing the penny machines all day? You should be ashamed of yourself for lying like that; you don't even have a bundle to lose!"

Well, they were on his case for the rest of the trip whenever he opened his mouth. Still, he seemed to enjoy the exchanges and eventually turned his attention to trying to win the two ladies over by sweet-talking them and amusing them until they reached their destination. The ladies got off the bus on Queens Blvd. around 56th Street, and Mr. Pitts even tried to get their phone numbers, but they wouldn't give him. They said, among other things, that he was "an old wolf and a crazy old fool!"

At the next stop, 72nd Street and Queens Blvd., some more passengers got off, leaving the bus half empty. At the stop after that, Continental Avenue and Queens Blvd., more passengers got off. Now there were only a handful of people left, including the Colonel. As the bus turned down Hillside Avenue heading toward 179th St., Jeff began to wonder about him and where he was getting off. As they came to the 179th St. bus stop, one by one, the passengers got off, including Jeff, because it was the last stop. He expected the Colonel to get off, too, but he didn't.

Jeff heard the bus driver say something to him.

"Hey, pops, this is the last stop! I'm taking the bus to the terminal."

He barely heard the Colonel's answer.

"I want you to take me to...and let me off there, please!"

"You know that's against the rules, pops!" the bus driver said.

And they kept on talking, but Jeff didn't hear the rest. It seemed that the Colonel, though, must have said something that made the driver decide to take him where he wanted to go as they drove off together and turned down Midland Parkway in Jamaica Estates, Queens. As Jeff walked along Hillside Ave. toward his home, he thought to himself that "Colonel Pitts is a strange character if I ever saw one! He got on the bus on Queens Blvd. when they left, and when they returned, he never got off but stayed on the bus past the last stop."

Two weeks later, Jeff decided to go back to Atlantic City and went to 179th Street and Hillside Ave. to meet the bus at 8:15 a.m. He met the same bus driver and decided to ask him, out of curiosity, about the Colonel. The bus driver said he would never forget the Colonel because he gave him $100 to take him to Midland Parkway near Grand Central Pkwy., which was only a few blocks out of the way, but for 100 bucks, he said he would have taken him anywhere! The driver also said he thought the old man was crazy at first, but when he returned to the bus terminal and told another driver what had happened, he told him that that was not the first time he had done that! In fact, several drivers said the same thing had happened to them. What's with this Colonel anyway?

Jeff was more than curious now and was hoping that the Colonel would be going to Atlantic City that week so he could find out more about him. But Colonel Pitts did not board the bus that Saturday, and Jeff had to wait until another time. A few days after he returned from Atlantic City, he was jogging on Midland Parkway early in the morning and saw an old man with a dog near Grand Central service road and Midland Parkway. He looked exactly like the Colonel, and Jeff was tempted to speak to him, but the man turned away from him and crossed the street. Jeff watched him as he climbed a stairway leading from the street level up a hill to a mansion that stood at the summit.

Jeff said to himself, "That son-of-a-gun!" and he shook his head. On his way back, he crossed the street, intending to pass by the stairs. He saw the mailman coming from the house and, just out of curiosity, stopped and talked to him.

"Good morning, sir! How are you today?"

"Fine," said the mailman, "I see you're getting your morning exercise!"

"Yeah, so are you with all the walking you must do every day!"

And the mailman smiled, nodding his head, and said,

"That's right!"

"I bet you also get to meet a lot of people on your route!" Jeff continued.

"Yes, and sometimes I meet some strange ones, too!" said the mailman.

"What do you mean?" asked Jeff, as if he almost knew what the mailman was going to say next.

"That old man, Dr. Jeffries, who lives in that fancy house, for example," the mailman said to Jeff, "is one of the strangest! He is very eccentric, you know. I don't even think he is a real doctor! Anyway, he doesn't practice medicine. He goes around impersonating different characters. If I didn't know him, he'd try to tell me he was a retired admiral or colonel or something."

"Colonel," said Jeff, "you mean he's not a retired colonel?"

"Of course not," said the mailman. "He never did a day's military service in his life! He's a rich, old eccentric who made money in real estate many years ago, and he lives by himself in that big house. Some mornings he'd get into a taxicab, and nobody would know where he was going, but he's not stingy, mind you! He's always generous to me around Christmas time!"

Two Saturdays after that, Jeff boarded the Funaway bus to Atlantic City, and, sure enough, when the bus stopped at Queens Blvd. and Continental Ave, the Colonel boarded it along with several other passengers. He sat beside Jeff and was his loquacious self as before.

"Hey, Sonny," he said to Jeff. "Going to try your luck once more, huh?"

Jeff looked at him long and suspiciously and slyly said:

"Yeah!"

The colonel then turned to another passenger on the other side of the aisle and started to tell him about the medals he got in the service, the different battles he had fought in, etc. Jeff then thought, "What a liar this Colonel Pitts is!" and he was tempted to blow his cover, but he didn't. The Colonel must have suspected that Jeff knew his true identity because, at one point, when he was telling the other passengers about his exploits, he looked over at Jeff and winked as if they were in 'cahoots' together. Jeff held back a smile and sheepishly thought, "What the heck, what harm can he do anyway?" and dozed off to sleep.

Sometime later, Jeff came to find out that that eccentric millionaire, though he traveled incognito using different aliases, was a philanthropist who helped a lot of poor people by anonymously giving them, through an un-named intermediary, large sums of money. His identity was kept a secret, and Jeff, for one, had no intention of changing that.

LOVE

JULIA

Julia Richards was only 19 when the Alvin Ailey Company came to Atlanta in 1972. At that time, she was already a talented dancer whose heart and soul were set on becoming a star. She ate, slept, and drank ballet and modern dance, emulating famous professional ballerinas and modern dancers such as Katherine Dunham, Josephine Baker, Judith Jamieson, etc. Julia performed with local dance groups, winning acclaim from local critics and theatre people. There was no doubt that she had a bright future as a dancer. It was only natural then for her to jump at the chance to audition for the Alvin Ailey Co. when they were in town. She was good enough to receive an offer to come to New York and join the company. But she and Jim Anderson, her fiancé, were in love with each other and were planning to get married. Jim realized, however, how much dancing meant to her, and he did not want to stand in her way, so they both agreed that she should take advantage of the opportunity even if their plans had to be postponed for a while. It was her chance to pursue her dream, and he would wait until she had given her career a chance to reach its full potential. When she felt the time was right, she would let him know. Meanwhile, they would correspond as often as possible. For three years, she never failed to write him regularly, at least once or twice a month; then, in 1975, her letters stopped coming. The first few months after he did not hear from her, he must have written her a dozen letters and waited in vain for an answer, but no letter came. When she had last written him, there was no indication that anything was wrong, nor was there any hint in any of the previous correspondence to cause concern. Now, however, he was completely lost for an explanation. Why hadn't he heard from her? What could be the reason she stopped writing him? It was affecting him and causing him to become more and more fearful and obsessed with the possibility that something terrible had happened to her. He could not work; he could not sleep at night; he was losing his grip on himself, wondering if she was all right. He could not continue this way. There was only one thing for him to do! He took a leave of absence from his job, packed his bags, and went to New York City to find Julia.

He arrived via Greyhound on a Friday evening in late July, checked into the New Yorker hotel, and, after considering his options, decided to visit the address where she had last written him from, 222 Edgecomb Avenue, N.Y. He found the super, who told him that Julia Anderson had moved out about six months before and did not leave a forwarding address. That news only frustrated him all the more. He returned to the hotel and spent most of the night thinking about what to do, where to go, and how to find her.

The next day he decided to go to the Alvin Ailey Co. headquarters in New York and make inquiries there. He checked the telephone directory and called to confirm their address, and then he went over to the management office. He was told that Ms. Anderson was no longer connected with the company, that over a year ago, she suddenly dropped out of the theatre and had not been seen or heard from. This left him greatly distressed, with nowhere to turn. Where could she be? Where did she go in this big city? What happened to Julia?

He knew that no matter what happened, he was not going to leave New York until he found her if it took him forever. With no leads to go on, he decided to hang around the theatre since there was still a possibility that maybe one of the dancers she worked with might be able to tell him something. After a week of hanging around the box office and mingling among the dance theatre people, he met Jeanie, Julia's girlfriend, while she was with the company. Jeanie and Julia used to spend a lot of time together; in fact, when Julia first came to New York, they roomed together for a while. Jim was glad that, at last, he had found someone who could tell him something about Julia. He invited Jeanie to go to dinner with him at B. Smith's restaurant on 49th Street on her day off.

As they sat in the restaurant waiting on their orders to come, she could see the anxiety on his face.

"You're my last hope," he said to her, "I have talked to the super where she used to live, and he couldn't help me; I went to the management of the theatre company, and they couldn't help me, either. You've got to tell me where Julia is!"

"Well, I'll tell you what I know," said Jeanie, "that's all I can tell you."

"Anything that will help me," Jim replied.

"Okay...I remember when she first came to New York City, she was green in a lot of ways as far as big city life is concerned and didn't have a place to stay, so I took her in as my roommate until she found a place. We got along fine! Her inexperience didn't seem to make any difference with her because she had that innocent boldness and naivety of a child that, in a way, I envied her for! She was refreshing, and I used to enjoy just being with her and watching her, most of the time teaching her how to act and handle herself in New York City. I would tell her, 'Don't do that, girl! We don't do that kind of thing here. You'll get into trouble; you have to learn how to act in New York, or they are going to make grits and cornbread out of you in no time in this fast town!' And she would just laugh and take it as a joke every time.

Anyway, she was full of excitement. She was loaded with talent, too, and had that gleam in her eye, you know, that ambitious, eager look that says, 'I'm going to make it no matter what!' Ms Toussaint, the choreographer, had liked her, too. She always said she could work with talented, ambitious young dancers because they listened and didn't waste time.' We gave a number of performances at the City Center and throughout New York, and Julia looked promising! She was going to be a star; I used to think.

Anyway, we roomed together for about a year in the village until one Monday evening when I came home, she had most of her things packed and told me she had found a place and was moving out on her own! Someone was coming in a little while, she said, to help her move her things, but she was waiting to see me tell me herself. She was sorry she had to leave like that, but it was what she wanted. I was shocked, of course, and as much as I tried to find out what was going on, she refused to tell me anything. She seemed like a different person whom you couldn't talk to, whose mind was made up, and that's that! About 7:30 p.m., some slick-looking guy...I mean...man whom she called her agent came by and helped her move her things. She thanked me for all I had done for her and said she would see me at the theatre on Wednesday, and they left."

"I can't believe Julia would act like that," said Jim. "Please tell me what happened afterward."

"Well, that happened a year and a half ago, a few months before she dropped out of the company. Of course, we saw each other at the theatre and at rehearsals after that, but we gradually spent less and less time together. It seemed to me that this was the way she wanted it because, for some reason, she didn't want to be too friendly with me anymore. One day when I insisted we have lunch together, I even confronted her about it."

"What's going on," I asked her, "you're acting very strange of late."

"You're imagining things," she said, "it's just that I am busy, and you are busy too these days!"

"Which was a lot of junk 'cause I knew I was right!"

"Fine," I said to her, "if that's the way you want it!"

And it wasn't long after that she left the company. That's all I can tell you...what's your name again...oh, yes, Jim. That's all I know, except to say that during the six months just before she left, the same dude...I mean...agent used to come around the theatre and pick her up, and they would leave together. I believe I heard her call him "Andy" or something like that."

By that time, the waiter had brought their orders, and they began to eat. She was very hungry, but he didn't seem to have much of an appetite. While Jeanie was eating, he was mostly thinking to himself, "It can't be true; it can't be like Julia to leave the theatre and disappear like she didn't care anymore! What am I going to do?"

As they left the restaurant, he gave Jeanie his address and phone number at the hotel where he was staying and made her promise to call him if she heard anything or if Julia should contact her.

A week went by; he checked the telephone directory; he called Jeanie every day to see if there was any news; he even went down to the local precinct and inquired about missing persons, but none of that helped. For two weeks, he wandered about the city, first in the theatre district, then Broadway, 8th Avenue, and the restaurants and clubs. No place was excluded in his search for Julia.

One night as he was walking along W. 42nd Street, about as discouraged as one can get, he couldn't help noticing the proliferation of cheap sex movie advertisements, freak porno houses, X-rated peep shows, etc. along 10th and 11th streets. He came upon a billboard with the announcement, "Live on-stage burlesque dancers, featuring Ms. Lulu La Tour from Paris, Ms. Georgia Peach from Atlanta, Ms. Ginger Gyrations from Hawaii, and many, many more beauties, both local and from abroad. Come in and see the shows starting at 7 p.m., 9 p.m., 11 p.m., and 1 a.m. Admission: only $10.00."

He wasn't really interested in burlesque, although he had never seen one, but he had nowhere to go and was restless and weary from walking the streets of New York City. Besides, they had a beauty from Atlanta, his hometown, in the show! He paid the admission and went in to see the 11 p.m. show. The theatre was all smelly with the odor of dead fish, urine, and marijuana that was easily detectable. There was whistling and shouting to get the show started as the theatre was packed with impatient patrons. At 11:10 p.m., the lights went out, and the stage spotlight shone on a female figure in black lace wiggling onto the center stage to the sound of some raunchy music. She was well endowed and, after a few bumps and grinds, started peeling off the little she was wearing. You could hear the "Ooooos and aaahhhs," whistling and hissing as the atmosphere sizzled. Ms. Lulu La Tour was in great form, it seemed, as she gave the customers an eye full of what they wanted. When she departed the stage, she was bumping and grinding so much 'till Jim didn't think her mother would recognize her anymore.

That opening number had them warmed up for the next dancer, who slithered onto the stage to the sound of soft, sexy mood music that had them in suspense and anticipation for the build-up that was to come. She moved like she had training, and she made every movement and gesture tell a story. As she came toward center stage and Jim got a good look at Ms. Georgia Peach saw that it was Julia! He couldn't believe his eyes! The woman on the stage was Julia. He ran towards the front of the stage, calling out, "Julia, Julia..." He started to climb onto the stage, still calling her name, when he noticed at a sidelong glance some burly goon rushing towards him to intercept him.

That was the last thing he remembered when he awoke in the alley feeling pains and aches throughout his body like a steamroller had run over him. As he tried to telegraph to his body (that seemed to disown him for a moment) a modest command to rise, it resisted stubbornly. He gradually gained the upper hand by summoning all his strength and managed to rise to his feet. Suddenly he realized that it was daybreak; the crack of dawn must have brought his full awareness back! "Julia," he said to himself, "Julia!" He crawled toward the theatre. He met a drunk on the street who probably thought he was either a bum like himself or he had been in a blitzkrieg and said something to him.

"Hey, soldja, which army you from? Here, wanna drink to slober you up?"

Jim ignored the charitable gesture and continued to make his approach toward the theatre. As he did so, he realized it was closed, and everyone had gone! He held his head with both hands and began to cry. After that, somehow, he made his way back to his hotel, and as he entered his room, he surrendered to the urging of his broken, tired body and mind as he flopped into bed, shoes and all.

He awoke around 11 a.m. that morning, not too happy to face the new day in his present state of mind. As he was turning his still aching body, there was a knock on the door of his room. He was wide awake now and wondered who it could be. He got up, opened the door and to his amazement there was Julia standing right before his eyes! He was staring at her like he was seeing her for the first time. She had to ask if he was not going to invite her in.

"Oh, Julia," he cried as he held her in his arms while closing the door behind them.

It was three and a half years ago when he last held her like this, and he didn't want to let go!

"I knew I shouldn't have let you go 3 1/2 years ago! Tell me, have I lost my Julia?" He said with tears in his eyes.

And she broke down, and she, too, cried in his arms. They stayed like that for a good while before anyone spoke again, then Julia started to comment about his rough appearance, like he wasn't taking care of himself, and how he seemed to have lost weight. He, in turn, noticed that she, too, had changed somewhat. She had matured a great deal and had filled out in certain places. She obviously was not the innocent little girl he knew back in Georgia, but he didn't care. He had found her at last, and that was all that mattered.

They lay in bed in each other's arms for almost three hours, with him not allowing her to talk and with her holding them back so as not to spoil those precious moments. They enjoyed the most beautiful lovemaking during those three hours that they laid together. She made him so happy that he seemed to forget everything else except that she was in his arms. Around 2:00 p.m., he said to her that he was starved and hadn't eaten anything since the previous morning, and he knew a little restaurant down the street where they could go and have a snack.

"That's a good idea," she said, "but I would rather you brought it back here so we could be more private. Don't you think that would be better?"

He agreed and told her to relax while he was gone; he wouldn't be more than 20 minutes. When he left the room, she began thinking to herself, how was she going to explain to him? He didn't let her speak before, but she knew that she would have to tell him everything. It was unfair not to! She had hurt him enough by not writing to him and by letting him go through what he did. No, she could not face him if she told him, but maybe, maybe, if she left a note! Yes, that was what she decided to do. After all, they had just spent three wonderful hours together, and she wanted only to remember him that way.

When Jim returned and found that Julia had left him again, the short-lived happiness he was feeling suddenly turned again to a lonely, empty feeling. If he was confused before, he was now totally lost and perplexed. Why? There was no answer. Then he saw the note on the dresser. He picked it up and read:

"Dear Jim,

You will always be my first, truest, deepest love, but I cannot hurt you anymore! By the time you read this letter, I will be out of your life forever. I could not bear to see your face when I told you what I was going to say.

The innocent little girl you once knew and were going to marry does not exist anymore. When I came to New York, at first, everything was going fine; but like so many others, I got carried away with the excitement and glamour, and somehow, I let my guard down. You see, I met someone who I thought was nice to me. Andy is his name. He was always there buying me things, taking me to clubs and places, showing me the bright and glamorous lifestyle. I just thought of it as having a good time at first, but it got more serious after a while, and before I knew it, I became pregnant! I didn't know what to do, and I certainly couldn't tell you! I was too ashamed! That's when I stopped writing. I said to myself that if I didn't write to you, after a while, you would forget about me and find someone else. You wouldn't want me then anyway. I was going to lose you, so it was better that way. I had to leave the Alvin Ailey Co. because, under the circumstances, my career as an Alvin Ailey dancer was over. I now have an 18-month-old daughter, Patricia, and I am taking care of her and myself by working as an exotic dancer. I don't deserve someone like you. This is a long way from Atlanta, Georgia, my love. Now you know the truth, and I don't hold you to any promises made in the past.

Goodbye,

Julia"

NADIA

An elderly gentleman sat alone at a table in Victor's Restaurant. His table was prepared for two with a place set facing him for a second mysterious dinner guest. After he had nearly finished the last course by himself and no guest came to join him, this caused the new waitress, who was dying with curiosity, to turn to the head waiter and inquire.

"Who is that gray-haired gentleman?" she asked the head waiter.

"He is Mr. Richards," replied the head waiter, "one of our regular customers."

"Was he expecting someone to join him for dinner?" asked the new waitress, who observed that his table was set for two.

"I don't think so," said the head waiter, "that's the way he always insists that his table must be arranged."

"That's very strange," rejoined the new waitress, "how long has he been a customer?"

"You know, come to think of it, ever since I've been working here, and that's almost seven years now! Most of the waiters and waitresses are new, just like you, so you wouldn't know, but senior staff have gotten used to him. I remember many years ago, he used to come into the restaurant, usually alone, ask for a table for two, and a little while later, a lovely young lady would enter the restaurant and join him. Almost every Sunday evening around 6 p.m., they had dinner together at that same table, and afterward, they would leave together arm in arm, and they always acted as if no one else in the restaurant existed. They seemed to be lovers, at least from the way they acted as far as I could tell."

"When was the last time that happened?" asked the new waitress.

"That's what's so strange," said the headwaiter, "would you believe that it was almost five years ago? Since then, I have never seen her again, although he keeps coming here every week alone and always sits there like he's expecting her to join him. He even puts a rose beside her plate every time. Sometimes I think he talks to himself!"

The new waitress thought the head waiter was pulling her leg. She found the stranger's actions so very unusual, to say the least, but since it didn't seem to bother anyone else but her, she stopped asking any more questions.

The scene and the conversation just described took place in Victor's Restaurant one Sunday evening in the year 1980, but to better understand the circumstances and what led up to such a strange occurrence, one would have to go back ten years earlier, to be exact!

It was on a pleasant Sunday morning in the early summer of 1970, when Phillip Richards was standing by a lake in Central Park admiring the ducks and their little ducklings. It was a lovely place to be, especially when it was quiet; somehow the lake, the birds, and the proximity of nature relaxed him greatly and gave him peace of mind. God knows the city was hectic enough and full of turmoil. This particular Sunday morning was so pleasant and peaceful, with the only people in sight being a few morning joggers in the distance and one or two other people besides himself who were walking by. As he sat on the park bench nearby, fully enjoying the rapture of that moment, someone came and sat beside him. It was a very lovely young lady about 26 years old, maybe 5'6", well proportioned, partly East Indian, of light brown mestizo complexion, pretty, dressed in a light floral print dress, her hair combed back in an attractive bunch, with a lovely mother-of-pearl comb adding to her coiffure. She had a delicately fragrant perfume that enhanced the freshness of the morning air.

As she sat on the bench, she spoke first.

"Good morning! How are you?"

And Phil, a little surprised but delighted, replied.

"Fine, thank you!"

"You know," she said, "I was watching you admiring the ducks, and I thought, what a coincidence, this is my favorite spot, and I love to watch them, too. Like most creatures of nature, they go about their lives so uncomplicated, so natural, so uncomplaining, and so contented!"

"Yes," said Phil, "unlike people who are always complaining about something and are never satisfied!"

"Then do you think that people should turn to nature to learn how to live? I mean, would we all be better off if we were like the ducks and the other creatures of nature?" She replied.

"To some extent," said Phil, "at least if we lived in harmony with nature and learned to appreciate it more, we might stop destroying it!"

186

"Yes, I know what you mean," she said, concurring with him.

And as she said that, she seemed to look far away as if a thought of something or somewhere remote had come into her head. By that time it had occurred to both of them that they hadn't bothered to properly introduce themselves.

"My name is Nadia. What is yours?" she said to him.

"Phillip!" he told her.

"Do you come to the park often, Phillip?"

"Yes!" said Phillip, "One day, I hope to move to the country where I can be surrounded by nature. If you had that choice, wouldn't you do the same?"

"Yes, I would. I see that we both have in common a love of nature. I like that."

And before he could ask her where she lived or if he could see her again, she got up suddenly with a hint of urgency.

"Oh, I am sorry, I really must go now, but I will see you next week at this same time here in the park. That is if you would like me to?"

"Yes," said Phillip, "I will look for you next Sunday."

And she disappeared as quietly and quickly as she had appeared. Phillip sat on the bench alone, feeling lighthearted and contented.

The next Sunday, he arrived at the park at the same time and sat on the park bench where they met. He was there at least a half hour and was beginning to think he would never see her again when she came walking toward him, dressed in a lovely green dress with her hair combed backward, cascading, the strands fastened at the top with a green band.

"I am sorry I am late! Are you angry?" she said as she sat down.

"No, of course not," said Phil, "I am very glad to see you!"

"Last week, you didn't tell me anything about yourself; are you married, Phil?"

"No," said Phil, "are you?"

"No, I am not either! What kind of work do you do? No, let me guess! Since your hands are so smooth and gentle, I bet you are an artist!"

"Yes and no," said Phil, "I am a school teacher, and I write a little."

"Yes, that fits my impression of you very well. Of course, you are going to want to know about me, too! I was...I mean...am an interpreter, and I like to paint. One day I will show you a painting I did of this lake and the ducks."

"Yes, I would like that," said Phil.

They chatted in the park a little longer than the previous time, and soon a few more people started to appear. A few couples were rowing in the lake, and it prompted Phil to ask Nadia if she would like to go rowing. She said she'd love to, and they spent a lovely time on the lake enjoying the relative peace and quiet and each other's company. From the first time they met, they had both felt an instinctive attraction to each other. Now it was a much warmer feeling that was developing between them. It was drawing them more and more to each other. They stayed together a long time in the park, and when she left him, he knew that he would have to see her again.

For four consecutive Sundays, they met in the park, and on the fourth Sunday, they were holding hands, embracing and exchanging a tender kiss or two or three on the park bench as naturally as if they were long-time lovers. Now it seemed as if they had always known each other, had always been close, and as if they were meant to be together.

If there was any mystery about it in the back of his mind, about who she was, where she was from, or where she lived, for instance, he was not letting it bother him in the least. But it shouldn't bother him anyway since she had not insisted on prying into his life except to ask what kind of work he did. It was enough that they had this instant attraction and cared very much for each other, and, furthermore, all the questions would be answered eventually, he thought, in due course as they got to know each much better.

On that fourth Sunday, when they were together before they parted, Phillip asked Nadia if she would have dinner with him that evening.

"I thought you would never ask." She said. "Of course, I would love to go to dinner with you!"

He told her he would come to pick her up at 6 p.m. where she lived, but she hesitated and told him that since she would not be home at that time, instead of her returning home to meet him, she would rather come straight to the restaurant and meet him there instead. He gave her the name and address of the restaurant, which she said she knew quite well, and they agreed to meet there that evening at 6:30.

At 6:30 p.m. Nadia walked into Victor's restaurant beautifully dressed in lavender with a silk scarf around her neck, her hair bunched at back with a lovely hair comb like the first time he had seen her. He stood and greeted her with a kiss and they sat absorbing each other more interested in spending the time doing that than ordering what they were going to eat for dinner.

"You look lovely," said Phil; and she returned the compliment.

"And you are the handsomest man I've ever seen!"

After a while, they got around to checking the menu and ordering dinner. They held hands and said sweet things to each other as lovers did while they waited for the food to arrive. Then for the first time, she said, "I know we've only met each other about six weeks ago, but I think I am falling in love with you, Phil!" and Phil kissed the palm of her hand and told her that he loved her with every fiber of his being. If they didn't eat anything after that, they would still have been filled. Fortunately, the food arrived, and they had physical nourishment.

After dinner, he took her to his apartment on 96th Street and Central Park West, and they made love the next day. Early the next morning, while he was still sleeping, she dressed and left him and left a note behind that she would meet him in the park the following Sunday at the usual time.

Phil was so much in love with Nadia that he couldn't wait to see her, to be with her, to spend all his time with her. The next Sunday, they met and walked through the park embracing. They sat on the park bench, kissing passionately and exchanging expressions of their tender love for each other. Later that evening, they had dinner and went to his apartment afterward. Before she left the following morning, he told her he wanted to see her more often, so she surprised him after that and came on her own to his apartment on several occasions. They would go to dinner each time they met at the same restaurant. Usually, she came alone and met him at the restaurant, except when they came together from his apartment. They started going to shows together, to the cinema, and to concerts, but they still always met in the park on Sundays except when it rained, or it was too cold, then she would come first to his apartment on those occasions. So at no time did Phil ever get to see where she lived. She always seemed to evade the question of his visiting her or taking her home or picking her up at her residence. He was curious of course, but he was afraid if he insisted, he would lose her. Once, she had said she lived somewhere on Central Park East, and when he attempted to accompany her home, she insisted and took a cab instead. Even though she said she wasn't, he began to think that she was married or that

189

she was living with someone, and that may be the reason for keeping him from coming to her home. When he asked her to marry him, she said she wanted to more than anything in this world, but that he must be patient, and, if he really loved her to wait 'till the time when she was ready, and that she would let him know. She asked him to trust her, to be patient, not to insist or pressure her in any way, that she would always come to him, that she loved him dearly and would always love him no matter what. She told him that he must believe her, that everything depended on it, that love was stronger than anything in this world, even death itself. He seemed to be a little puzzled but satisfied with her answer and never insisted or questioned her again.

Their love affair continued for about a year, and on her terms One day, when she came to meet him at the restaurant, she gave him a package as a gift. When he opened it, he saw it was a painting of the lake with the ducks and their ducklings. It was a beautiful painting, which he later took home and hung on his living room wall as a permanent fixture. After dinner that evening, they went to his apartment, and during lovemaking, she said she always wanted to remember him the way he was that evening, that it was the most beautiful time they had spent together. Even though he was happy, in his mind, he was afraid of losing her. She assured him that he would never lose her, and they went to sleep in each other's arms.

Early the next morning, she left while he was still asleep and wrote across the mirror, "I will love you forever...Nadia!"

The following Sunday, he went to the park and sat on the park bench, half expecting her to come and half expecting her not to. The latter was the case. The following Sunday was the same. He kept going there Sunday after Sunday, but she never came. About the fifth Sunday, when he went there at about 8:30 a.m. and sat on the bench, he found a mother-of-pearl comb in the place where she used to sit. He didn't know what to think. Was it hers? Did she come there before him and leave it there for him as a keepsake? He took it with him as he sadly left the park that day.

By a strange coincidence, one day at his school, there was a heated discussion among his colleagues about an article in the papers dealing with the lack of safety in Central Park and about all the crimes and killings that had taken place there over the years. He did not agree with them that the park was so unsafe because he went there all the time and didn't find that to be the case. One of the instructors said that he had done some research on the history of crime in the park and that he had facts and evidence to prove it. He produced statistics that disturbed Phillip. He even showed copies of old clippings dating back to 1945. It was one of these clippings that attracted Phil's attention, for it was a story about a murder that had happened in the park in 1945, and it said: "Young, attractive, East Indian woman murdered in Central Park at about 8:30 a.m., the morning of Sunday, May 18, 1945." Then he tried to read the name of the victim, but that part of the article was too blurred. Further on, it continued, "She resided at 222 Central Park East at the time of her death..." After seeing the photograph in the article, he was not sure of the victim's identity because it was too faded and blurred. "Anyhow," he thought, "If there was even a slight resemblance, that was only a coincidence since she was East Indian. Furthermore, the clipping was dated 36 years ago, albeit the murder had taken place near the same location where they met! But that didn't prove anything because she would have to be a 63-year-old woman at the time he met Nadia and not someone young in the flesh. Anyway, his mind did not want to believe that that person in the clipping could, in the slightest, be his Nadia. "Of course, that could never be," he said to himself, "for how could such a thing even be possible?" Yet he found that he could not dismiss it entirely, as impossible as it seemed.

Then he remembered something else...'She had said to him that love was stronger than anything in this world, even death!' What did she mean... if he even had given it a second thought! Only one thing to him was certain: he met and fell in love with a beautiful young lady in the flesh named Nadia, who was real, and her love was real, and the time they spent together was real. That newspaper article must be about someone else since that person could not be Nadia. But even if it could be, and it cannot be, what is true beyond all doubt is that she had appeared in his life and entered into his heart for two years and then mysteriously disappeared. That little doubt had entered his mind for only a moment causing him to entertain the unthinkable, and in that brief moment, he asked himself, "What other explanation can there be? If she was not a ghost, then maybe she is a heartless adventuress who just wanted to have a romantic affair with him, and her sudden disappearance was her way of ending it." That seemed to explain why she didn't let him escort her to her home. He never knew where she lived; he never met her relatives; she always appeared mysteriously. And so what if that picture in the article is really her? What if the unthinkable were really true? In that case, she would have to be from another time reincarnated, a spirit that materialized and made him a promise that she would always love him and come back to him. In the meantime, he has his precious memories; he has her comb; he has her painting that she gave to him. No, no, she is real alright! She has to be real! And if she is not an adventuress, she will keep her promise. Therefore he will go on treasuring the moments they had together which were real. And one day, he believes sincerely, she will return as mysteriously as she did when they first met, and they will be together again.

The elderly gentleman got up to leave the restaurant, and when the waitress went over to his table to clean up and set up for the next customer, she noticed that the rose had vanished and although she may have imagined it, she could have sworn that there was a whiff of perfume lingering behind in the seat across from where Mr. Richards sat, but that was impossible since no one was sitting there...

THE ORGAN MUSIC

The last mass was over, the congregation had dispersed, and he had just driven off in his car when he remembered he left his umbrella beneath the pew where he sat. It had started to rain slightly and he was reluctant to leave it behind so he turned around and headed back to St. Catherine's. When he arrived, the doors were already locked, and the church was empty, so he went around to the back, to the entrance of the rectory, and rang the bell. Father James let him in.

"Father, it is only a trivial thing, but I left my umbrella!" He said to the pastor.

"If you did, then I'm sure it is still where you left it," said Father James. "Come with me."

And they both went from the rectory that passed through a passageway behind the altar towards the hall, with Father leading the way. As they entered the hall, Fred could hear an organ playing so beautifully that it flooded the hall up to the rafters. The music held him spellbound. It was playing even though there was no one visible at the organ. He stopped in his tracks and listened, motionless. Father James picked up the umbrella and turned to him.

"Here it is; see, it is safe and sound."

It appeared that Father James did not hear the music issuing from the organ, as he did, or else why would he act unconcerned as he came toward him to hand him his umbrella? No, he didn't hear a thing.

"Are you alright?" remarked Father James. "Is everything alright?"

"Yes, Father, thank you very much," replied Fred.

As they passed the altar on their way back through the passageway toward the rectory, he kept looking back, for he could still hear the sad and beautiful organ prelude as if played by the hands of a master organist. Aware that Father had not heard the music, he did not say anything to make himself seem unbalanced, for what else would Father have thought of him if he told him what he heard? Therefore, he kept it to himself as he departed from the rectory, confused and mystified.

That was Fred Ames' first visit to St. Catherine since he moved into Queens from Deer Park, Long Island. He decided to return the following Sunday and several Sundays afterward to attend mass. The next Sunday, he lingered behind after the last service, kneeling in the pew after everyone had left. When Father James saw that he was still there, he asked him to leave through the rectory when he was ready to go, for the ushers were closing the doors. He remained there for almost an hour as if hoping to hear the music again to convince himself that he did not imagine it. He would recognize that music if he heard it again because he knew the piece. It was Bach's Toccata and Fugue in D minor, a most sad and hauntingly beautiful piece of music that moved him whenever he heard it. He continued to stay after service every Sunday, but he never heard that music again.

It had been two months since his paranormal experience, and he was beginning to put that phenomenon behind him as possibly some kind of hallucination of his. But one day in the early summer, he was visiting his sister, Rachel Eves, who had recently moved into a new home in St. Albans more than six months ago, and there were a few of her friends and neighbors there as well. They were gathered in the living room and were mostly talking about the latest social gossip and recent events to bring each other up to date, especially Rachel, on what was going on in St. Albans. They talked about people and incidents that happened in the past, sometimes even a few years ago. At one point, Sue Allen, one of two neighbors Rachel had met a few months ago and had invited to her home, spoke and asked another neighbor, Mary Collins, who was also present, about a person whom they both knew who used to live in the neighborhood.

"Do you remember Margaret Jones? She used to live near you, Mary. Whatever happened to her? I haven't seen her in quite a while now."

"O, she moved back to North Carolina with her husband, who retired. That's where they are from originally," said Mary.

"And what about your good friend, Mrs Richards?" inquired Mary. "I know you two were very close. Didn't her husband pass away last year? What happened to her after the funeral?"

"Yes," said Sue Allen, "her children came, put the house up for sale, and took her down south to live with them. She sent me a postcard last week."

And so the gossip continued, which to Fred was very boring at first, but his interest was quickly awakened when the subject of the conversation changed.

"O, by the way," said Mary to Rachel, Fred's sister, "I know you're not a member of St. Catherine. You go to St. Pascal, not far from here; anyhow, you must have heard about what happened over a year ago last March in St. Catherine Parish. It was all over town."

"No," said Rachel, "I moved here near the end of last year, so I wouldn't be familiar with things that happened before I moved into the neighborhood; but I would like you to tell me about it since you have been very active in that church."

Fred was now sitting on the edge of his seat listening intently when he heard Mary say, "St. Catherine." He remembered vividly the strange experience he had that first Sunday he attended mass there two months ago during the Easter season.

"Well," said Mary, "as you may know, I used to sing in the choir at St. Catherine; and I don't mind saying that we were one of the best choirs in Queens."

"Yes, yes," said Rachel, "but tell me what you started to say about something happening there a year or so ago last March."

"Very well, let me tell you what happened. About a year ago, It seemed like one of the ladies in the choir, Ms. Rhoda Gunning, was carrying on a love affair with the choirmaster, Samuel Towers. She wasn't the only one, though, that was involved with him. Samuel was a middle-aged man in his fifties, and he had a twenty-seven-year-old young thing, Ms. Lynn Dunn, living with him in his house in South Jamaica at the same time while he was involved with Rhoda Gunning, a 34-year-old female member of the choir. It looked to me like one woman wasn't enough to satisfy him. I tell you, that twenty-seven-year-old must have been one damn jealous woman, as it turned out, but what I still can't understand is why he exposed his affair and himself like that! He should have been more discreet, in my opinion. You know, all three of them were attending the same church at the same time. The young woman would be sitting in the congregation, praying, so to speak, or observing, while her rival was singing in the choir with her man, who was the choir director and organist accompanying the choir. And she knew for some time that they were having an affair. I wonder what was going through her mind at the same time when she was praying!"

Mary paused for a moment to catch her breath.

"On one particular Tuesday, I remember it so well because it was during Holy Week, March 29, 1994, and they were there, all three of them, in the church that evening praying and singing and rehearsing for Easter," resumed Mary, "and after the choir rehearsal that evening Lynn Dunn, Mr Towers' live-in mistress, approached her unsuspecting rival in a gesture of friendship in an attempt to resolve their differences like good Christians, amicably, so to speak, by inviting her to come home with them so the three of them like grownups could discuss it and try to resolve their situation."

Here Mary paused briefly a second time to clear her throat. Meanwhile, in Fred's mind, he was thinking, *'How foolish and simple we human beings are! How can such an encounter end in an amicable, peaceful way? Someone has to get bruised. Someone has to suffer and pay the price. And why could none of them see the danger? This was not safe, nor was it neutral ground. If things should turn badly, how would one extricate oneself? But then, as humans, often we do not think with our heads, but with our hearts, and fail to take the proper precautions.'*

"The unsuspecting Rhoda," continued Mary, "went along, and the three guilty souls, two perhaps trusting and one perhaps with sinister intentions, proceeded to the residence of Samuel Towers and his mistress. Once there, they now began to try to hash out their differences, or, in other words, resolve their triangle and make it a duet with one of the three being excluded and made a grievous loser. You don't want to know what happened next in the scene that followed, I beg you."

"Yes," said Rachel, "you can't stop now when the plot is just heating up. Go on and finish the story before you make me mad!"

And sitting on the side, anxiously waiting for the denouement, Fred could not have concurred with his sister more.

"Alright… alright," responded Mary. "After several accusations and recriminations back and forth, a loud and bitter quarrel ensued. Then Rhoda declared that Samuel loved her, and Samuel declared that he chose Rhoda over Lynn, his live-in mistress, whom he then told that their relationship was over and that she was no longer in the picture."

Fred, sitting there, listening to this, was thinking, *"Poor Samuel, he must not have known of the lesson taught by the truism, 'Hell hath no fury like a woman scorned' -- William Congreve, 1697; nor of the lesson in the axiom, 'The female of the species is more deadly than the male' – a poem written by Rudyard Kipling in 1919. In any case, all men should be aware of these things.'*

"I don't like where this is going," declared Rachel with perceptive anticipation. "This sounds like bad, bad trouble to me."

"You are right," said Mary, "for, unbeknown to both Samuel and Rhoda, Lynn had found out that Sam had a gun hidden in the house, and just before she went to church that evening, she found the gun and put it in her pocketbook. So she was preparing for this possibility, even while she was in church -- she did not intend to lose this argument. At the moment when it was clear to her that these two, especially Samuel, were going to make her the loser and the fool, the heat of anger and revenge overwhelmed her. She pulled out the .38 revolver from her pocketbook, and that was going to be her equalizer. Fearing for their lives then, the other two did whatever she demanded while begging and praying for their lives; but the steel was in Lynn's veins now. Filled with revenge and hate, she made them kneel, their backs to her, and while they knelt trembling, praying and begging for their lives, she fired a bullet in the back of each of their heads in quick succession – bang!!!…bang!!!... and it was over!!!"

Mary paused.

"How horrible!" said Rachel, "How horrible...and what did she do then, shoot herself?"

"No…she calmly went to the telephone," said Mary, "called the precinct and reported to them over the phone that she had just killed a man and a woman and they should come and arrest her for a double murder. The police didn't waste any time getting there. When they arrived, they found her standing outside with the revolver still in her hand, which they took from her, and she gave herself up without any resistance."

"What a pity," said Fred, "out of this sad event, two people lay dead, and three lives were shattered because of an ill-fated triangle and the wrath of a woman scorned."

It was then that he found the courage to mention his paranormal experience in St. Catherine and the organ music he had heard. Mary was taken aback emotionally when he told her.

"Bach's Prelude and Fugue in D Minor -- that was his favorite piece!!" said Mary, "He always played that solo on special occasions, especially around Easter. What are you saying?"

"Just what I told you," said Fred, "and there is no way I could have made it up. Before tonight, I never knew anything about any tragedy, nor about the organist and his playing that music. All the same, it is one of the saddest stories I have ever heard…that's all I have to say…just like the organ music."

THE MAN WHO HATED LOVE

There he sat one evening in his apartment in Queens, N.Y., slumped over his desk, clutching tightly in one hand the letter he had received earlier that day in the mail, which he had just finished reading. He felt depressed and angry, but it was not so much due to this one letter, so much as it was to the accumulation of all the broken relationships he had experienced in the forty years of his life. This letter, finally, was the last straw -- he swore this time that he was finished with love. "If only I hadn't been so foolish, so gullible, and so easily deceived!" he said to himself. But perhaps his real tragedy was the fact that he had looked for love too many times in the wrong places and for the wrong reasons; or that he hadn't the slightest idea in the first place of the true nature of love. Bitter and distraught, he raised his head from the desk, looked up to the ceiling, and cursed, "DAMN LOVE!!!...I HATE LOVE!!!" and crushed the "Dear John" letter in his hand and threw it across the room. Thusly, he sought to relieve his agony.

What he did not know, however, was that his utterances were overheard, even in the privacy of his own apartment. Call it his conscience, but a voice in the room replied.

"Surely, you don't mean what you said?"

"Yes, I meant every word!" he shouted back as he looked around to see where the voice was coming from.

Again the mysterious voice spoke.

"How can you say that? Love is the greatest thing there is."

"It is not!" he answered. "It is a hoax! A fraud! One is a fool to believe in love! I hate love!"

"That's a terrible thing to say," rejoined the voice, "the human heart was made to love."

"Then damn the human heart! I curse, love! I wish I never loved, never was loved, and never love anyone again!"

"What a pity!" said the voice as it faded away, leaving him in his state of wretchedness.

Soon, he got up and dragged himself to bed, full of anguish and frustration and with a splitting headache. He tossed and turned for a good while then he finally fell fast asleep.

He had hardly lost consciousness when already it became morning. He dragged himself out of bed, followed his daily routine and showered, dressed, ate breakfast as usual, and prepared to leave for work. Before leaving the apartment, however, he walked into the living room, and it was totally transformed! The walls were completely bare! On it, there were no longer displayed framed pictures of his grandparents, his mother, father, and sister hanging there — they had all vanished from the wall before his eyes as if they never existed. Momentarily he thought his mind was playing tricks on him, but he soon shrugged that off as if it were a hallucination, and, since he seemed to be running late, ignored it and grabbed his briefcase and left the apartment to go to work.

As he walked out of the building, he felt a strange sensation! Physically everything seemed the same, and yet he felt different, for somehow he had changed! His thoughts, his consciousness, and his feelings now were not the same -- as a matter of fact, the transformation was so complete that he had a different memory, a different sense of awareness, a different past (So much for granted wishes!). As he walked across the plaza, pigeons scattered before him and took to the skies. Even the squirrels noticed something strange about him, and they scurried frantically away and up the trees. None of this affected him, but the little creatures knew they would have been trampled upon by him had they not escaped. He crossed the plaza and walked towards the subway without a smile and with cold indifference to the rest of the world.

Riding on the rush hour train seemed more natural to him now with all the cold and heartless stares that beamed at him, which he, too, returned in full measure. Like a mechanical robot, he felt nothing, not even the toes he stepped on or the bodies he elbowed without a wince or word, and vice versa. In about an hour, he arrived at the office where he worked in downtown Manhattan. It was a civil service job, one he was well suited for -- he was a tax auditor with the I.R.S., and he had the right temperament for it, cold, uncaring, calculating, heartless! It seemed he had built up a reputation, and the poor taxpayers he dealt with knew that with him, they didn't have a chance, for many were already ruined by him through the years. He had no heart! Well, maybe he had a physical one that pumped blood, but it felt no tenderness, no kindness, no affection, nor compassion. It was as cold as snow and as hard as granite. "Ice," they called him; even his co-workers called him by that name, for he never smiled, never socialized with anyone, and had no friends or loved ones. People used to wonder if he was always that way if at one time he wasn't human, kind or charitable, or loving, but as far as anyone knew, he was always like that.

The only person he might have called a relative was a sister he once had. When he was born, he was found abandoned as a baby. Both he and his twin sister were raised together in an orphanage where they named him Frank M.T. Hart (Hart House was the name of the orphanage). He never knew his parents, for they were too anxious to rid themselves of him and his sister at birth, and both of them went as a package from one foster home to another. The fact is, since he was born, he was a strange child who never showed the slightest affection or love or kindness to anyone, not even to his own sister, and when they later grew up and were on their own in their twenties, he never even acknowledged her as his sister. She lived alone in a broken down one-room cold flat somewhere in Brooklyn and was always frail and sickly. She died in her twenties of consumption and a weak heart, and he didn't even shed a tear or even attend the funeral, for he had no feelings nor compassion. In fact, she might have lived longer if he had cared for her as a loving brother; but that was not his nature – he had no heart! He treated her death as if she had never existed. "Let the weak help the weak," he said, "and the sick the sick; only sentimental fools have hearts!" What did it matter to him anyway who suffered, who ate, who starved, who lived or died? And he went on his way, alone, even in a crowd, uncaring, without emotion, a robot with ice water in his veins.

One evening after work, as he left the office and was walking along Broadway, he passed an old blind man sitting near the curb with a cup in his hand, begging in a humble voice.

"Spare some change, sir! Help a poor old blind man, please, sir!"

The blind man stretched his hand out with the cup but was inadvertently blocking the path of Frank as he tried to go by. Frank, with a show of contempt, knocked the cup out of the blind man's hand, and as he went by, the blind beggar called out after him.

"You, Frank N. Hart, you should be called Frank "No Heart!!" You have the curse of the damned upon you! You are more wretched than I! I am sorry for you!!"

Frank heard every word, and for the first time, he felt a slight tremor in his armor. He looked back scornfully, nevertheless puzzled that this blind fool whom he never saw before in his life could call him by his name, "Frank N.

Hart," speaking some nonsense about a curse besides. He was puzzled at first but soon dismissed it and went on his way.

The next day he had to work late and left the office at about 8 p.m. When he walked out into the street, he did not see the blind beggar. Had he seen him, he would have demanded to know how he knew his name, for that still remained a mystery to him. A few blocks away, he stopped in a little coffee shop for a cup of coffee and an evening paper. As he sat at a table alone, drinking his coffee, someone touched him on the shoulder. Startled, he turned and saw a gray-haired old lady standing over him.

"Kind sir," she said while handing him a pamphlet with some scripture written on it, "would you care to donate something to the church to help the poor?"

He seemed to ignore her.

"You don't have to give anything if you don't wish to, sir, but you may keep the pamphlet if you like," which she placed on the table in front of him.

He gave her a cold stare and a loud, uncharitable response.

"Get away from me, you gospel peddler! I don't need your damn salvation! Leave me alone!"

"God be good to you, sir!" the poor old lady, still trying to be charitable, said and walked away from him, feeling more sorry for him than she felt insulted.

When he got up to leave, he picked up his newspaper and didn't realize he had also taken the pamphlet with him, folded inside the pages of the newspaper. He got on the train in the downtown part of New York City, heading to Queens.

It wasn't really very late, about 8:45 p.m., but the rush hours had already passed, and the train was not so crowded. Somewhere between Lexington Ave. and Queens Plaza, three dangerous characters boarded. They were youths, two of whom were in their teens and one in his early twenties, wearing jeans and trousers sagging down below their waists, shirts hanging out of their pants, and caps turned backward, but they had no good intentions. They acted very sinisterly, sizing up everyone in the car and huddling together as they stood near the exit. Suddenly, two of them went to the opposite ends of the car, and one stood in the middle. Then they announced to everyone not to make a move or do anything stupid, that it was a stickup in progress. With guns brandished, they told everyone to take out their wallets and purses and drop them in a bag carried by one of them. One man resisted, and they shot him and told everyone else to let that be a lesson, that they would get the same if they breathed too hard or gave them any trouble. They soon approached Frank N. Hart when one of them, the one in his twenties, suddenly uttered something.

"Well, well, look who we have here! Hey guys, this here is 'Ice,' the meanest, most heartless m.....f....r in Queens. I once saw him kick an old lady's butt for stepping on his shoes! He wouldn't lift a finger to help his own sister, let alone his mother, if he had one. He wouldn't even show kindness to a dying man! A lot of people hate his guts. Yeah, Mr. Tax Collector, what you got to say for yourself now?"

While Frank was shaking in his seat, one of the other two, the youngest one, spoke.

"Let's waste him! If he is that mean, he doesn't deserve to keep on breathing!"

Then the other teenager responded.

"I bet nobody would miss the s. o. b. We'd be doing everyone a favor!"

Then the oldest one put the gun to Frank's head, but before he could pull the trigger, the second oldest spoke to him.

"Hold on a minute, K.J., let's have some fun first!"

Turning to the people on the train, he said the following.

"Which one of you would like to change places with this 'scum bag'?" Nobody answered, and he continued, "Alright, if you won't die for him, then which one of you would crawl and beg for his life?"

After a few seconds elapsed, he said something to the one holding the gun.

"K.J., let me have the pleasure!" and he took the gun from him, cocked the hammer, holding it to Frank's head, and said to the people in the car:

"This is the last chance. I swear if no one begs for this bastard's life, I am going to blow him away!"

Just at that moment, the blind beggar, who happened to be sitting quietly in the same car and heard everything, stood up and addressed the gunman.

"Wait! Wait! Don't shoot!" said the beggar.

"Yeah, what he ever do for you, blind man?" the youth with the gun retorted.

"He is my friend! Please don't hurt him!" said the blind beggar, "If you want to shoot somebody, I'll take his place, shoot me instead!"

"You mean you'd die for him, blind man?"

"Yes," replied the beggar.

And at that very moment, the little gray-haired old lady, who was also on the train, sitting opposite the blind beggar, stood up, for she, too, had pity on the tax collector.

"You might as well shoot me, too! This man has done you no harm; the Lord will thank you not to touch a hair on his head, you hear me? Take what you came here for, and leave this poor man alone!"

It took a lot of courage for her to say that, risking her own life, both she and the blind beggar, but they did it anyway.

Then the robber who had the gun to Frank's head said,

"I wouldn't believe it; somebody actually cares about this son-of-a-b…. and, turning to Frank, "You can thank those two I don't pull the trigger," and to his friends, he said, "Come on; let's get off this train!"

And as the train rolled into the station, they jumped off and ran up the stairs, and were gone. By that time, the conductor had become aware of what had happened from the commotion and screaming and summoned for help. In the meantime, the muggers made their getaway just before the police and an emergency team arrived at the next station, where they removed the injured man and took him to a hospital. After a brief investigation, the train continued on its route.

By now, Frank, who sat trembling through the whole ordeal, did not know what to say or do.

"Why did that beggar whom he had treated so meanly say he was his friend and offered to give his life for him? And the old lady, whom he insulted and called those awful names, why did she, too, stand up for him?" he said to himself.

He had been so cold and mean and heartless for so long that meanness was all he ever expected in return from anyone. Those young punks could have easily taken his life, and what was that they said about him?

"Ice... the meanest, most heartless m......f....r in Queens, he doesn't deserve to keep on breathing! Nobody will miss the s.o.b.!" So that's what everyone thought of him? Maybe they were right," he thought.

He looked at the blind beggar and wanted to say, "Thank you," but he didn't know how; it was not in his vocabulary, if ever at all, and such words had never before come out of his mouth. But the beggar must have understood a lot more than Frank imagined, for he smiled as if to say:

"I know...I know...it's alright. You don't have to say anything."

Then Frank looked at the old lady sitting across from him, and he almost managed to say thank you, but the words just stuck in his throat. At l69th St. Station, she got off, but before she left, she said something to Frank.

"God still loves you, son. You'll see."

Unlike the restaurant encounter, this time, he said nothing to her as he watched her depart from the train.

The train was now approaching the last stop, his stop, as he remembered that he still did not know how the blind beggar knew his name. He turned to look for him diagonally across the aisle where he was sitting, but the beggar had vanished! He was no longer on the train. He was nowhere.

"That is impossible!" he thought, "He was just sitting there. Where? How? When...?"

He could not understand it, for he never saw him get off the train unless the blind beggar could see, and he opened the door while the train was moving and jumped off!

When the train finally came to the last stop, the conductor announced:

"Last stop, last stop, everybody off!!"

Frank N. Hart walked off a puzzled and confused person. He managed to get to his apartment, though slightly disoriented and very confused. He deposited his briefcase on the floor and dropped the newspaper on his desk. As he did so, the paper unfolded, revealing the pamphlet the old lady had placed on the table in the restaurant. In clear print, it read:

> "Love is the greatest gift. If you spoke
> in tongues and knew every language there is
> in all of heaven and earth but didn't love others,
> you would be nothing. If you had the gift of prophecy

and knew all about what was going to happen in the future, knew everything about everything, but didn't love others, you would be nothing. Even if you could speak to a mountain and make it move, you would still be worth nothing at all without love. ..."

Further on, he read:

"Love is patient and kind, never jealous or envious, never boastful or proud, never haughty or selfish or rude. Love does not demand its own way. It is not irritable or touchy. It does not hold grudges and will never even notice when others do it wrong. It is never glad about injustice but rejoices whenever the truth wins out. Love bears all things, believes all things, hopes all things, endures all things...Love never fails. All the special gifts and powers from God will someday come to an end, but love will last forever."

And at the bottom of the pamphlet, in bold letters were written:

"NO GREATER LOVE HATH ANY MAN THAN TO LAY DOWN HIS

LIFE FOR A FRIEND" and written below that,

"...FOR GOD SO LOVED THE WORLD THAT HE GAVE HIS ONLY

BEGOTTEN SON THAT WHOSOEVER BELIEVETH IN HIM SHOULD

NOT PERISH BUT HAVE EVERLASTING LIFE..."

He finished reading the pamphlet that had a strange effect on him, and at that moment, his whole wretched life flashed before his eyes, and he hated himself.

No longer sure about anything, he lay in his bed and tried to sleep. Something kept him from sleeping. He kept tossing and turning with perspiration covering his entire body; then he cried out half asleep and half awake:

"Who am I? What am I? What am I living for? Nobody loves me! I love no one! I couldn't even say thank you to those two people who saved my life. Better I had never been born! No one will miss Frank No Hart. O God, let it be that he had never been born! Let it be...that...he..."

Suddenly... It was morning... and he had the strangest sensation, a weird feeling as if he had been somewhere else, filled with nightmarish recollections of a terrible dream he had about a stick-up on a train, a blind beggar, and an old woman. In fact, it was so real. It was as if he really was somewhere else and had been transported back from a different life in a different world back to the present one. He had never dreamed of anything like that before. It was as if he had traded places with someone else in a parallel universe for what seemed like a lifetime but was, in reality, less than 7 hours. Thank Heaven it was only a dream, and he was now himself again! Somehow he had managed to get a little sleep between the tossing and turning most of the night, but now that he was awake, among other things, he had an enormous appetite. He freshened up, dressed, and ate a hearty breakfast. Just as he finished, the telephone rang! He picked up the receiver.

"Hello!" he said.

"Hello Frank! It's your sister!" the voice on the other end replied.

She called him to see how he was doing and if everything was alright with him. His sister!! It seemed like a miracle, for she wasn't dead after all!

"Sis," he said, "is that really you? You're really alive? O, sis, I love you so much!"

"I love you, too, Frank," she replied.

He was so happy to hear her voice that he told her to keep on talking, that her voice was heavenly, that he hoped she lived to be a hundred, no, two hundred years old! She laughed and said he was crazy, but she loved him, too, and they talked awhile about their parents, about how they missed them, and they made plans to go home together for Christmas to spend it with their parents and relatives and have a happy family reunion.

When she hung up the phone, he walked into the living room and looked up at the walls. There were the pictures of his grandparents, his mother, and father, and his sister prominently displayed where they had always been. He felt like a changed person, however, a new man, with a new lease on life, for the man who had wished he had never loved or was never loved or will never love again, the man who cursed love and damned the human heart, was no more! Never again would Frank No Hart reappear, and Frank Newhart (for that was his real name) would never make the mistake of callously mistreating that most precious possession that he had.

From that day on, he was always conscious of and cherished dearly his sensitive, vulnerable heart. In fact, he opened it to the world, to people, to nature, to let the world have it all, only this time he really knew what love was, how to find it, how to give and receive it -- and every human need affected him emotionally, the plight of the sick, the plight of beggars on the

206

street, the plight of the handicapped, the plight of the homeless, the pain and suffering of others. He was filled with compassion and a greater, more spiritual love than he had ever known. He empathized with others in both their joy and pain, even in their frustrations.

"There, let me help you with that package!" "O Miss Jones, you shouldn't do that heavy work. I'll do it for you!" "I don't have much, but here's a sandwich, etc."

And he would give away his lunch to the homeless person on the street corner. He was always giving away something to relieve or satisfy someone else's need, whether it was money, food, his time, his labor, but especially his love. And it brought him much happiness. He was even kind to the dogs and cats in the neighborhood; he fed the pigeons in the park; he gave the squirrels nuts, and whenever they saw him coming, all the animals eagerly approached him without the slightest fear or reservation. He came to be known and loved by everyone and every creature for his kindness and compassion. He was a very happy man, and I doubt that anyone or anything could ever break his heart again, for he found the true meaning of "LOVE."

REUNITED

He stood on the 102nd floor staring out at the world, at the city streets, buildings, lights, streams of red and white lights moving in opposite directions on the roads and parkways, at a depth of the starry skies, at the bridges in the distance lit up, the glimmering waters of the Hudson joining the Pacific, and the shadowy shorelines that formed a dark silhouette against the sea and sky. He stood there feeling loneliness, detachment, and emptiness inside. He could hear the words still ringing in his ears, "Druscilla!...Druscilla!..." Out there was a huge and complex world, a world of awesome contradictions, social boundaries, cultural diversities, corporate structures, power brokers, vested interests, political intrigues, graft and corruption, a world of good and evil, virtue and vice, greed and envy, cruelty, and kindness, a world of wealth and poverty, a complex world, a hard and uncompromising world. He thought that he had come to grips with that world, that he had dealt with it on his terms, that he had "made it" with an iron will, never letting weakness or sentimentality rule him, with a take-no-prisoners, a me-first-and-to-hell-with-everybody-else attitude, with a lie, steal, pretend, say-what-others-want-to-hear, wear-whatever-mask-will-do attitude. And it was this philosophy that brought him all his success, so he thought. Yes, he was a successful businessman, a corporate executive who made it to where he was through ambition and selfishness. But he may have paid a high price, too, for that success!

A long time ago, he had made a decision, a choice, when he came to a crossroads in his young life. At age 21, an only child whose parents had died a year earlier in a plane crash, he was about to be married to his 19-year-old sweetheart. Preparations were made, and everyone was waiting at the church. The bride had arrived and joined the crowd of waiting people, but they didn't know then that the bridegroom, Carl Stevens, had already taken off in another direction and was never to be heard from again. It was quite an embarrassment for the girl, Druscilla Harley, and her family, who were extremely disappointed, but more puzzled and confused. There was seemingly no warning or indication that this might happen, and when it did, everyone searched for Carl Stevens in case he met with foul play, even the local sheriff and his staff, for days until finally, someone who was at the bus depot on the day of the wedding reported they saw him boarding a greyhound bus heading West. This was later confirmed by the taxicab driver, who dropped him off at the station. There was no question that the young lady's life was ruined after that, particularly since, unbeknown to Carl, she was a few weeks pregnant and was planning to tell him on their wedding night or later. Now he was gone! Who would have thought? Who could have known? Of course, to prevent any further embarrassment, her parents, once they found out about the pregnancy, sent her away to live with her grandparents in Ohio, where she gave birth to twins (a boy and a girl) and where she raised her two children, Priscilla and John, as a single parent. She never married and devoted her life to her children. This was by choice though there were many suitors, but she could never say yes again. She carried the hurt inside her for a long time and, in fact, never recovered from it.

All this time, Carl had fled to California, where he struggled for a time in the advertising business selling ads, and anything else, while honing his take-no-prisoners-way-of-life skills, which he perfected when he relocated to New York City. In New York City's rat race, he mastered the art too well. There, he found his niche when his ambition helped him rise to V.P. of a large advertising firm. Later when the firm was taken over by the Miller Brewing Co., he went even higher until he became 1st Vice President in Charge of Advertisement and Sales. Of course, he didn't do all of this with talent alone, he seduced, with the sole purpose of exploitation, and married the daughter of the owner of the advertising company when he came to New York City, which got him the promotion to Asst. V.P., in the first place, from where he rose to V.P. It was a marriage of convenience, so to speak. All this time since leaving Atlanta, more than 25 years had passed. He was now a successful businessman, married into a fairly well-to-do family, a marriage which bore no children; however, since his wife, after many diagnoses and treatments by specialists, was found unable to conceive due to a biological problem.

No matter what, his life was busy all the time, taking him to the four corners of the globe, running advertising campaigns, attending Board of Directors Meetings, advertising conventions, luncheons, national sales conventions, etc. It was at one of these conventions in Chicago when it happened for the very first time. In the middle of his keynote speech, a voice in the audience suddenly shouted:

"Druscilla, Druscilla! Remember Druscilla!"

He had not heard that name in 25 years, and it was like a bolt that jolted his memory. He paused for a second while the security people removed the person from the hall. Somehow he continued his speech to the end, but later in his room, he thought about the incident, and he thought about Druscilla!...

The incident was repeated in St. Louis and San Francisco and finally in New York City. He was speaking at a dinner in the Twin Towers and was talking about the corporation as being a closely knit family, run like a family, where everyone's well-being is important and their contributions vital to the success of the company; then, out of nowhere the voice in the audience shouted:

"You have no family! Remember Druscilla!"

This time he instructed the security guards to hold the man in a room nearby until he had finished his speech. He made light remarks to the audience about the heckler that it was his competitors who had put him up to it.

"They'd do anything," he said, "to get an edge in this business, but we're going to stay No. 1!"

After the speech, he went to where the guards were holding the man, and, to his surprise, he saw that it was Mr. Harley, Druscilla's father, who had broken down.

"Why did you do it? She was pregnant besides...Why? If only I had the nerve!!"

(Mr. Harley apparently had never forgiven him and was planning all these years to get revenge if he ever found him--now that he did, he lost his nerve!) The security guards took away from him the gun, which he flayed at them, but he apparently didn't know how to use it or didn't have the heart to. Then Mr. Harley broke into tears! Carl told them to see him safely out of the building but under no circumstances to harm him or arrest him either. And as they dragged him away, he could hear Mr. Harley loud and clear.

"I hope God makes you pay for it!"

He took the elevator and came to where he was now standing on the 102nd floor. Only now, perhaps because he was much older, for age and time have a way of changing one's perspective, or perhaps because he came to realize that having a high position in any company in itself is not happiness at all if you never loved anyone, never knew the pleasure of being loved, of having children, and of having a real family, for he had married only for convenience, as a means to an end, not for love. Only now, as he stood there looking out at the vastness, did he begin to realize that his whole life and philosophy were flawed. Only now did he begin to think about the past!

He remembered when he was 16, and she was only 14, and they first met in High School. They were the perfect couple on campus, always together, dating, going to parties, picnics, games, and dances. Everyone who knew them considered them as joined forever. It was a foregone conclusion that someday they would be married to each other. They were from the same community and went to the same State College. He was a senior, and she was a junior, and they were about to be married. Getting married in a small town was a natural thing for a young lady soon after graduating from High School or College. Most of the married couples there, including her parents, had done the same thing before her. She looked forward to being a wife and mother, and while college was fine, it wasn't absolutely necessary. Marriage was; besides, she had another reason for not wanting to put it off. She was looking forward to the wedding, and he likewise seemed to be, or maybe he thought he did, but perhaps that was more because it was expected of him - - for, after courting a girl so long, you'd better have marriage in your mind. However, in Carl's 20th year, when both his parents were killed, that had a severe impact on his mind. He started to change inwardly and to think differently about life, his life. Indeed, his uncle and his uncle's wife had helped him and encouraged him to finish college, and everyone was very nice. Feeling a little sorry for him, but deep down, a restless seed began to germinate.

Little by little, it grew into a desire to get away from this drab old southern town set in its ways of living. Apart from his hating his parents for dying, he began to lose trust in the world he knew, their world, and its conventions, and he wondered what it would be like to strike out in a different direction. He said nothing, however, to anyone, not even to Druscilla.

Druscilla and her family, meanwhile, were already making preparations for the wedding. He was senior only days away from graduating, and Mr. Crown had already made him an offer to work in his real estate office downtown. Even Mr. Harley was ready to give him a job in his hardware store. Druscilla didn't suspect any real change in him and attributed his latest attitude to his bereavement though it was almost a year. It seems, though, that his decision to act must have come very suddenly, even to himself, on the early morning of the wedding. He started to get dressed, then suddenly changed his mind and made some excuse to his uncle that he had to pick up something and would be right back. And that was when he lit out for California.

"Hey, what the heck, they'll soon forget about me, anyhow, and she'll find someone else to settle down with..." he thought.

Now, as he stood reflecting on these things in the past, the words of Mr Harley sank in.

"Why did you do it? How could you? And she was pregnant besides!!"

"Pregnant!! He must be mistaken; she wasn't pregnant at all! If she was, why didn't she tell me? No, she wasn't pregnant at all!"

Then he thought again, "Was she...?" The implications of this hit home like a ton of bricks! Now, here he was, close to fifty, feeling sorry that he had no family, no children around him. What if it were true? What if, all those years, he was a biological father to someone and didn't even know it? O, that's a hard one to swallow, and, in his act of abandonment long ago, what pain he must have caused? Only at this moment did he seem to possess an awakened conscience when for 25 years, he had none. It caused all kinds of misgivings and second thoughts to stir, not to mention a new feeling for him, guilt! So that was why Mr. Harley came after him to shoot him when he lost his nerve! And Druscilla, what became of her...and his child? Sometimes, one has to wonder, maybe success isn't all it is made out to be if there is no one to succeed for but yourself, and there is no one to carry on your name!

At that moment, his associates began to wonder where he was when one of his assistants remembered seeing him get on the elevator. The elevator operator took his assistant up to the 102nd floor to look for him.

"Mr. Stevens," said the assistant, "So here you are. We were all looking for you!"

"Oh, Mark, it's you! Was I gone that long?"

"Not really, sir, about 20 minutes, but we really should be going. Your chauffeur is waiting downstairs for you."

"Mark," said Mr. Stevens, "tell me, you're a young man. Do you have a family?"

"Why, yes, Mr Stevens. Mary and I have two lovely children, 4 and 6 years of age, two girls."

"That must be wonderful, Mark, how I envy you! You're a very lucky young man!"

"Why thank you, sir."

And they came down the elevator, rejoined their other associates, and they all left the building together.

That night at home, he told the whole story to his wife, who, for the first time, saw a human side to his nature that she had never seen before. He was actually vulnerable for the first time, deeply troubled with his conscience, and genuinely sorrowful. It awakened her maternal instincts, and she tried to console him.

"After all," she said, "you were too young and confused at the time; besides, you did not know! But now I think you should try to find them, both the mother and the child. You must try to make up to them somehow."

"Yes," he said, "I must try to find them!"

The next morning by coincidence, Mrs. Stevens had turned on channel nine, and an interesting program was in progress about people trying to find their lost relatives, parents, and children whom they had.never seen or had last seen many decades ago! Some people were given up for adoption, for instance, and were looking for their biological parents. On the show, there were two very interesting young people, a young lady and a young man, who were guests on the show and who, at that very moment, were making a plea to the TV audience and viewing public to please call into the station if they had any information about someone they believed to be their father, but whom they have never met. Some of the circumstances they talked about fit her husband's story to a "T." They even mentioned his first name, Carl, a name they said they heard their mother call many times, sometimes in her sleep.

"Carl," they said, "if you can hear us, please call into this station."

And a telephone number was flashed across the screen, which Mrs Stevens wrote down. Then she called her husband.

"Carl, come quickly, something you have to see on the TV screen. Come quickly!"

When Carl came into the room and looked at the television, he saw a beautiful young woman and a handsome young man, sister, and brother, in their middle to late twenties, who spoke again:

"Dad...Carl, if you are listening, my mother's name was Druscilla Harley of Atlanta, and we are her only children, twins, your son, and daughter. Please, we beg you, call this station. We need to meet you and hope you would like to meet us, too! There's so much to tell you. We made a promise to our mother that we would find you. Please call!"

Carl was watching the TV, and when he looked at their faces and heard them speak about their mother, he knew there was no doubt whatsoever that they were Druscillas and his children. Suddenly this iron-willed man, this

213

unsentimental, self-disciplined, unemotional man, started to cry in front of the television set. His wife picked up the telephone and called the station. They took his name and telephone number and announced to his children that they had just heard from their biological father, who was living in New York City and was anxious to meet them. The studio then made arrangements for them to meet that same evening, and they videotaped it at the Stevens' home.

It was a very emotional meeting, a grown man crying and begging his children to forgive him, which they did, for they were very glad to know him at last. They told him that their mother had never married and had passed away a few years ago. She had forgiven him for what happened 25 years ago, for they were too young at the time, she said. All the time, she only told them good things about him. One thing she made them promise was to look for him. She was sorry that he had not known all these years that he had a son and a daughter. She had wanted so much to tell him on the night they were to be married and not before the wedding. She told them that she was sure that once they met, he would love them, and she would rest better if she knew they had found each other at last.

Carl Stevens, whether deserving or not, was a lucky man indeed that he had such good children whose mother was so forgiving. They were never taught to hate him. Now, with time, they would come to know their father, and he will get to know them. He was a transformed person from the day he met them, and he became more loving and caring than ever before, especially to his wife. They both now had a family in Druscilla's children! With time, they all grew very close, and when grandchildren came along, they pampered and spoiled them all the more.

I suppose the only loser in this story was Druscilla, but maybe not! Her life was filled with the love of her children for 25 years, and Carl's was empty all that time where love was concerned! It was because of Druscilla that he finally came to know love, and it was through her children and grandchildren that the two of them, in a way, were reunited.

THE RING

As he sat in the airplane above the clouds, his mind began to travel back in time. He was a little boy again, not more than ten years old, and he had just come in from the playground where he and other boys and girls of the neighborhood played softball and kick football almost every day after school. Their playing field was usually the school ground or the open spaces between the tenement houses in La Boca C.Z., where he grew up as a child. On this particular day, it was important that he arrive home on time, for it was a special day. As he walked into the house, his mother was there to greet him.

"You're a good boy for coming home on time, now go and wash up and come to the table to eat your supper!"

He looked at her and smiled, "Yes, Mommy, but afterwards, I have a surprise for you!" And he ran to the bathroom, scrubbed himself clean, and then came to the table for dinner.

There were happy faces at the table -- happy, smiling faces of his father and mother, his two brothers and two sisters; and there, too, was his favorite dish, stewed chicken with peas and rice, which was all the more delicious with the special flavors his mother used. After dessert and everyone was more than satisfied, his mother turned to him.

"Now, Henry, what was the surprise you had for me?"

Henry ran to the bedroom and returned with a little package, which he gave her.

"Happy Birthday, Mommy! I love you, Mommy!"

"Why, thank you, Henry," she said as she opened the package. Inside was a gold-plated ring with a beautiful rhinestone set on its crown. She tried it on, but it was too small to fit on her fingers.

While she was trying on the ring, Henry said, "We read a story in school today about mothers, and afterward the teacher recited a poem called "Somebody's Mother!" I felt so glad you are my mother. I wanted to buy you something, so I took the money from my savings bank and bought you this ring, but I didn't know it was the wrong size!"

"It's a beautiful gift," she said, "even if it is too small; I will always cherish it regardless, and I love you, too, Henry! You are a good boy, the best son a mother ever had!" She hugged him and kissed him, and it made him very happy.

For almost two years after that, a day never went by unless he showed some outward sign of his love. He would offer to help more than usual around the house; he would draw pictures in school of her and bring them home; he would never leave home without kissing her on both cheeks; in short, he was a model son though he was only ten years old.

As time went by, however, he became interested in things away from home. There was softball, movies, pals, hanging around bigger boys, camping, seeking out new adventures, etc. He was still affectionate but not like before. In his teen years, as his hormones started acting up, he became interested in girls and parties and the usual things that teenage boys do. He had long forgotten about the ring! The only rings he thought about now were the friendship rings he gave to girls he liked.

Chores around the house were becoming a burden he would try to get out of if he could. But his mother understood such things; after all, he was a growing boy who must learn about the world and become a man. She saw that he did not lack for anything, nothing but the best for her, Henry, her "wash belly"!

When, as a young man, he left home to live and work in another town, she anxiously waited for the days when he would come home on weekends to take special care of him. He was her pride and joy! When he was gone, all she worried about was her Henry, how he was getting along, whether he was eating well, and if he was happy. When he came home, he wasn't fat enough for her, and she took good care of that with her special home-cooked recipes.

Soon he didn't come home on weekends, but she understood, for he was a very busy man, a very important man, and, she said, he would see her when he could. A few years went by, and one Friday evening, Henry came home, this time to tell her he was going far away to a foreign country where he could go further in his career and achieve the things he wanted out of life. Ever understanding, she told him, "Follow your star and be the best you can be. That's what I want for you!" So he left and went away to the land called "America" to follow his star.

In his third year abroad, while a senior in college, his father passed away, and he took an emergency leave to rush back to Panama for the funeral. It was a sad occasion but a happy one, too, for his mother got to see her "washbelly" once more! And after a brief stay, however, he returned to the U.S. to complete his studies. During the next few years, he continued to write

216

home often, every week, in fact, then his letters became fewer and fewer, and eventually, they stopped. The years just seemed to go by swiftly after that, and before you knew it, he was in his late thirties and studying and working very hard to become a successful school administrator. He never went home again, and his mother never saw him again, although she thought about him and asked about him and prayed for him. He was ever on her mind, and not a day went by that she did not ask, "How is Henry doing? How is my son? Tell him I love him!"

Meanwhile, Henry had become a top executive of an educational institution, working day and night. Any thought of home he put aside, "One day," he said to himself, "I'll go home again!" But that day never came, and more years went by until what seemed like yesterday turned into 40 years since he had left home. He was always too busy! Never seemed to have time! Panama was too far away! He made up excuses, too many excuses to himself, until one day, sitting in his office quite alone and feeling sad, he thought about home, his mother, and his childhood. "Surely it was just yesterday," he said to himself. "It can't be 40 years already!" And in his mind, he saw himself running into his mother's arms to tell her how much he loved her, and then the guilt welled up inside. "Lord, what if I never get to see her again?" The conscience of the little boy pushed aside so long, overwhelmed him. Nothing else mattered now; he had to see her, to see for himself how she was.

It was in early spring, about 2 p.m. in the afternoon, when he sat at his desk in his office and decided to write a long letter to his sister and brother in Panama who were taking care of their mother, for she was getting old and her sight was very poor. He said they could read the letter to her, and he poured out his heart in it to her. He closed the letter by telling them of his plans to come home for a visit later that summer, that nothing would prevent him from doing so. On his way home, he mailed the letter.

Now, by a strange coincidence, his sister had sent him a telegram at about the same time he was writing his letter, and the telegram was waiting for him when he arrived home that evening. The telegram informed him that if he wanted to see his mother alive again, he had better come quickly because she had suddenly taken seriously ill. In fact, she was dying and was asking for him, calling out his name:

"Henry, tell Henry I am fine, not to worry, he mustn't worry! He is a fine boy, the best son a mother ever had!"

As he read those words, he could bear it no longer. His heart just broke into a thousand pieces, and he sobbed uncontrollably.

That is how he came to be on that emergency flight that evening in the spring of 1989 heading for Panama, thinking about the past and wondering, 'When did he stop being that little boy'? He couldn't remember. How he would have loved to turn back the clock!

Finally, at about 7:30 p.m., the plane landed at Tocumen Airport, Panama City, and his brother, who awaited his arrival, took him straight to their mother's home in "Parque Lefevre" as fast as they could go! All along the route, Henry kept saying, "Hurry, hurry, I hope we're not too late!"

When they arrived, they saw people standing downstairs. All they said was, "Hurry!" and moved aside to let them pass. As they ran up the stairs and entered the house, there were people there as well, and as Henry and his brother approached the bedroom, the people who were standing around were crying! They told him that his mother had just passed away only a minute ago, and her last words were, "Henry..." He ran to her, completely out of control of his emotions, and cried like a baby, begging her to forgive him. They tried to console him but it didn't help. Then he kissed her on both cheeks and held her hand. He noticed her left hand was clenched tight, even in death, as he tried to open it. When he managed to open it, he saw in the palm of her hand the "ring" he had given her fifty years ago, when he was a little boy. She had kept it all these years close to her heart and never parted with it, even to her very last breath.

Epilogue:

O to look on my mother's face
as she lay in her final rest,
And to think of my life that she gave,
And of all of her love that was mine,
And to think of her gentle hands,
Of her self-sacrificing ways,
And of all that she did just for me
That I never could repay—
It is too much, too much for words,
And too great a debt to bear!
 ...August, 1989
  Parque Lefevre, Panama
 J.W.E.

THE LOVERS

It was dawn, and somewhere on the banks of the Ganges River near a place called Sangam not far from the city of "Allahabad," a small group of men gathered on the shore as they watched a boatman offshore steer his vessel while a holy man seated in the boat, tilted a receptacle once, twice, three times, each time casting ashes into the river. As he did so, he chanted:

"Receive, O Mother Ganga, these sacred remains of two lovers. Joined now their ashes; may the Great Spirit give them peace, and may their souls be eternally united in paradise. Receive, O Mother Ganga, these sacred remains…"

The dark crystals fell on the surface of the tranquil river and slowly sank into her bosom, and as the last remains were cast, a gentle gust of wind blew over the boat and scattered wide the remaining ashes. It was as if the wind also was paying its last respects like the visitors who stood on the shore.

On another day several years ago, far away in a country called America, late in the springtime when fresh flowers were blooming, and the sun was not so harsh, a similar gust of wind, perhaps the same one on its travels around the earth, blew and sent a silken scarf floating. It fell at the feet of a young man as he walked across the square. He rescued it and, pleased with its bouquet, turned to return it to its owner. As he turned and his eyes met hers for the first time, he was happy that the wind had blown and that fate had brought him there to that place at that moment in time, for the one whom his eyes beheld was beautiful. Her long black hair, her delicate features, her beautiful eyes of amber, her smile, the bangles on her hand, her graceful figure, her lovely silk dress, they were all so neatly put together.

"I believe you dropped your scarf. It is such a lovely scarf, too!"

"Thank you," she said, smiling at him as she approached a step closer to retrieve the errant scarf, "you are very kind."

"It is my pleasure," he responded, "are you a student at the university?"

"Yes, this is my first semester. And are you?"

"Are you what?" he said as her beauty distracted him for a second.

"Are you a student, too?"

"Yes, I am a senior in Biochemistry. What is your major?"

"Biophysics," she replied, "I am thinking of possibly a medical career."

"That's interesting," he replied. "I am going to be a doctor one day."

Their academic interests struck a common chord, but even without that, she was already struck by this handsome young man who was so bright, who spoke so well, and who was East Indian besides.

"Forgive me," he said as they walked toward the building, "I didn't even introduce myself properly. My Name is Shakeem Devi Budhu!"

With pleasure in her eyes, she said, "And I am Kumarie Sacrani. I am late for my physics class; it was nice to meet you, Shakeem!"

And before she could dart off, he asked, "Will I see you again? May be for lunch?"

"Yes, at one o'clock!" replied Kumarie.

"I will be waiting right here," he said, pointing to the bottom of the stairs where he stood and watched her disappear into the building.

At one o'clock, he was there waiting, and he did not have to wait too long when at 1:10 p.m., she came to meet him.

"How was your chemistry class?" she asked as they walked toward Broadway together.

"It went well, thank you. How was your physics class?"

They talked as they crossed Broadway and made their way to a little East Indian restaurant. It was small and cozy, and they found an empty table where they sat and continued their conversation.

Since he was a senior at Columbia University and he was much more familiar with the institution, he shared with her the intricacies of how to get around, where everything was located, what she should know about the campus, etc. She was gratified to have someone to relate to who was a source of support, especially someone to whom she felt so attracted to. After lunch, he walked her to her class, and they parted with the knowledge that they would be together for lunch the next day as well.

They saw each other again during the next few days and agreed to continue seeing each other on a regular basis. After the first few meetings, their conversations became less and less academic as they talked about the future, their personal lives, social activities, hobbies and interests, etc., discovering more and more how much they had in common. Already the bond between them was becoming stronger.

"Do you live in the city?" she asked him.

"No, I live with my family in Manhasset, L.I. Where do you live?"

"I live in Rego Park, Queens, with my parents," she said.

"What part of India did you say you came from?" asked Shakeem.

"I didn't say! I was born here in America!" said Kumarie, "but my family is from New Delhi. Were you born in India?

"No. I was born here, too. My parents came from New Delhi before I was born."

"Do you think it is right for us to adopt the ways of this country since we were born here? My family is always telling me I should not think like Americans," said Kumarie.

"I believe," answered Shakeem, "where we were born does not change the fact that we are East Indians. That is our heritage, and we must pass on the traditions, customs, and culture of our people to our children."

"It is alright for you to say that, but do you know that by our customs and traditions, I should not be making dates with you without my family approving in advance?"

"Yes, of course, that is true. I know that in India, these things are arranged and approved of in advance by one's family, but maybe it was our destiny to meet the way we did. For that, I am glad we are in America!" said Shakeem.

"So you do agree, then, that we should adopt the ways of this country?"

"Not exactly," said Shakeem, "we should take the best from both worlds."

"Do you also believe that women should be equal to men?" she asked, knowing how the old customs were in India.

"Yes, I believe they should be equal, although some things a woman is better equipped to manage."

"Like what, for instance?"

"Well, like having babies, for instance."

222

And they laughed and joked about it, saying what a pity men can't have babies, too, then they would know how a woman feels in childbirth. Then Shakeem said to her, as they were returning from lunch, "This evening, I will wait for you. I could go part of the way home with you. Would you like that?"

"Yes," said Kumarie, as in the back of her head she was hoping that one day soon he would also ask to meet her parents, and maybe, too, both their parents could get to meet each other.

That evening he waited for her after her last class, and they took the train into Queens together. All along the way, they sat holding hands, communicating with furtive looks, sighs and smiles, flirtations, and silly remarks, the way young people who are falling in love for the first time do.

Before she reached her stop, he said, "Kumarie, I told my parents about you. Wouldn't it be nice if our families could meet? I'd like to visit your home one day soon."

Strange he should say that, because every day since the first time they met she could not keep from telling her parents about him and how wonderful he was, and they insisted that they should meet this young man and his parents before she could take him seriously. So when he said what he did, her heart was so pleased that she couldn't wait to tell them.

The day he visited Kumarie's home, he brought her a gift, a silk sari, and a scarf for her mother, Mrs Sakrani. That Saturday evening, he met Kumarie's parents, sister, brother, aunt, niece, and nephew. They were all eager to meet this young man whom Kumarie had spoken so much about. Needless to say, they were very pleased with him.

"My mother and father send you their best regards," he said to Mrs. Sakrani, "and one day, they would like to meet you."

"Thank you," said Mrs Sakrani. "Did you say your last name is Devi Budhu?"

"Yes, my father and mother came from New Delhi, where my father was a clerk in the government office."

"Is your mother's first name Chandra?"

"Yes."

"I know your mother! We went to primary school together. This is a wonderful surprise!"

And she was pleased with him and happy to know he was both Hindu as well as the son of a childhood friend from the mother country. She insisted on him calling his mother on the phone, which he did, so she could talk to her. They were emotional and talked for a good while.

Kumarie, in the meantime, seeing that her family liked Shakeem so much, was overjoyed. Her heart was now so happy that after that, she dreamed about him day and night, anxious for the time to pass quickly so she could be with him again. And each time they met, their relationship grew stronger and stronger still. They were now madly in love and were together not only at school but on weekends, holidays, and on festive occasions as well. Their parents had approved of their seeing each other, and they visited each other's homes often.

They made it a point, although comfortable in American society and ways, to hold on to their deeply religious Hindu culture. They prayed together and pledged their undying love for each other.

"Shakeem," she said, "will you love me forever?"

"Yes, Kumarie, I will love you till I die," he replied.

"Oh, Shakeem, won't you love me in the next life, too?"

"Forever and ever," said Shakeem.

"And I will love you till eternity!" replied Kumarie.

The two of them declared their love and pledged that they would never part. They told their families. Shakeem proposed marriage, and the two families arranged a joint celebration, at which time they would become officially engaged.

The Sakranies had many East Indian friends who were close and were like family, as is the way in closely-knit Indian communities. Tanweer Persaud was one such friend. For years he knew the family and came there often. Married, with a wife and three children, his friendship was taken for granted.

Mr. Persaud, however, who lived in Jamaica, Queens, was a quiet, mysterious man who did not have a good reputation. He was regarded by his neighbors as "anti-social" and unfriendly. To them, he was a secretive, mean-spirited, suspicious character who spied on them and caused problems by reporting them falsely to the landlord.

Mr. Persaud, it seems, acted differently when he was around the Sakranies. Nevertheless, whether presuming upon his friendship with the Sakranies or

224

presuming more than he had a right to, he took a fancy to Kumarie. He had known her most of her life and had watched her grow into a beautiful young lady and must not have been satisfied that he was already married but sought the affection of the much younger Kumarie, which of course, she denied him. He continued, nevertheless, expressing his interest in her and pursuing her affection persistently. He became obsessed and determined. He even threatened her.

"You will be mine, Kumarie, or no one else will have you!"

Kumarie did not take him seriously and thought that when he saw her and Shakeem together, he would be reasonable and realize that there was no chance for him in her life. That is why one evening at a social gathering of friends and family, she introduced them to each other. He was jealous, of course, but hid his feelings towards his rival, Shakeem. In his twisted mind, he still thought that he could make her his.

Meanwhile, Kumarie and Shakeem continued to enjoy their blissful courtship.

"Shakeem," she said, "I can't wait until we are married! I will make you very, very happy!"

"Yes, Kumarie, we will be the happiest couple ever!"

"After we are married," said Kumarie, "could we go to India, to Bombay, New Delhi, and sail on the Ganges River?"

"Yes, we must go home to our roots," said Shakeem, "and know the place where we came from. I would like that very much!"

The day came when the families announced the engagement of Kumarie Sakrani and Shakeem Devi Budhu at a social gathering at the Devi Budhu residence. The two young lovers were radiant, she in her silk sari and he in his businessman's suit and tie. Since the engagement ceremony was semiformal, his western dress was acceptable. Shakeem knew, however, that at the wedding, he was going to wear the traditional "Jorajamma and Cakhat" and Kumarie the traditional "Sari and Sirbandi," and that their wedding outfits were already being made and everything was well in hand.

At the engagement, there was the traditional array of mango leaves and dried coconuts, fruits and soft drinks and candles, etc. When everyone was gathered, a brief ceremony was conducted, and the two happy people exchanged rings, and they danced all night in each other's arms Everyone was happy for them and said, "They are a perfect couple!" The engagement party, as stated, was held at the Devi Bhudus; however, one person was conspicuous by his absence. That is because he was not invited. That was Mr Tanweer Persaud.

The next day when he learned of the engagement party, something inside his brain snapped, and, on that night, as Shakeem lay in his bed at his family's home, around 11 p.m., the doorbell rang. When he answered the door, he saw an angry-looking man standing there at the entrance with something in his hand.

"I have something for you!" said the man.

Shakeem could see the shape of the dark metallic object that he brandished in his hand. It was a semi-automatic rifle! Instinctively Shakeem tried to close the door as he sensed the sinister meaning and turned to seek cover, but the man fired through the door and forced his entry, continuing to fire a barrage of bullets into Shakeem Devi Budhu's body. Shakeem died there in the hallway riddled with machine gun bullets. The killer was Tanweer Persaud!

The following morning, when Kumarie heard the news, she fainted. When they revived her, she was still hysterical and remained distraught all day, screaming and calling out her lover's name, "Shakeem!!...Shakeem!!!..."

Two days after it happened, she was more distraught than ever, and her depression and sadness grew frighteningly worse. Her parents, fearing she would do harm to herself, had her confined to her room for her own safety. Later that morning, her older sister, Nadine, who was the last person to speak to her alive, called her on the telephone, and Kumarie spoke some frightening words to her.

"I am going to be with Shakeem…he's waiting for me…I cannot live without him!!… Goodbye, Nadine!!"

And with those words, while her sister was pleading over the telephone:

"No, Kumarie … don't do it, Kumarie!!"

She plunged through the window of her bedroom, eight stories high, to the grounds below to her death!

The two families, friends, and the whole Indian community were shocked and deeply saddened by the double tragedy that came just weeks before what was to have been a happy wedding day. The wedding dress and suit were already made, and there was so much promise of happiness that now was not to be. But although they could not be married in life, they would be in death, for the families decided to have the wedding ceremony anyway, while the two lovers' spirits were still on this earth. Their bodies were dressed in splendid wedding outfits, a beautiful silk bridal saree for the bride, Kumarie, and a finely gold-embroidered sherwani 2-pc suit for the groom, Shakeem. They lay magnificently side by side as the priest conducted the wedding ceremony, and incense and flowers were laid at their sides. The wedding rings were placed on their fingers, and they were pronounced husband and wife. If not in life, they would go into paradise as Mr. and Mrs. Devi Budhu. After the ceremony, they were cremated together, and their ashes combined and sent to India to be cast into the bosom of the Ganges River.

Their wish to return to their homeland after they were married was now fulfilled as the last of their ashes dissolved in the sacred waters of the Ganges River. Slowly, the boatman plied his oars toward the shore, he and the holy man having finished their mission. When they reached the shore, as they disembarked from the boat, both they and the group of men that had gathered on the shore soon departed. Evening approached, and the river was left alone to itself, flowing peacefully with its secrets and sacred essences of those whose earthly remains had come to a final rest within her sanctuary.

Epilogue

Shakeem and Kumarie could not live without each other, and so when Shakeem was tragically murdered, Kumarie committed suicide so that in death, they would be together. Although they died tragic deaths, be not sad for them, for they died with the certainty that their love would live forever.

I believe that on some dark nights, if you look up to the sky and see two bright stars twinkling close together in the heavens, or on a clear summer day, if you see two sunflowers kissing in the sun or two lovebirds soaring sublimely in the skies, or a rainbow against the sky and you are moved, be not surprised for it is Shakeem and Kumarie that you see, expressing their love for each other, inseparable forever.

Eternal Love
(Dedicated to Shakeem and Kumarie)

O Shakeem, Shakeem,
True lover of mine,
Sweet is your love today;
But will you love me when I'm

feeble, old and gray?

O Kumarie, O Kumarie,
when we grow old and gray
our bond will be secure,
for, when we face that day
I shall but love thee more.

O Shakeem, Shakeem,
Sweet is your love I know;
but if I shake and bend,
and barely see, even so
how will you love me then?

O Kumarie, O Kumarie,
know that my heart shall see
you then the same as now,
though countless years may flee
and we are old and bowed.

O Shakeem, Shakeem,
My lover true, think not that I offend;
but though you love me now,
all things, I fear, must end!
And when I'm dead and gone,
How will you love me then?

O dearest, dearest Kumarie,
Our love shall never die!
If even we have changed, Kumarie --
As all things shall with time --
yet time will not the cheater be,
my love, for you and me
as swift as it may flee!

O Shakeem, Shakeem,
Sweet lover of mine,
How shall I know 'tis thee,
How shall I know, O love divine,
If we are changed, tell me,

If we are not the same
tell me how love shall be?

O Kumarie, O Kumarie,
O dearest one, if thou,
a thousand years from now,
should be a bird I'll be the wind
that bears you up
in flight and soothe your wings.

O Shakeem, Shakeem,
your words and pledges sweet
are worth my sleep with thee;
my life is now complete
as long as you love me,
no matter what shall be.

My dearest Kumarie,
Ten thousand years shall pass,
the first just as the last --
If you're an angel, I'll be your sunshine
That warms your face divine;
If you're a rose I'll worship at your vine
And be charmed every hour
Ten thousand years and more!

O Shakeem, Shakeem,
True lover of mine,
I cannot wait to see
Or share such bliss with thee!
Tell me again, true lover,
That it may dwell in me
Tomorrow and forever!

Kumarie, my love, Kumarie,
O dearest, dearest one,
If I'm a sunflower, you'll be my sun;
If I'm a bee, you'll be my honey;
If I'm a song bird, you'll be my song;
If I'm an oyster, you'll be my pearl!
You'll be the rainbow in my world,

My treasure and my happiness
As you are now, and I'll be blessed
Ten times ten million times, you'll see,
And though eons go by,
When you shall say to me,
Do you still love me now?
Just like a star, Kumarie,
The brightest in the skies,
You'll sparkle in my eyes
And I'll be answering still,
"Yes, yes, my love, and always will
for all eternity!"

HOPE AND DESPAIR

JACKIE'S CHRISTMAS PRESENT

It was a bitterly cold day, and the symbols were everywhere. Strings of lights and decorations ringed the buildings and rooftops, tinsels, bells, and wreaths were in the windows, and even the trees outdoors were bedecked with lights. It was a day when the world should be happy, when peace and brotherhood are supposed to reign, and people are supposed to be kind to each other. It was Christmas day!

Somewhere, away from the freezing cold, away from the blistering snow and the biting winds, was a bright and happy place, somewhere a warm and comfortable place, with plenty to eat, with the smell of freshly baked cake in the oven, with the windows and rooms beautifully decorated, the Christmas tree lights blinking, presents all pretty and neatly wrapped under the tree, just waiting!

As the sounds of Christmas carols filled the air, ushering from the radios, echoing in the streets, and the shouts of "Merry Christmas" came from everywhere, a family gathered around a tree, anxious to open their presents. There was mommy, daddy, sister Annie, and brother Billie, even Sheppe, the family dog, full of the Christmas spirit. Yes, it was a happy place that day in the apartment. Jackie had every reason to be happy; she even knew which present was hers before daddy announced it. She knew the three-foot Barbie doll townhouse with accessories would be her present. Why, she must have pointed it out to her daddy and mommy a hundred times when they were in the store before Christmas. It was the only present she wanted. She just knew that's what she was getting! Annie and Billie wanted a rocking horse and a choo-choo train, and they were beside themselves when they got their wishes and more besides. So when Daddy announced that the Barbie doll townhouse was hers, she wasn't too surprised, but of course, she was very, very happy.

After the gift-giving, there was a late breakfast on the table as they sat, joy beaming from their faces, to have their morning repast on that 25th day of December. Jackie was full of expectations, but she was so hungry! Why she should be so hungry, she did not know, but her stomach ached with hunger pains, especially when she saw the juicy slices of ham and cheese, eggs and grits, buttered muffins, fresh fruit cake, and eggnog on the table! She would make fast work of it, she thought, if only daddy wouldn't take so long with the prayers! Soon he stopped praying, and Jackie reached for a piece of fruitcake that her mouth was watering for...but the cake seemed so far away...and so hard to reach! Why couldn't she reach the cake?... She strained to move her hands... and could hardly move them. With all the strength in her little body, somehow she managed to get a small piece into her mouth. It tasted like snow!! Cold as ice!! Suddenly she felt cold, her whole body numb and stiff from the cold! Then a chill wind blew across her face! At that same moment, a voice that seemed far away spoke:

"Lord, help us; she must be completely frozen, lying there in the snow like that!"

And another voice spoke:

"Is she dead?"

"No, I don't think so!" Replied the first voice, "I thought I saw her eyes move a little, but she must be close to being dead, poor thing! I wonder how long she has been lying there!"

"We can't leave her there! Let's take her home with us," said a third voice, "we live just a block away from here! We can call our friend, Dr. Foster, from our house."

"Yes, we can't, for the love of God, leave her here!" the first voice rejoined.

It was Christmas morning, and in the Masons' home, a life hung in the balance. Mrs. Mason kept going back and forth to the kitchen to bring fresh water and whatever else was required. The doctor worked feverishly, trying to keep the little patient warm and alive.

'Would she live? Did they find her in time? Was it too late? What does it matter, anyway, to a society that has so many homeless, unwanted children already if one more such life were snuffed away? What is it about a society that would allow such tragedies? After all, it was not her doing that made her homeless; that brought her to this predicament! What could a 12-year-old do to deserve such a fate? There are too many victims of poverty and indifference already to create another one.'

Those were the thoughts that motivated Mr. and Mrs George Mason. Perhaps, too, their action was the only kindness this 12-year-old victim had ever known, but was it already too late? The doctor wanted to remove her to a hospital, but the Masons refused and would not hear of it. They were ready to stand by that decision! All day, then, they worked on Jackie and kept a close watch over her condition.

Ten hours later, on Christmas night, the smell of freshly baked cake from the kitchen registered on her olfactory nerves. It reminded her of the dream she had had while she laid in the snow. Then she opened her eyes and looked around and saw a room and windows just as she had dreamed them, beautifully decorated, Christmas tree lights blinking in the other room, presents under the tree! Then she heard the sounds of Joy to The World playing...ever so sweetly playing...and she thought she was in Heaven! Only in Heaven or in her dreams could these things happen! She looked again and saw a little boy and a little girl, and a little dog, staring at her lying in the bed, and she heard Mrs Mason's voice.

"Oh, thank God, she is alive! She is alive! She is going to live!"

The doctor instructed them to give her some warm soup for now that she was going to be alright, not to worry! The family gathered around her, full of warmth and love. They held her hand, they kissed her forehead, they wished her a merry Christmas...and Jackie started to cry! So did Mrs Mason! Then little Annie whispered something in her daddy's ears, and Mr. Mason went into the other room and returned with a package. He laid it beside the bed so Jackie could see it. It was...a Barbie doll townhouse!

"This is for you," he said, "from all of us."

And Jackie was so happy! "This must be Heaven," she thought. "This must be Heaven," while the Masons sang for her, "Silent Night, Holy Night!"

THE PIGEON LADY

It was a quiet Sunday morning, except for the intermittent flow of traffic going north and south along the island that divides Midland Parkway traffic – no one knows why they gave it that name, Midland Parkway, since it is not really a parkway but a local street in Jamaica Estates about ten blocks long, extending north from Hillside Ave. across the Grand Central service road and ending at 188th Street. At any rate, on this pseudo parkway, vehicles could be seen traveling even on a Sunday morning, though not as heavy as during the week when all the busy working people are about, and the busy commercial world is astir! It was, nevertheless, a relatively quiet morning several summers ago when most people were still in bed at 7:15 a.m., and, after convincing himself that it was only Sunday and he needed more rest, Carl Edwards hastened back to bed and slept until about 10 a.m. On this particular Sunday morning, when he finally awoke, he came into the living room, turned on the T.V., sat on the sofa, almost reclining, and started to look at the Sunday morning news. On the window ledge, there were two pigeons cleaning and pruning their feathers and cooing away. Suddenly they darted off the window ledge and flew away. Carl rushed to the window to see where they had flown in such a hurry. Looking down from the 6th floor toward the street, he saw pigeons flying from all directions and converging on the island in a clearing near a huge tree. There, he also saw an old grey-haired woman who seemed raggedy in appearance with a bag in her hand. She apparently was the reason for the flight of the pigeons who swooped down from everywhere, from the trees, from the tops of buildings nearby, from ledges, etc., like rockets with aero-dynamic swiftness and agility and unerring accuracy to the spot where the old lady stood that was soon overwhelmed by hundreds of cooing birds. As the old lady scattered handfuls and handfuls of breadcrumbs, rice, peas, and corn on the ground, the sea of pigeons, busily but orderly, pecked at the bountiful meal that rained down from her generous hands. Some pigeons landed on her shoulder (One even attempted to land on her head, but it did not bother her!), some at her feet, but they all found room somewhere, and when she saw that the more timid ones on the fringes were not fast enough or aggressive enough, she tossed a liberal supply in their direction, and the swarm spread out so that all the pigeons, strong and weak alike, had enough grain and crumbs to peck at. For a full half-hour, this feeding frenzy continued until the old lady's bag was empty. She said something to the pigeons, then turned and slowly walked away, leaving them to finish clearing the scraps, which they did impeccably, as she crossed the street and disappeared into one of the buildings.

235

That Sunday morning was the first time that Carl observed the old lady and the pigeons, but what he saw must have been happening long before he became aware. Anyway, he had only been living there two months, and by the time he usually left the house at about 8 a.m. to go to work on Mondays through Fridays, it was too late to see them. After that Sunday, however, he made sure he did not miss the pigeons' breakfast feeding. Some mornings he observed other species of smaller birds (who were in the minority) join in, likewise the local squirrels who seemed curious mostly until the pigeons pecked at them to keep them at their distance. The old lady appeared to caress certain pigeons at times who would never try to shun her, and Carl wondered what she was saying to them when she talked to them. One morning he deliberately left the house at 7:30 a.m. and passed close by them on his way to purchase a newspaper by the subway stand, which was nearby. He overheard her speaking to the pigeons.

"Come, children; look what your mother brought you today! Come, Myrtle, Sarah, Jane, I know your little babies have to be fed, so eat up all you can now! O Miriam, you naughty thing! Stop pecking at my hair!"

And when one of the frisky males tried to molest one of the females the way they often do with their strange dance around them, the old lady would shoo him off.

"Naughty, naughty Freddie, not now, don't you see she is eating! Shoosh away, you naughty boy!"

The pigeons would act like they understood every word she said, and she seemed to know the language they spoke, so it was a mutual thing. Carl felt a certain empathy with the old woman, seeing that she cared and took the time religiously to feed and look after the pigeons, while very few people seemed to even notice them or care what happened to these creatures!

"Thank Heaven for people like her!" he thought to himself as he passed her by.

He even turned toward her and said, "Good morning," very pleasantly while waiving in her direction.

"Good morning, sir. How do you like my children?" The old lady replied.

Carl returned her smile while nodding his head as he moved on.

That evening when he came home from work, he thought about the raggedy old lady, who she was, and what made her do what she did every day without failure, almost like an unflagging maternal duty and personal responsibility.

236

The majority of people in the world are too selfish and too busy with their own pursuits and daily lives to even care about each other, much less about pigeons. And the pigeons, they fly around us, walk around us every day picking up whatever they can find in the streets like the city's scavengers, and most people do not give them a second thought, and in fact, even find them a nuisance in many cases. Carl may not have felt that way, and he had not given it much thought until he saw the old woman who seemed genuinely to love the birds and who acted as if she was fulfilling a sacred mission.

"Alright, so there are people who love pigeons," he thought, "and she was one of them, so what of it!"

But he could not dismiss her so easily. Why did she go out of her way? What was her reason? Was she going to do this for the rest of her life? He could see doing this once or twice, but not every day! After all, it costs money for the food to feed them. Nobody was paying her to do that. Anyway, he went to bed thinking about it and was never quite satisfied he had figured it out.

Apparently, he was not the only one who observed the old lady in the mornings feeding the pigeons. He discovered this one Saturday morning when he ran into "Old Jim." That was what the neighbors called him. Old Jim lived in the same building as Carl, and he always said hello to him whenever he passed him by. That Saturday morning, Old Jim was sitting on a stump by the curb resting after his early morning walk when Carl came out of the building.

"Good morning, Old Jim," said Carl, "how are the legs this morning?"

"Oh, all right for an old man! Got to keep them pumping, you know, or they are going to give out on you! What about you, do you do any exercising?"

"Yeah," said Carl, "I go to the gym sometimes…look here, Old Jim, I don't mean to change the subject, but there's something I want to ask you!"

"Take your best shot, kid. Ask me anything!"

"Jim, you see that old lady across the street feeding the pigeons?"

"Yes, I see her. What about her?"

"I mean, who is she? Why does she feed the pigeons all the time? I've been watching her every day now for weeks, and she's there at the same time every morning without failure. Why is she doing it?"

"Soulmates!" replied Old Jim.

"I don't understand!" said Carl.

"She gave her soul to the pigeons, and vice versa!"

"I still don't understand!" said Carl.

"How long you say you've been living here?"

"About three months."

"Then you couldn't know."

"Couldn't know what?"

"Well, you see, it's like this," continued Old Jim, "I've been living around here for some forty years now, retired and everything, and I don't intend to move. I've seen just about everything that's happened 'round here. Do you see that building on the corner there by Hillside Ave.? I have seen a man get killed in that building once. His ex-woman shot him dead right there in the lobby as he was coming out of the building. Sucker must have mistreated her real bad, so he just got what he deserved. What apartment do you say you live in, 6F?"

"Yeah, I live in 6F. What about it?"

"That's another one. A woman poisoned herself in there. Just got tired of living, that's all! But you don't have to worry; that happened ten years ago! Her spirit isn't coming back there!"

"Old Jim, while you scaring the heck out of me, tell me about the pigeon lady!"

"Oh, I'm sorry, friend, don' mean to scare you or nothing. The pigeon lady, yeah, I like that name. So you want to know 'bout the pigeon lady, eh!"

"Yeah, tell me about her!"

"All right, all right already. You see her there; take a good look at her gray hair and all that. She's about eighty, my friend, about the same age as me. We go back a long way, her and me. Forty years ago, when I moved here, she was living on the top floor, room 8b, in that building across the street. Then, she wasn't alone; she lived there with a man she called her husband. She was a fine-looking woman and could dress to kill! She don't look like nuthin' now, but I tell you, she was fine then. I had my eyes on her myself (I even made a pitch once, and she turned me down!), but of course, she was married, or so everybody thought. Her husband used to show her off when they went strutting 'cause he knew he had a good thing! He fussed about her 'cause all the fellows found her very attractive. For several years they lived like a perfect couple, and you never would suspect anything. They even had a baby together. It was perfect until one day, her so-called husband left her and went back to his real wife somewhere down south. Left her, you hear me, with a 4-year-old daughter to take care of besides, and they never saw him again! She tried to pick up the pieces and get along without him after that, just her and her little girl, but after a while, she started seeing other men. I guess she was trying to find a father for her little girl or a husband, but none of them seemed to work out, although she kept trying. Then after the accident happened, life just went downhill for her."

"What accident?" asked Carl.

Jim paused for a moment and looked at Carl, who urged him to continue with the rest of the story.

"One day," he continued, "she went out to meet one of her male friends and left the little girl alone in the apartment. She had probably done it before, and nothing happened. But this time, somehow, somebody must have known she was away and got into the apartment! People say the intruder must have tricked the little girl into opening the door because the door wasn't broken, nor were the windows forced. Anyway, the intruder raped the little girl, murdered her, and took whatever he wanted from the apartment. When she returned later that night and saw what she saw, she went crazy! Clear out of her mind! She screamed so loud you could hear her screams several blocks down the street! All the neighbors came rushing, too, to the apartment and did what they could, but of course nothing could comfort her, especially when she knew it was her fault for leaving her daughter by herself. Life is full of irony. All the neighbors said that they would not have minded keeping her daughter if she had only asked them; but they never showed that lady any kindness or tried to befriend her. They even shunned her after her husband left her and said unkind things about her. Then after the terrible tragedy they had the nerve to say how they would have helped when in fact they never tried. People! I tell you they are something else! Anyway, someone did call the police, gave the mother a sedative, and called an ambulance to take her to the hospital where they kept her for a week under observation for shock, hysteria, and possible psychiatric examination and treatment. They kept her a few days longer and finally when they sent her home, a couple of the neighbors stayed with her for a while to keep her calm and help in whatever way they could. She kept asking for her baby, "Where's my baby! Where's my baby!" and kept blaming herself for what happened. It was sad! I tell you, friend, life is hard for a single woman out here especially with children and no other adult around! And to see her go through that tragedy, I was sorry for her. She never looked the same after that and went completely downhill, losing weight, losing interest in everything, getting careless with her appearance, staying inside that apartment all the time by herself."

"That's a very sad story, Old Jim," said Carl, "What…" but before he could end his sentence, Jim continued.

"I haven't finished the story yet, friend; you'll understand everything better when I am through. It seemed the neighbors felt she was alright enough to take care of herself again, and after a week or so, they left her by herself again but made sure they told her to call them if she needed them, and they also took her phone number to call on her from time to time.

What they didn't know is that although on the outside she seemed alright, the pain and brooding and the guilt remained deep inside. That is why early one Sunday morning, she climbed up on the rooftop (No one knows how she got up there!) and sat on the ledge looking down eight stories below. She had left a note in her apartment stating that she had no more desire to continue living and was going to fly away out of this world to be with her daughter. As she sat there in tears, building up her inertia to dive off the roof, who knows what thoughts were going through her mind? I'm sure she thought about her little girl, how she was so pretty, and so innocent! She was all she had in this world. She was so happy and had her whole life before her. Why did God let this happen? Now she was alone; she had no family, and, God knows, very few friends if any. She had tried to live her life as well as she could, but no use, and now the end that awaited her seemed all the more inviting. She would welcome it gladly.

Just at that moment," continued Old Jim, "when she set herself to leap to her death, was the very same moment that a flock of pigeons flew over her head and landed beside and around her on the rooftop. They cuddled next to her cooing and touching her, cooing and touching her as if to say, "Do not jump! Do not jump! We need you!" Some even sat in her lap as the cooing continued, and a watershed of tears poured out of her being as she sat on the ledge with the pigeons surrounding her. That was when she gave her soul to them, and they gave theirs to her. They saved her life. They gave her a reason for living. Yes, Pigeon Lady, that's a good name. You can call her the Pigeon Lady alright. The pigeons are her children; they are her whole life now."

When Old Jim was finished, Carl was speechless and tried his best to hold back a tear. "Thanks, Old Jim," he said, "thanks for telling me about the pigeon lady!"

KARLA

On a certain corner on Hillside Avenue, Jamaica, Queens, every day at the same time, rain or shine, snow or sleet, you'll see him standing there, waiting. He will wait two, three hours watching the subway exits, glancing at the faces passing by. He will not move from that corner until well into the evening, after dark, when all the crowds have dispersed. Then, drooping and with soul-sad eyes, slowly he would walk away into the night...until the next day.

Each day at 5:30 p.m., without failure, he comes, and waits! Sometimes the look in his eyes brightens, he raises his hands in a friendly gesture, he moves toward a passerby...but, no, he quickly returns again to his former stance, the gleam faded, to stand and wait as he had done, day after day, until the darkness comes.

So many people go by! They come from the subway in droves and droves. Many have friends and family waiting in cars to meet them; many join the long lines at the bus stops awaiting transportation to their homes some distances away. Each day they pass him standing at the corner and do not even know he is there. He does not beg, he does not stop them with outstretched palms, he does not make a sound, he only stands and waits. He watches and he waits and never leaves 'till well past eight. When he does, he walks away with body drooped, with faltering gait, off into the shadows of the night! He droops not only from a saddened state of mind, but also from the weight of years, years of waiting that only take their toll.

It is another day! It is nearly 6 p.m....and there he is, waiting and wondering, "Will she come today?" There was a time, however, when he didn't have to wonder, when he didn't have to wait too long, when two spritely feet would quickly dash toward him, when his heart would leap, and his soul would know no bounds for joy to tire quenching, as her blithe, soft and shapely form would melt within his bosom and his open arms, when those eyes, beaming with happiness, would make the rest of the world to him seem dull, how he lived just for those moments of happiness when she was in his arms! How he thrilled with ecstasy from the moment he saw her dashing across the street to be with him, to fill his life with unspeakable joy!

They first met one day in May. The beauty of that late spring day had not escaped him as he left work to take the train bound for the city. When he reached his destination, he hurried through the streets of mid-Manhattan, across 5th Ave, to the Metropolitan Museum of Art to catch the famous art

241

exhibit. He arrived at the museum in time and was wandering through the corridors when he suddenly saw her admiring an El Greco painting, and he walked up to her and said:

"Don't move; I would like to paint you just as you are against the Greco background. It will be my masterpiece!"

She turned and, pleasantly surprised, asked,

"Are you a painter?"

"Why, no," he said, "but I would paint you if I were, 'cause you are prettier than the Greco."

She was flattered, of course, and he took advantage of the opening to introduce himself.

"My name is Raymond Denis," he said, "and yours?"

"Karla St. Clair," she replied.

"Is El Greco one of your favorite painters?"

"Yes."

"Mine, too. He uses shadows and depths so magnificently!"

"And color," she added, "his use of light and color is amazing!"

They continued to walk through the museum admiring all the paintings and enjoying each other's company. The time went by so quickly they hardly noticed until the museum was about to close and everyone was being ushered toward the exits. As they were leaving, reluctant to part, he asked her where she lived.

"Forest Hills, Queens," she said.

"That's great," said Raymond, "I live in Jamaica Estates. We can take the same train to go home."

They took the subway to Queens together and all the way they engaged in conversation. She told him she was a secretary for a law firm in Manhattan and he said he was an accountant with an agency in Queens. The rest of the conversation was mostly light and trivial in their effort to amuse themselves and become better acquainted. Karla got off at Continental Avenue, Forest Hills and he continued to 179th Street and Hillside Avenue, but, before they parted, she gave him her telephone number and he gave her his.

That was the way they met. Of course, it was only the beginning for they saw each other again and continued to do so quite often until the spark that had kindled became a full bloomed flame and developed into very strong feelings for each other. Sometimes he would go to her place in Forest Hills where she shared an apartment with a girlfriend, but usually she would come to his place where he lived alone. He would be home long before her and would be waiting at the corner of Hillside Avenue when she got off the train at l79th Street stop to meet him. She would come straight from work and meet him there each time around 5:30 p.m. She was such a pretty thing with long flowing hair, clear brown eyes, smooth brown skin, and a dimpled smile that was so heavenly it could put flowers to shame.

"Sweetheart," she said, "I couldn't wait to see you! A day is much too long!"

"I know," he said, "even a minute seems too long away from you!"

Then, arm in arm, they would walk away, two happy lovers. He would take her to his 'place' not far from there, and they would spend many blissful hours and evenings together, with her staying over sometimes until the next day. Many times they would go out to dinner or to a show. In the next few summers, they both arranged their vacations at the same time and took trips together. They went abroad to places like Mexico, Paris, Barbados. It was one summer in Barbados that he proposed to her.

"Karla, I love you very much; will you marry me?"

"Yes," said Karla, "I thought you would never ask!"

And they were as enchanted with each other as two people in love could ever be. When they returned home that summer from Barbados, they planned to be married the following spring, for she wanted to be an Easter bride.

"Easter," she said, "is my favorite time of the year. The flowers are so beautiful then. Let's have plenty of flowers at our wedding, in a garden. I would like that!"

Raymond smiled, for he loved to see her happy and a garden would be fine with him. So now the summer was over and time kept creeping by. Cold December came and went, January and February, too. They never changed their way of meeting by the subway station after work whenever she came by his apartment. If anyone saw them when they met, they would know that these were two people who were meant for each other.

Now there was plenty of planning to do and arrangements to be made, invitations to be sent out, etc. etc. They contracted a wedding planner and everything was being taken care of in its proper course as March and April came around. They had even decided where they were going to live after the wedding, for they had planned to move out to Long Island as soon as they could find a house. But first things first, the wedding, then the honeymoon, then they would go house-hunting!

April came around on schedule, as well as time and destiny! The whole world seemed to move on schedule, and Karla and Raymond could not wait to exchange their marriage vows. Two weeks before the wedding was to take place, Raymond waited by the subway for Karla as he had always done. He stood by the corner and waited past 5:30 p.m. going on to 6, then 6:30, and still no Karla! He was becoming concerned, for she had never been this late before. He knew his Karla and trusted her completely. What could have happened? What could be keeping her? Then, at exactly 6:55 p.m., someone dashed out of the subway, and it looked like Karla! The person looked everything like her, the same spring coat and hat, the light quick steps; yes, it was Karla, for she called out to him as she dashed into the street, "Raymond! Raymond!" She called out, not seeing the crazy, reckless, speeding sports car that ran the red light just as she was dashing across! Raymond saw her and tried to warn her, "Karla, wait!!...Karla!!..." was all he could say as he dashed into the street to try to save her, but it was too late, too late to change the course of that fateful evening as the speeding car struck his Karla down and sped away. She lay dying in the street, cradled in his arms.

That was twenty years ago one day in the spring, the day and time are etched forever in his brain as he makes his daily pilgrimage to that eventful spot. Perhaps he goes there every day now, hoping somehow that his Karla will come back to him, hoping to see her dash from the subway exit once more and leap into his waiting arMs Perhaps he goes there because a part of him remains there forever and draws him back there. He still hears her call his name, "Raymond! Raymond!" He looks across the street for her, to see her as he stands and waits...but Karla does not come. Sometimes her name is on his tongue, "Kar..la? Kar..la?..." as if wishing she could hear him. He keeps on coming back, perhaps because tomorrow he will meet her there, perhaps someday. Who knows, perhaps one day in the springtime, when all the flowers and gardens are beautiful, and the earth is alive again, his Karla will call and he will go to meet her. So, for now the years go by, and one day, at last, the long, long wait will be over for the lover who stands and waits.

FAITH

ANGELIQUE

In 1956 Henry came to live with his sister Helen and her husband, Bertran Martin at 25 Irving Place, Brooklyn, N.Y. They lived in a 3-family house where the landlord occupied the first floor, Helen and Bertran Martin the second floor and a younger couple occupied the third floor above them. The apartment was a two bedroom apartment in a wood framed house that must have been a few hundred years old. Henry had just emigrated to the U.S. from the Caribbean and had great expectations; however, this story is not about Henry or his sister, it is about "Angelique", his cousin!

About a year after Henry moved in with his sister, his cousin Angelique, who also emigrated from the Caribbean, came to stay there until she could find a place of her own. She was given Henry's room and he had to sleep in the living room on the convertible sofa bed. At that time Henry was going to school at night and was working as a clerk in the day somewhere in Woodside, L.I., for a German import- export co. He had heard of his cousin, but this was the first time he ever met her. She was simple in her appearance, gentle by nature, calm, very humble and soft-spoken with a kind of personality that seemed to quiet you in her presence. She said, "Hello, Henry, I am so pleased to meet you!" in a soft but pleasant voice and with a warm smile. He estimated at the time that Angelique must have been about 55. She had one suitcase and a little bag both of which contained all of her worldly possessions.

Angelique was not a worldly person, as he came to know, and that was by choice not by circumstance. Instinctively he knew that if she was going to find happiness, it was not going to be via this world's physical pleasures, and it was not going to be in a spousal relationship either. He, who was filled with great expectations of worldly pleasures, of meeting women and perhaps getting married, and of becoming wealthy, could not understand that! He was fascinated anyway by her calm, peaceful demeanor and her celibate nature.

Each morning Angelique was up early, reading her bible and praying, and it wasn't long before Henry realized that she was very religious. In fact, religion was her whole life, as he would discover. She would offer to prepare breakfast for the family, and she could cook as well as the best. Breakfast would be ready by the time everybody had showered and dressed so that they were always assured of an excellent repast and of being on time for work. She had a way of preparing plain and Spanish omelets that made them come out neat and appetizing! She taught Henry how to make omelets, because, until then, he always made a mess of the eggs and could never get it to come out neat. So thanks to her he became an expert at omelet making!

As time went by, Henry continued to have an obsession about Angelique. How come she had never been married? Never had children? And where dating or male-female relationships were concerned, it seemed that that part of the heart, if there's such a thing that is responsible for physical love for the opposite sex, in her was dead and gone forever! She loved people, but in a different way. She was always most unselfish, compassionate, and kind to everyone; but her heart was dead to sensual love. Henry used to tease her and ask her why she didn't date men, or go to parties, or wear sexy clothes, etc.; and she would only say, "That's not for me, I am happy the way I am. I have given my heart, body and soul to the Lord!" "Well," Henry thought to himself, "I do believe that the Lord wants us to mate and have a family, too!" He couldn't accept her way entirely and his obsession was not satisfied.

Finally, the day came when Angelique found a place of her own and left the apartment. It happened that she got a position with the Christian Mission Church a block away and she was to live upstairs above the church in her own apartment. She would be as close to the church physically as you can get. Spiritually she became a church "sister" and a lay preacher, too, and went on retreats and trips, etc. She lived and breathed for God!

Henry saw her after that but not as often as before. One Saturday morning he visited her at the church. She was interested in how he was doing, if he was happy, etc. She fixed him a snack and some lemonade and they chatted; in the back of his mind he wanted to bring up the subject of her celibacy again, but he couldn't. She seemed so contented and at peace with herself. Besides, some of her peace of mind was rubbing off on him, too! It was a pleasant visit.

Back at the apartment, since Angelique moved out, his sister gave him back his room which he reorganized and redecorated to match his personality. About a week after visiting Angelique, he cleaned up his room and changed the bed sheet. While he was rearranging the bed, he happened to rotate the mattress 180 degrees because it was sagging on one side. While moving the mattress, he noticed a small black book underneath it. He couldn't imagine what it was doing there and who could have placed it there. Out of curiosity, he opened the book. Inside, he found an old photograph of a very young lady, not more than 19 or 20 years old! She was very pretty! The back of the photo said, "I love you, Joe," in Angelique's handwriting and, "I am yours forever" with her signature: Angelique. There was another photograph also with her posing with a handsome man much older than she was, perhaps in his 30s.

247

They made a handsome couple. She appeared to be in love and very happy by the way she looked at him. Further in the book was a letter that was dated May 13, 1932, which was 35 years ago! He opened the letter and read its contents which said:

"Dear Angelique:

It hurts me to write this letter to you like this. I hope you do not hate me for it. I know I promised to marry you and make you my wife; but that cannot be since I have a wife and family of my own. I am sorry if I led you to believe otherwise. I am returning the photographs we took. Please forgive me!

Goodbye,

Joe"

Somewhere on the bottom of the letter was the impression of a teardrop that had apparently dried and left a slight smear. Reading the letter just filled Henry with sadness to think of what Angelique must have felt when she was 19 and had read it for the first time. Now, he understood the part of Angelique that shut the world of flesh out, that said no more will deception pierce this flesh, no more will this heart be broken. He understood better, then, why she never married, and never wanted to; why she turned to the only life she cared about, a life in the church. As he closed the book he said to himself, "God bless you, Angelique. I hope you will be happy in the life you have chosen, because God never hurt anyone!"

THE WOODEN HORSE

In the summer of 1976, I was in the Village in New York City trying to find a specialty shop that deals in antiques carved out of wood, particularly hand carved chess sets made of African mpingo hardwood. I had been referred to a chess shop in the Village on 3rd street in New York City, and, as I was walking on 3rd street going west, I saw in the display window of another antique store the most beautiful miniature wooden horse on a stand striking a magnificent pose on its hind legs. I was attracted to the statuette by its resemblance to a wood carving I once owned and was so proud of until my heart was broken when I lost it several years ago while moving from Brooklyn to Long Island, N. Y. and when I finished unpacking the wooden statuette was missing. It was a personal gift from childhood and I never found it again. There must be in existence numerous carvings of miniature horses by any number of sculptors; but this one, I thought, seemed almost identical to mine. I went into the store and asked the storekeeper if I could purchase it, but, unfortunately, he told me it was already sold and he was about to remove it from the showcase and there wasn't another one like it in the store. He said he was sorry he couldn't oblige me and offered to show me other items, but I wasn't interested. I thanked him and left. I continued further west on 3rd Street to the Chess Shop, or Chess Forum, I think it was, and purchased a chess set made of teak wood since they didn't have any made of mpingo hardwood as I had wanted.

When I returned home that evening, I couldn't stop thinking about the wooden horse in the window that had reminded me so much of the one I once owned as a child and had somehow misplaced or lost. For a long time after I first noticed it was missing, I searched everywhere, trying to find it but all in vain. The sight of the wooden horse in the window rekindled in me the impetus to repeat the exercise once more, so when I returned home, I looked again in every corner, every closet, every box and piece of luggage. Still, it was clear that my little wooden horse was lost forever. In my search this last time, however, by a stroke of luck, I found in a box of old papers the original sketch of the sculpture with a note that was written some forty years earlier by the artist himself who had sculpted the horse for me. It said, "John, here is a sketch; the horse will be finished in a week or two." It was signed: William Greenidge. The sketch, the note, and the horse in the window also brought back vividly some of my childhood memories.

I began to daydream and found myself sitting once again on the middle staircase of house 1071 Trinidad Street, La Boca, Canal Zone, where I once lived. I was eight years old, the youngest of seven siblings, and I was allowed to watch the older boys and girls playing on the grounds between buildings 1071 and 1073. They usually played games in the yard during the dry season in the evenings after school or on holidays, or during school vacations. Our parents liked it when we played in the yard where we lived because at least they knew where we were and if they needed us where to find us. Sometimes you'd hear them call out our names, and if you were a little hard of hearing, someone would let you know:

"Boy, don't you hear your mother calling you? You'd better get upstairs in a hurry if you know what's good for you!"

(And if you didn't move quickly enough either your dad, if he's home, or your mom would come after you with a strap!) I was given boundaries at that time and was restricted mainly to the building where I lived, 1071 Trinidad Street (Gold Street) and the area on both sides of Trinidad Street, as far south as the end of the block bordered by San Domingo Street and as far north as Barbados Street at the opposite end of the block — which I think was as far as my mother's voice could carry. Barbados Street crossed Trinidad Street and went east and west. Eastward it ended at the La Boca ballpark where all major community sports activities took place. The row of houses on our block from south to north consisted of 1075, 1073, 1071, 1069 and 1067 on the east side of Trinidad Street. These were the last row of houses on the eastern border of La Boca. East of them was a tank farm that was fenced off from the town. Beyond that fence was taboo to us.

Returning to the time when I sat and watched the older boys and **girls playing games on the grounds between the houses, sometimes they** would ask me to join them in their games when they were shorthanded and needed someone to fill in, then they didn't mind my being too small, and that made me feel important. They would play games like:

(1)"FOR WE ARE THE ROMAN SOLDIERS" (A war game between the Roman and English soldiers:

"Have you any bread and wine, bread and wine, bread and wine... Yes, we have some bread and wine, bread and wine, etc...

> Will you give us some of it, some of it, some of it...
> No, we'll give you none of it, none of it, none of it...
> Then we'll send for the policeman, the policeman, etc...
> We don't care for the policeman, the policeman, etc....
> Then we'll send for the sorefootman, the sorefootman, etc...
> We don't care for the sorefootman, the sorefootman, etc...

250

Then we'll have to fight for it, fight for it, fight for it...,
for we are the Roman soldiers..."
(Here, the two sides then attack each other, and the mock war
begins);

(2)"BINGO (A farmer had a little dog, and Bingo was his name: B-i-n-g-o,
B-i-n-g-o, B-i-n-g-o, and Bingo was his name –- A ring is formed, and one
person is in the center. As the ring moves in one direction, the person in the
ring walks around in the other direction touching one player at a time while
spelling the letters B-I-N-G-O. The last person touched becomes the next
one in the center;"

(3)"CHICK, CHICK, CHICK...ME NO WAN' NO CORN (A game in
which the Hawk tries to steal one of the Hen's chicks as he calls to them:
chick, chick, chick, and they respond: me no wan' no corn;"

(4)"RHYTHM" (Seated in a circle, players establish a rhythm by slapping
their thighs, clapping, and snapping their fingers then one person begins by
calling out a letter, and the next player says a name which begins with that
letter, and states a letter for the next person to do the same and so on); but
the game I liked best was:

(5) "HOT BEANS AND BUTTER COME FOR YOUR SUPPER" (a game
in which everyone covers his/her eyes while a belt is hidden. When the
person hiding the belt shouts HOT BEANS AND BUTTER COME FOR
YOR SUPPER everybody starts looking for the belt while the one who hid
it gives clues: hot, hot or cold, cold or warm depending on how close
someone comes to the belt. When the belt is found the finder whips the first
person he can catch who then becomes the next person to hide the belt, etc.).

Of course, the girls would sometimes play by themselves on the sidewalk
games like "hop scotch", "skipping rope", and "jacks" while the boys would
play "chupon", "platillos", and "marbles" sometimes 'under the cellar.'

Then there were the adult games and sports. The adults would engage in
various semi-professional spectator sports in the ball park, such as cricket,
baseball, softball, soccer, track and field, and the whole town would come
out to see them compete. Our older brothers and sisters, and sometimes our
parents, would be there, so we eight-and-nine-year-olds didn't have to worry
that our parents were concerned about our whereabouts. Not that we didn't
play "hooky" some of the times, but when we did we always paid the price
when we came home.

251

In our building, 1071 Trinidad St. (also known as Gold St.), one of the families that lived upstairs was the Greenidge family. Mr Greenidge worked for the Oil Handling Plant as an Oiler, and he had three sons, William, Clarence and Victor. Victor later became a famous professional baseball pitcher both in Panama professional league and in the United States Negro league. He once beat Satchell Page in the Negro baseball league. But in my account, here I am more interested in William, his brother, who liked to carve things out of wood. I always saw him with a carving knife chipping away at a piece of wood but I was fascinated one day when I saw, in his hands, what was a plain old piece of wood had turned into a beautifully carved bird. On another occasion it was a rabbit and on another it was a small toy boat. So, for a while he was the most interesting person on the block to me. That is, until I chanced to walk under house 1073 and saw the most amazing thing taking place.

Mr. Hubert Lord, a Barbadian who was employed as a painter by the Mechanical Division in the Canal Zone and who lived with his family on the second floor of 1073, was actually a boat builder in his spare time and was in the process of building what looked like at least a 15-foot boat. The frame was propped up by several sturdy supports, and the sides were almost completed. It looked magnificent. I had never seen anything like it before. He was building it for a wealthy white American who lived in Balboa, Canal Zone, and who knew of his boat-building skill enough to pay him to build this masterpiece. And I am sure he was getting it very cheap compared to what he would have to pay for it on the market! Anyway, while I was marveling at this creation by the hands of an underpaid silver worker of the Panama Canal Zone, I felt proud of him and his workmanship. One day, I was impressed by two of my older neighbors. I felt like I wanted to do something creative with my hands then, although I didn't know what or how, and I started to pick up a piece of scrap wood lying on the ground. It was a 1ft. square piece of wood, by 6 inches thick, that was lying there, and I asked Mr. Lord if I could have it. He said he didn't know what I would do with it, but if I wanted it, I could take it. I sure wasn't going to build a boat with it, or anything like that for that matter, but I just felt good taking it anyway. I would figure out what to do with it later. But somewhere deep down in my mind, I already knew. As an 8-year-old, I did not yet have the power to create anything with my hands or my mind, but I saw what these two men did with theirs, and I wished that I could do half as much. Nevertheless, I took the piece of wood, and the next day, I went to my upstairs neighbor William Greenidge with it, and I said to him:

"I have seen what you can do; I know what you can do with your hands and your carving knife. Inside this piece of wood, I know there is a horse, a beautiful wild horse standing on its hind legs, if I could only set it free! But will you please set it free for me? Will you carve that horse from out of this wood for me? I know that you can do it. Please, I beg of you!"

He looked at me astonished and with a look of compassion, the way one with experience looks down on an innocent 8-year-old with only a child's imagination and a child's faith. Yes, I put my faith in him, for I believed then that he could carve anything in this world with his hands, and so, in my mind, what I was asking seemed like it was nothing for him to do. How could he, William Greenidge, the magician, then disappoint me? He was overwhelmed for a moment, I am sure, before he spoke.

"Of course...of course, I'll sculpt a horse for you," he said. "Give me the piece of wood, and don't worry." He said this, knowing that he had never carved a horse before.

The next day he gave me a sketch of the horse, and when I saw it, I knew he had read what was on my mind. Two weeks later, when I came home from school that evening, my family and I had just finished eating our supper, the doorbell of our apartment rang, and my mother answered it. It was William Greenidge, and in his hand, he had a beautiful miniature wild stallion standing on its hind legs. He spoke to my mother.

"Please give this to your son, John, for me. It came out of the piece of wood he gave me two weeks ago when he asked me to sculpt a horse for him."

My mother thanked him and asked how much he charged for his work.

"There is no charge, Mrs Evans. Your son had so much faith in me and my ability I just could not disappoint him. It is a gift for the gift of faith he gave to me."

Nevertheless, my mother, being the kind person that she was, asked him to wait for a minute, and she went inside. She returned with a hefty piece of a fruitcake she had baked earlier and gave it to him. He thanked her and left.

I had cherished that wooden horse and had it for forty years before I lost it. Today I don't know what became of William Greenidge, the sculptor, whether or not he went on to sculpt professionally. I only know that because of both him and Mr Hubert Lord, the master boat builder, a little 8-year-old dreamer had gained an appreciation for art, for skilled craftsmanship, and for the value of a block of wood and the power of faith.

REDEMPTION

THE HOUSE OF THE LOST

Only the broken in spirit are found
here in the House of the Lost.
It matters not from where they've come,
how high or low, or at what cost,
how great the sins they're guilty of,
here in the House of the Lost
they are deemed still worthy of being loved
and redeemed by the blood of the cross,
for God sent a shepherd from above
to gather them in the House of the Lost.
...John Weldon Evans

Chapter I: Mark Henderson's Journey

Nineteen sixty-eight was a year of tension and turmoil in America. In the news the Tet Offensive (1/30 – 4/8), the largest military operation of the Vietnam War, launched by 80,000 North Vietnamese Army troops, had taken place against American forces; the My Lai massacre (3/16) of 500 Vietnamese civilians by U. S. troops had occurred; the American protest movement against the unpopular Vietnam War was at its peak; Dr. Martin Luther King, Jr. was assassinated in Memphis, Tennessee (4/4); Robert Francis Kennedy, N.Y.S. senator and promising presidential candid ate, was assassinated in the Ambassador Hotel in San Francisco (6/5); the Democratic National Convention's five-day riot (Aug. 25 - Aug. 30) between 100,000 anti-Vietnam War protesters and Chicago Mayor Daley's 11,900 police force joined by 7,500 Army troops, 7,500 Illinois National guardsmen, and 1,000 secret service agents had taken place; the Apollo 7 rocket was launched from Florida (on 10/11) for an 11-day journey to orbit the earth 163 times; Richard Milhous Nixon was declared the winner of the U.S. Presidential election (on 11/5); and of course, the Vietnam War from which the U. S. was desperately seeking to extricate itself was at its peak and would not be officially over until 5 years later, January 27, 1973, at the Paris Peace Accord Conference. All seven of these major events, except for the peace accord, had happened during that year, the year Mark Henderson was wounded-in-action and lay in a coma in the Atlanta VA long-care medical center.

On the day he was brought to the Atlanta VA hospital, November 21, 1967, unconscious and almost dead, he had been evacuated from Vietnam to Andrews A.F. Base and then to the Atlanta VA Medical Center. There he lay in a coma from his injuries on the battlefield near DAK-TO, where he was found near death by a field medic. He was first taken to a local army treatment facility in Vietnam, was cleared for release (ROS) back to the U.S., and evacuated to Atlanta, where he would receive neurological, TBI, and PTSD treatment. Due to the severity of his injuries and the unlikelihood of a full recovery, his war days, of course, were over.

While he lay there in a coma in Atlanta VA Medical Center, doctors were not even certain if he would ever regain consciousness or recover from his injuries. His next of kin, his mother, a registered nurse, his father, an ex-marine from the Korean War, and his brother came to visit him regularly and could only watch helplessly as he lay there with all those bandages and tubes connected to him and pray ever so hard for a miracle. Their prayers were answered approximately one year later, November 2, 1968, when he showed

256

the first signs of awareness by movements of his eyes and fingers. Then he was able to move his arm and tried to speak his first words since returning from the near dead. His parents, Mr and Mrs Henderson, and his brother, David, were so elated when he looked at them and spoke for the first time since the tragedy occurred.

"Mom… Dad… David…" he said as he recognized them.

"My son, my son," said Mrs. Henderson with tears of joy in her eyes, "Thank God He has answered our prayers!"

His father called for the nurse immediately to come and attend to him quickly. The nurse summoned the doctor, who came to his bedside and examined him while trying to keep everyone calm.

"You're a medical marvel, Mark Henderson," said the doctor after examining him, "you've been away from us for a very long time, but now everything will be just fine. Try not to exert yourself too much. The nurse will give you something to help you get your strength back."

Then he turned to the family.

"This is the best sign we've had since your son was first admitted. Most of the physical damage he suffered has been healing, and our main concern, the injury to his head, is now showing signs of healing as well. We are going to move him to another room tomorrow so that family and friends will be able to visit with him more comfortably. Right now, he'll need plenty of rest and rehabilitation for the medication and treatment to be effective."

His mother kissed his cheek, his father and brother held his hand, and they said good night until tomorrow, which could not come soon enough. They left knowing that their son would be well again, which they had waited for and prayed for, for so long.

During the next two weeks, only the family was allowed to visit with him as they were trying to limit his stress and excitement until he was strong enough. Gradually he began to show signs of being himself, conversing though slowly and for short intervals with his family, who had so much they wanted to say to him and to hear from him, but they were careful not to bring up the subject of the tragedy too soon and talked only about immediate family matters and friends. His aunt and uncle sent their love. Some of his former high school friends came by to visit. Many sent their regards and get-well cards that had piled up and could now be shared. Even some Army brass came by to pay their respects. But there was so much in the news and so much that had happened in the country during the past year! Well, in time, he would certainly be able to catch up with everything. For now, though, if any accidental remark was made about the war, he would be silent and seem to lose the thread of what was being said as he seemed to have no memory of that subject, not even of how he came to be injured and in the hospital. They usually changed the subject quickly if it had anything to do with the military or the war and said everything would come back to him in due time, and he was not to try to think too much about such things. Seeing his family, though, and being with them again, he had so many questions to ask that he did not know where to begin. *Did dad get to visit his ailing brother in California?*

Did he get his leg fixed? Did he get the station wagon he always wanted? Did David get the new job he was applying for? Did Jimmy, his two-year-old nephew, learn to talk as yet? And what about Martha, his ex-girlfriend? Did she get married yet?

Speaking about Martha Jacobs, his ex-high school girl friend, they had broken up at the start of their senior year in '64 over a jealous argument, and they were both too stubborn and immature to admit either one was wrong. Just after they broke up in '64, Martha, probably in an attempt to spite him, started dating Harvey Colson, a popular high school rival from an upper-class family. Mark had hated Harvey Colson because he was so cocky and sure of himself, and no wonder he was a spoiled brat with all the advantages his well-to-do parents could afford to give him. He had all the girls chasing after him, and when he had the chance to move in on Martha, that's what he did. The two of them were still dating when she entered nursing school in the fall of '64, and somehow she got engaged to be married to him but later changed her mind and broke off the engagement when she realized she was not really in love with Harvey. She finished college in '68, and that summer, when she learned about Mark's near tragedy, she came to the hospital to visit him almost every week while he was in a coma, and she got to meet his parents. She had stayed and prayed with them on several occasions for his recovery until a few weeks before he regained consciousness, when she had to go to Boston to stay with a sick aunt for a while. She had even left a note with Mrs. Henderson for him in case he recovered before she returned. Mrs. Henderson had read the letter to Mark, which she thought would help to cheer him up:

"Dear Mark:

If you are reading this letter, it means that all of our prayers have been answered. I prayed every day for you to get well and believed in my heart that one day God would bring you back to us so you can continue with your life. I almost made a mistake and married the wrong man, but God helped me to see the truth before it was too late. I only hope that we can be friends again and that I may be a part of your life in some way when you get well. Hope to see you when I return from Boston. Martha."

After his mother read the letter to him, he was pleased because he remembered Martha and how much he had liked her back in high school. He looked forward to seeing her again and would keep the letter and read it to himself whenever he was feeling lonely.

Several weeks later, he was well enough to go home to Decatur, Ga., to recuperate under his parent's care, and with regular visits by a nurse assigned to him, and of course, his mother was also a nurse, making it two nurses caring for him.

It was now December 1968, in the middle of the Christmas season, and no better time to be home enjoying the warmth and love of family and friends, Christmas cheer, and a good Christmas dinner. There was so much to be thankful for, especially at Christmas time which made him realize how lucky he was.

On Christmas Day, he and his family had just finished eating a sumptuous Christmas dinner when the telephone rang. It was Martha. She had sent him a Christmas card but wasn't sure if it got there in time. She called to wish him a speedy recovery and to wish him and his parents a happy holiday. She mentioned that she would be back in Atlanta sometime in January and was looking forward to seeing him. Martha asked if it was alright for her to come by to visit when she returned, and he insisted that she come, and he wished that it was sooner. So the call added immensely to his yuletide cheers.

Soon the New Year, 1969, came and found him getting around with a walker and gaining strength enough that it wouldn't be long before he would no longer even need one. Sometime near the middle of January, Martha, who had returned home by then, called and asked if it was alright to come by to visit the following day. Mark insisted, and the next day, the second Saturday in January, was the first time they saw each other since they broke up almost five years ago. Mr. and Mrs.

Henderson and Mark had insisted that she come over for dinner that Saturday evening, and when she arrived, and he saw how pretty she was, his eyes lit up, and it was apparent that the old flame was still there and that it only needed a little fanning to get going again.

During dinner, while they were conversing, Mr. and Mrs. Henderson inquired about the well-being of Martha's parents and family.

"Are you an only child?" asked Mrs Henderson.

"No, I have a sister, Mildred, who is a little younger than I am."

"Did your father ever serve in the military?" asked Mr Henderson.

"Yes, he served in the Korean war when he was a young man back in 1950-53. From what I know, he was an NCO attached to the 25th Division."

"Do you know what regiment or company he was assigned to?" asked Mr Henderson.

"He told me once that he served in the 77th Engineer Combat Company. He was proud to have served with men like Lt. William A. Benefield and Lt. Chester J. Lenon, both of whom received D.S.C.'s for heroism," said Martha.

"I should have known your dad," said Mr. Henderson, "we were in the same division. I was in the 24th Infantry Regiment. Those were all segregated black units that had some of the bravest soldiers to wear a U.S. Army uniform, even though, at the time, we were denied proper recognition for our services. And believe me, the Army was officially integrated by President Truman back in 1948, but they took their time implementing desegregation. It wasn't until 1954 when the entire Armed Forces were fully integrated, and today they are still taking their time with eliminating racial discrimination in this country, in spite of all the protesting that's been going on."

"Steve," Mrs. Henderson interrupted, "this child doesn't want to talk about such things. Remember what we agreed to?" She was referring to their agreement to avoid bringing up discussions about the war for Mark's sake.

"Yes, honey," he said to his wife and to Martha, "I am sorry, Martha, for getting carried away like that. Maybe we can get to meet your dad some day?"

"My dad passed away a few years ago," said Martha, "It's just me and my mom and my younger sister. But I am sure they would also like to meet you one day."

"I am very sorry about your Dad," responded Mr. Henderson, and he said very little after that.

Mrs. Henderson asked Martha if she was still in school or if she was pursuing a career.

260

"I just finished nursing school," said Martha, "and I expect to start working in a week as an RN at Emory University Hospital."

"That's a top-ranked hospital, #1 in the state of Georgia," said Mrs Henderson, who is a registered nurse herself.

"Yes, I was very fortunate to be among those in my class who were offered a position there after graduation. Not to change the subject, Mrs. Henderson, but this casserole is delicious. You must give me the recipe, please."

Here Mark interjected his two-cents for the first time into the conversation.

"Wait until you taste her peach cobbler for dessert," he said. "That's my favorite."

And it wasn't long before they were all partaking of the best Georgia peach cobbler you ever tasted.

It was a most delectable dinner and dessert. After dessert, Mr. and Mrs. Henderson started to clear the table, and Martha offered to help, but they wouldn't hear of it. And they said to Mark and Martha:

"Why don't the two of you go out and sit on the porch? You must have a lot you would like to say to each other without the two of us getting in the way. Besides, we have some things we'd like to take care of in the meantime. Mark, take the young lady outside and entertain her. You haven't seen her in 5 years; you must have a lot to talk about."

The two of them withdrew to the porch, and she helped him reminisce about high school and all the friends and classmates they used to know. Such pleasant memories induced by the thrill of seeing her again came back to the surface as fresh as if it were yesterday. What a difference a few years of maturity can make. He was no longer a light-head schoolboy, and he saw her now as an excellent candidate for a more serious and lasting relationship. And she realized, too, that she had made the right decision when she broke off her engagement with Harvey Colson. Mark was always her preference.

Now that they had renewed their friendship, they began seeing each other again. They went for walks in the park regularly, which was what he needed to gain back his strength, and in her spare time, she came and sat with him and talked about a lot of things, and occasionally they went to a movie or dined out together in a local restaurant.

His health was improving, thanks partly to Martha and especially to being home with his parents again. It was impossible to keep him entirely isolated from what was going on in the world since the news was all around them every day. As things started coming back to him and his memory continued to improve, he began having flashbacks and started to ask more and more questions. One evening as he was coming to grips with his memory of the past, he was sitting alone, wondering to himself what had been going on here in the land of the free and the home of the brave during his absence. Of course, he had asked himself that question before, but now he was deadly serious. A whole year out of his life had passed of which he had no knowledge, although he could remember a few things that had happened prior to 1968. For instance, he recalled: In 1967, *Lyndon B. Johnson was the president of the United States; Dr. Martin L. King, Jr. was the leader of a protest movement; and Robert Kennedy was the Senator from New York who was thinking of running for the next presidential election in 1968; and wasn't there a war going on? Of course, there had to have been...* I must have been a soldier in that war...that must be the reason I was in a military hospital... It was getting near 6 p.m., and the evening news was on the TV. They were discussing the presidential inauguration of Richard M. Nixon that took place earlier that morning and were playing excerpts of his speech. *Yes, I remember Nixon.* Mark said to himself *he was Dwight D. Eisenhower's vice president (1953-1961), and he ran for president and lost the election to Eisenhower's successor, John F. Kennedy, in 1960. So now he and the GOP are taking over again!* At that moment, Mrs Henderson told him the news could wait that it was time for him to eat supper, and she calmly turned off the TV and asked him to join his dad and her at the dinner table.

Regaining his memory completely was a long and painful process. Little by little, month by month, the past was coming back to him, every detail. Until it did, his mind had blocked large doses of memory from his consciousness. During those long months when he was home recuperating, his nights were filled with nightmares and hysteria that would awaken him suddenly in his sleep whenever his subconscious mind flashed back to the past, especially to the terrible killings on the battlefield and the stench and heat of the jungles of southeast Asia. But the brain is a remarkable mechanism that has a way of healing itself over time, and his memory kept improving remarkably.

One of the things in his past that came back even sooner than the dreaded Vietnam tragedy was the eight weeks he spent in basic training down in Fort Polk, Louisiana, and that memory helped put a lot of things into perspective. His thoughts were now clear to him about that time, and he remembered the first day when he arrived at Fort Polk. It was March 12th, 1967, and he remembered the feeling of excitement and anxiety, the anticipation, the prospect of a great adventure, the swearing-in, the induction process, the haircut, his army issue of uniform, boots, and later an m-14 rifle and field equipment. They were all boys from all parts of the U.S., averaging in age from 21-23, and they would soon become men. They had to rise every morning at 5 a.m. to begin basic training in the rugged terrain and hills of Fort Polk, Louisiana, a simulation of the terrain of South East Asia. They were drilled eight hours a day every day on the firing range, on the confidence course, the obstacle course, the high beam, climbing down ropes, doing push-ups, running for miles, undergoing rigid physical combat proficiency tests, and, if you failed you had to start over again until you passed the course. Routine inspection took place every Saturday in the barracks. During those eight weeks, everything counted towards passing.

As far as personnel were concerned, there was this Sergeant Dexter Dixon, his drill sergeant, and what a mean son of a gun he was. His meanness must have been in his genes when he was born. He was mean and hard, especially to both Mitchel Goldberg, Mark's buddy, and Mark, who were in the same basic training class of new recruits in Company B. In the beginning, Mark didn't figure him out, but later he came to find out that Dixon had a strong bias against Jews and blacks, even though he himself was black. He was what they call an Oreo Negro who wished he was white and adopted white hatred just as if he were a white racist. He always seemed like he was picking on them, especially and pushing them to the limit. He would embarrass them every chance he got during training drills to try to break their spirits. He would give them demerits whenever he could, forcing them to do extra drills and pushups and assigning them to the worst tasks deliberately. He would get into their faces and into their heads and would make them angry enough to want to take a swing at him, so he could either hurt them physically or have them thrown into a military prison. He gave them no rest or peace if there was such a thing, and often used vulgar and derogatory language when speaking to them. He would address Mark as nigger and Mitch as kike. It was obvious to Mitch and Mike he didn't like them, and the feeling was mutual. In a way, his actions towards them, as well as the fact that they were both from two of America's most discriminated minorities, caused them to gravitate toward each other. Often when the two of them were alone, they would talk about what they would like to do to him. They knew that Serge had a drinking problem, and sometimes he would return to base at night after a late binge and stumble back to his quarters barely sober. They thought of lay waiting for him on one of those occasions and beating him to a pulp, but it never happened. They were only venting their anger.

Mark remembered, too, the time when they returned from their two-week home leave after completing basic training, and since they had a two-day wait because of a delay in their flight overseas to Vietnam, he and Mitch had gotten a temporary pass to go into the local town where they were in a local bar/restaurant and were aware it was getting late and they had to get back to the barracks by 11 p.m., so they were having their last beer when they heard the sergeant's voice.

"You kikes or niggers or both, better get your asses out of here. You know what will happen if you are late getting back to barracks."

Of course, nothing would happen. Was he going to cancel their tour of duty in Vietnam? They didn't think so! He was just using his usual tactic and was trying to pick a fight with Mitch.

"What's a sissy kike like you doing in my unit, anyway? You should all be lined up and shot. Hitler had the right idea. And as for you, Nigger..."

At that instant, a superior officer walked in, and Serge jumped up, kissing up to him, and saluted him and vice versa, then the lieutenant addressed the three of them.

"Is everything alright with you boys? It's getting a bit late to be off base, don't you think?"

"Yeah," dug in Serge, "I was just telling them the same thing. This is their last drink, anyway."

Mitch and Mark were only too glad to leave Serge's unwelcomed company and took off to go back to the base. The next day in the afternoon, news came that their flight would be leaving for Vietnam early the following morning at 0300. That meant confinement to barracks and lights out early for all front-line bound units.

So far, after his fourth year at home recuperating, Mark regained his memory of almost everything that happened during basic training in Fort Polk, March 12, 1967 – May 12, 1967, and a lot of other things were also clearer now inside his head. He remembered the MAC flight from Fort Polk to Cam Ranh Bay U.S. Air Force/Navy base and Army Processing Center in South Vietnam, and, after being processed there, they were transferred by a C-130 Hercules aircraft to Camp Radcliff at An Khe in the Central highlands. There they received Team Academy training on things they had to know for their survival in the jungles of Vietnam and in guerrilla combat against the VCs, a mandatory course for all troopers assigned to the 1st Cavalry Division.

From An Khe, they were transported to Landing Zone English, a large base camp close to the town of Bong Son. Here they were issued M-16s, ammunition, grenades, flares, c-4, and claymore mines, called a typical load. From there, they were taken by Huey helicopter to the field location, where they met the Company Commander and 1st Sergeant, who assigned each one to a platoon. Then they met their platoon leader, their platoon sergeant, and finally, their squad leader. After all this journey and ordeal, and after trying to get as far as possible from demon Dexter Dixon, who should be their Platoon Leader? Yes, it was the Devil himself! *In Vietnam, though,* thought Mark, *it might be different because just as their lives might depend on him, his might also be in their hands; after all, they all had live ammunition out there and a common enemy. Nevertheless, you could never trust that sick-o serge. The last thing he said to them when they were going on their first deployment was:*

"Alright, you lazy bums, this is not boot camp. This is the real thing, and the VCs aren't playing either, so you'd better be alert at all times! Got that, knuckleheads?"

He said that looking straight at Mitch and him as if it was a threat meant particularly for them. Mark knew he was always going to be on their case, and they knew, too, that he went lighter on others, especially his girly-faced, handsome young white recruit with whom he was friendly from basic training. *Anyway,* thought Mark, *this is Vietnam, and we'll see how the cards are dealt out here.*

Now that his brain seemed to be functioning close to normal again, his recollections of his Vietnam tour were getting clearer than ever. He was now trying to reconstruct the sequence of events in his mind. *After we landed in Cam Ranh Bay in May 1967, on June 6th, our battalion units were deployed to provide base security and to conduct search operations in the area surrounding An Khe. Then the mission changed to deploy north of Quang Ngai Province and conduct a reconnaissance in force in the Song Re Valley. This was a Viet Cong stronghold. Our forces came under intense fire from the moment we landed in this hornet's nest, and our battalion had to be airlifted by Caribou aircraft back to Landing Zone English Base. During September 17-18, our Battalion was then moved from LZ English to a Special Forces camp west of Qui Nhon; eventually, by the end of September, to the rolling hills west of Tuy Hoa. North Vietnamese Army (NVA) threats for a while seemed to have faded. Our battalion was scheduled to return to LZ English within two weeks, by October 14, and it was during this brief lull in action that Mitch and I came upon a startling discovery involving Sergeant Dexter Dixon. There, in the bushes near Tay Hoa, under cover of trees and thick brush, at dusk one evening in late September 1967, we came upon Sergeant Dexter Dixon engaged in what we couldn't believe we saw.*

Sergeant Dixon was humping on his favorite recruit like nobody's business. War or no war, Vietcong or no Vietcong, they were going to town, and the Serge was getting it off. When he and his lover realized that Mitch and I had seen them, they hurriedly tried to straighten themselves up, but it was too late. Now Mitch and I had the upper hand on the S.O.B., and he knew it.

"You boys had better not say anything about this, you hear, if you know what's good for you," *was all the feeble threat he could manage towards us.*

His days of intimidating us were over. Now we had something damaging that we could use against him. We bided our time and measured what we would do with the information, whether we would blackmail him or report him. Nevertheless, by this time, it was October 14th, and the 2nd Battalion had returned to Landing Zone English. We began conducting combat operations in Bon Son until we were deployed to Dak To, where the U.S. forces were expecting a big push by the NVA and VCs.

In late October 1967, military intelligence had knowledge that the NVA was preparing to attack US military units and installations in Dak To, located in Kontum Province near the regions where South Vietnam, Laos, and Cambodia meet. Reports had it that more than five enemy infantry and artillery regiments totaling 12,000 enemy troops had encircled the U.S. 4th Infantry Division and were building up and getting ready to attack.

Their main goal was to inflict heavy casualties on the U.S. military in order to expose U.S. troop vulnerability and the NVA capability. To counter this, several U.S. units were sent to reinforce the 4th Division. They included at least 5 U.S. cavalry divisions, four brigades, and four battalions, besides hundreds of B-52 sorties, thousands of tactical air sorties, and hundreds of thousands of artillery rounds to pound on the enemy. It was expected that this encounter would likely be the largest battle between the VCs and U.S. forces up to that time. Unfortunately for Mark and Mitch, November 19, 1967, the date of the outbreak of the battle, was fatal for Mitch Goldberg and near-fatal for him Mark Henderson.

"There is one detail that is still not very clear to me," Mark thought to himself. *"All I can remember is that during the Dak To battle, Mitch and I were holding a defensive position facing the enemy who was attacking from the west. As the shooting started, we were sure we were well hidden and safe from enemy fire, and, as far as I can remember, our position was never overrun by the enemy, so whoever shot us had to have done so from behind. We never saw it coming nor had a chance to defend ourselves. Mitchell was shot first, he was riddled with bullets, and by the time I could turn to see who*

266

was doing the shooting or to try to defend myself, I was riddled with bullets, too. It happened so fast. I remember the blinding flash and the burst of machine gun fire. I can still see my dead friend lying there and the bullets ripping through me when I thought I, too, was going to die. It tears a big slice out of me now that the memory of it has come back to me. Aside from sadness, it fills me with wild doubts, suspicions, and a feeling of unspeakable anger. What if it wasn't the Vietcong that did it? Then who could it have been? Who...?"

It was now 1978, and Mark had fully recovered, or at least up to 98% of him, and he was venturing out on his own, travelling to the VA office and conducting his own business and was a great joy to his family and friends to see him in almost perfect health again. He and Martha had discussed the possibility of marriage, but he would not commit to her and told her he would not hold her to any commitment to him either, but if she agreed to wait until he was fully healed and until all the ghosts of his past were behind him, then he would ask her to marry him. Of course, much time had already passed, and he would require still more time, but Martha was very patient and did not pressure him and told him she would always be there for him whenever he was ready. There was one particular ghost that bothered him the most and that he and he alone knew about, and that continued to linger on his mind. It was the memory of the murder of his friend, Mitchell Goldberg, and the almost successful murder of him as well, by an assailant or assailant unknown. By now, though, he had come to the unmistakable conclusion that the killer had to have been Sergeant Dexter Dixon, his arch-nemesis. To a single-minded purpose, therefore, he now committed himself, and that pledge was to find the sergeant and resolve this unfinished business – and settle the score.

Mark started tracking down the records and history of his company and his platoon in Vietnam: whether they were all alive or dead, who was and who wasn't. He was going to find them and see if they had any information that would help confirm his conviction. Of course, he had a photograph of his platoon that he had kept, and that turned out to be helpful. The army records showed that more than half of the platoon was wiped out, and the remainder had been discharged from the army. But of course, as it turned out, the evil Sergeant Dixon was one of those who survived the war. For some reason, he had left the service either due to early retirement or a disability condition.

After learning all he could from the army personnel records and from other sources about Dexter Dixon, it did nothing to change Mark's decision and mission. In fact, it reinforced it. Dexter was a psycho, it seemed to him, or else at least he was depraved, but he was still a murderer and had to pay for what he had done.

Before Mark left Atlanta, he made sure that Martha understood that there was no other female interest in his life but that there was something he had to take care of before he could be free of his past and would be able to marry her. It was only fair that there should be no barriers in the way of a happy life together. He would be leaving Atlanta for a while, and when he returned, if she was still there for him, he would ask for her hand to make a life together. Martha trusted him and promised to wait. He told his parents, and they also wished him success in closing the tortured chapter in his life.

Chapter II: Dexter Dixon's Journey

In his search of the military archives to find out as much as he could about Dexter Dixon, Mark had turned to a very good friend who worked in the army personnel records division and who was able to access Dexter's records secretly and showed a copy of the Sergeant's confidential files, personal history, and psychological profile to him. Dexter was born in Northeastern Philadelphia back in the 1930s. His parents, Raymond Dixon, a white man, and Sue Ellen Baker, a Negro from Georgia, had fallen in love and moved to Philadelphia to get away from Jim Crowism and race hatred to try to start a life as a mixed-race couple. In the South, the whites looked down on whites who mixed with blacks, and the blacks looked down on blacks who did the same with whites. Where Sue Ellen and Raymond were concerned, both of their families disowned them when they broke forbidden laws governing cohabitation and marriage between the races. Raymond's parents were poor southern whites who were horrified by their son's involvement with a black girl, a "nigger" as they referred to her. In fact, Charles Dixon, Dexter's grandfather, was so horrified that he cringed with hate and almost puked; likewise, his grandmother, Eva Ann Dixon, became paralyzed at the thought of a nigger child in their pure-blood southern Dixiecrat racist white family. On the other hand, Sue Ellen Baker, a Georgia-colored girl, caught hell from her side of the family, too. In fact, they threatened to disown her if she brought any white baby into this world. So when she became pregnant with Dexter, she and her white lover decided to move far away from the South.

The two of them left the south and moved to northeastern Philadelphia, where their son Dexter was born. But even there, certain problems eventually caught up with them. First, Dexter grew up not having a true sense of his identity – he was too white to be black and too black to be white, and too mixed to be anything, and this haunted him in his youth as well as later in his adult life. Second, after living in northeast Philadelphia for a few short years, both Sue and Raymond came to find out that being a mixed couple in the north in those days was no different than in the South, and Raymond couldn't handle the isolation, living in two conflicting worlds at the same time, and the nigger lover name-calling by whites. Even worse, he couldn't handle the pressure of being ostracized by his own white family and white friends. The price became too high for him, and finally, he abandoned both Dexter and his mother and returned to the South. Sue Ellen had to work hard as a waitress to support both herself and her son. She enrolled Dexter in a local public school, where he had a hard time adjusting socially. He developed an attitude that made him think that because his skin was lighter, it made him a little better than his darker classmates, and they, in turn, ostracized him and shunned him. He didn't remember much about his father personally, only that he was white, and when Dexter tried to understand why he had left them, he figured it out for himself and blamed his mother's race as the reason – although he never said this to her. From his adolescence and teen years, he started sucking up to white people and thinking that they were the master race and he would be better off trying to be like them.

He managed to complete high school in 1954 and had a fascination for the soldier's uniform for military strictness and the stiff authority of command. Although the Korean War was over, nevertheless, he enlisted in the army to become a career soldier. But even in the military, he seemed to be full of self-hate and still carried with him his identity problem. His superiors, however, always thought of him as a reliable and loyal colored soldier, and that helped him eventually to reach the rank of sergeant by the time the Vietnam War was well underway in the late 1950s. They could always count on him to volunteer for the hardest, toughest assignments, and he was always anxious to impress them that he was worthy of their praise and their acceptance (Although they never regarded him as their equal.) In the same way that he looked up to them and they praised him (like you praise a loyal and obedient pet), it gave him a sense of worth and stature in their eyes from which he acquired self-value and purpose, and maybe, he thought, one day he would become like one of them as well, if he were to be the best sergeant possible. This translated into the strictest and harshest he could be over the soldiers under him, especially the non-white recruits. He loved pushing them around. Dexter Dixon, unfortunately, despite all those thousands and thousands of servicemen and army officers around him performing military duties every day, drills and combat duty, despite being in crowded barracks or army gatherings, he was still as lonely as he always was before entering the service ever since he was a teenager. Maybe that is why he turned to drinking so much – to kill the loneliness. He had no one, no girlfriend, no wife, and his mother passed away a few years after he enlisted.

So aside from being a soldier and drill serge, his personal life was a mess. After 20 years of soldiering and concealing his tragic identity crisis, as well as other insecurities and emotional issues, even the army couldn't do anything more for him; in 1968, after many injuries from the war and after his emotional disabilities began to surface, the army was glad to offer him an early retirement. If Dexter Dixon was lost before he joined the service and the army only provided him a temporary period of escape and a temporary sanctuary, he was now set loose again back into the same world where in the past he had lost his way and could not find out who or what he was nor where he fit in. He was a loner and became a wanderer and a prisoner in his own skin, trying to find a way to escape.

Chapter III: Dr. Bernard Drew's Journey

Bernard Drew was born in 1928 in Manchester County, New Hampshire, and was an only child whose father, a private practice physician, and whose mother, a professional dancer, were estranged from each other when he was a child in elementary school so that he grew up in a broken home. He lived with his father and seldom saw his mother, who, after the divorce was final, walked out of their lives and returned to the theater and her dancing career. He seldom ever saw her again. Bernard was very bright and did well in school, in Jr. High, High School, and college, although he developed some emotional insecurities and resentment toward both of his parents for the broken home situation. His grades in school gave him intellectual self-confidence and independence, but socially he envied those classmates whose home lives were happy, intact, and secure. A sense of emotional insecurity and incompleteness led him to feel that he was different.

At nineteen, he attended Dartmouth College in New Hampshire, described then as "the drinkingest" of the Ivy League schools. While there, some of that culture rubbed off on him, and he was only too willing to participate in the many fraternity drinking parties and sprees during his Dartmouth years. He found ways of dealing with it, however, and never allowed the habit to interfere with his studies. He successfully completed Dartmouth College and went to Cambridge, Massachusetts, where he applied to and was accepted into Harvard University Medical School to fulfill his ambition to be a doctor. He graduated from Harvard in 1955 and did his internship at N.Y. Presbyterian Hospital, where he joined the medical staff.

It was Bernard Drew's desire more than anything to be a surgeon, his preference for neurosurgery, so when he had completed his medical internship, he applied for and qualified for a neurosurgery residency at Presbyterian Hospital where, in 1963, after seven years of residency, he was certified and joined the staff of neurosurgeons at Presbyterian. It is certainly true that he was bright and talented, which his post-graduate work at N.Y. Presbyterian indicated. It is notable, too, that in the twenty years since he left Dartmouth College, alcohol never became a problem for him, although he did his share of social drinking more often than not.

In 1964 in New York City he ran into one of his old Dartmouth College chums, Gary Underwood, who was now a junior Wall Street broker. He was a social bon vivant and a member of the Union League Club of New York City. The club sponsored regular exclusive parties and social events and to one of these events, a New Year's Eve Gala, his friend invited him to come out and have some fun, meet some people and ring in the New Year, 1965.

When he arrived at the party and was checking his coat Gary was there to greet him.

"Bernie, you rascal, I'm glad you could make it."

"I'm glad you invited me," said Bernard, "I remember those wild cocktail parties back in Dartmouth. So this is what a high society party looks like."

And as they entered Gary introduced him to several people including the club president and his wife, and the chairperson of the event and his wife. Then he took Bernie to the table where his party had already been seated and introduced him.

"Bernie, Let me present you to my charming wife and to a friend of ours. This is Eva, my wife. Eva, please meet Bernie Drew, an old college buddy of mine."

"Hi, I am Eva Underwood, and this is Mary Collins, a very good friend of Gary and me."

"Hi," said Mary, and they all sat together at a table for four in this elegant-looking club.

"Mary teaches at Hunter College. She is an English professor," said Eva to Bernie. And to Mary, "Bernie is a surgeon at Presbyterian. I thought I'd save you both time by helping you to get acquainted. (Smile) Now let's have some fun."

There was a top band and a vocal soloist and an emcee providing the entertainment for the evening. Everyone had their noisemakers and holiday hats and was in a festive mood. Even the stiff shirts were letting their hair down tonight. They literally danced their booties off and partied till their spirits were high.

"Are you enjoying yourself?" Bernie asked Mary.

"Very much, I'm having a really good time. And you?"

"Very much," said Bernie, "it was a great idea of Eva and Gary to invite us…I couldn't imagine missing all this fun for anything."

Of course he really meant that she had something to do with it, because he felt very attracted to her.

"Yes," replied Mary, "I can't thank Eva and Gary enough." She really meant to say, thank them for bringing you and me together; but she didn't have to say it, they both knew what the other one meant to say, for the feelings were mutual. As the clock approached midnight and the Time Square ball started to drop, ...5...4...3...2...1..., the hall exploded into the biggest uproar as the band started playing Old Lang Syne and shouts of Happy New Year echoed across the room with noise makers and horns blowing and the confetti flooding everywhere. And in the heat and joy of it all, Bernie and Mary embraced wishing each other a Happy New Year... and they kissed for the first time. And that was how he came to meet Mary Collins, his future wife.

After a one-year courtship they were married in St. Thomas Episcopal Church, New York City and celebrated their reception in the same club where they first met, the historic Union League Club of New York City. They purchased an upscale cooperative apartment on the Upper East Side of Manhattan where they began their lives as a married couple after their honeymoon. For their honeymoon they had spent a week of bliss on the beaches of the Bahamas soaking up the Caribbean sunshine when they were not enjoying the comforts of each other in the privacy of their bridal suite accommodations. It was a wonderful and enjoyable honeymoon. Mary made him forget the loneliness of his past and gave him the happiest experience of his life.

Returning to New York City, they blended right into the social atmosphere. They started socializing regularly as Dr. and Mrs. Drew, and Mary joined a few social clubs in addition to her membership in one or two sororities. While he was not a smoker, she smoked heavily, and they both drank a little more than average, but these habits never seemed to be a problem. Married life made him a very happy man and they were both very contented and very much in love. In her he found the love and emotional security he had always needed. She spoiled him every chance she got. They did everything together and were each other's best friend. Despite their being apart while fulfilling their career obligations, they took every opportunity to call each other two or three times a day and otherwise spend every moment of their lives together, going everywhere, to shows, concerts, eating out, staying at home often reading and sharing their thoughts and experiences, supporting each other in everything each one did, travelling, creating an inseparable bond between them. For him, Mary at last had given him something that he had long envied others for from childhood when he observed other children who belonged to a happy and secure home life, for the maternal love and companionship she provided him filled that emotional void completely.

By 1971 his career as a neurosurgeon was going very well; in fact at 43 he was considered as one of the hospital's most promising neurosurgeons. He had performed numerous successful operations affecting the nervous system such as head traumas, brain tumors, spinal diseases, strokes, meningitis, etc. He gave lectures at the university and wrote numerous papers and articles.

In 1973, however, seven years after their marriage, his world suddenly collapsed when an ill-fated accident occurred. He was having a rough day, and it was nearing late afternoon when an emergency case requiring immediate surgery was rushed into the hospital. At that same time, a call came through for him telling him that his wife was the patient who was just rushed from Hunter College, where she had collapsed during a presentation after complaining of a severe headache. He rushed to the emergency receiving area and accompanied her up to the operating room immediately. She had suffered a massive brain aneurysm that had ruptured, and she was in a coma. The situation was very serious. He would let no one perform the operation on her but himself. The moment she was brought into the operating room, it was busy with doctors and nurses working frantically to seal off the aneurysm and repair the affected blood vessel to try to save her life. He did everything he could, summoned all his skill and knowledge, all his surgical ability; but it was already too late and the damage was too severe — he could not save her life. Her heart stopped beating and nothing they did could help. His wife died on the operating table. "Why? ..." he asked himself. "What good was it that he was a surgeon? What good was all his training and his technical skill if he couldn't even save the one person he loved?" He was filled with unbearable sadness, guilt, and remorse and he blamed himself. No matter what anyone did or said to console him, the pain still remained.

After the funeral he took some time off to grieve before returning to the hospital to resume work. It seemed like no one and nothing could console him. Gradually he withdrew more into himself and became less and less outgoing. Over the next few years he tried to camouflage his growing depression by a steady dose of overwork at first, but gradually the reverse took place, for that wasn't working. He began to slacken off and was passing up cases to other neurosurgeons time and again. He started to become careless about his health, and his attire, and was forgetting things. Then he started to take time off regularly and this pattern of behavior began to be noticed. He was called before the Board and their concern for him and the quality of his work of late was at issue. He was granted a leave of absence to take care of his personal problem.

While on leave, the problem only got worse. He was no longer able to control or hide his addiction to alcohol. He became a slave to his addiction. One drink was never enough to kill the pain, and the 2nd drink only led to the 3rd and the 4th, etc., until drunkenness and numbness seemed to relieve somewhat the emotional pain, at least for a little while, so he had to remain in that state to overcome it. The drinking habit was easier now for him, and it was easy for him to sink into alcoholism, for he was already a habitual drinker from his college days. Only then they called it social drinking and binge boozing, but now the trauma of suddenly losing his beloved wife drove him to the brink of oblivion. Wherever he went he found a source for his craving, which was not hard to do. Time passed and he never returned to work. He abandoned his practice, disappeared, and ended up drifting from city to city, town to town, bar to bar, sinking deeper and deeper into oblivion.

Chapter IV: Reverend Evan Michael's Journey

Evan Michael, whose parents were of Canadian descent, was born in Bay Village, Boston, Massachusetts, on May 15, 1948. His grandparents were immigrants from Ontario. In his own words, he relates the following:

My parents, Joseph and Marianne, were second generation immigrants, and were very hard working people. They owned a hardware store which they both operated and they had two sons, Orville Michael and me, Evan Michael. Orville was more practical and followed in my father's footsteps, learning the hardware business while I was always involved with the church.

When I was a teenager I became an acolyte in St. Stephens Catholic Church and also an active member of its youth program. I always felt drawn to the needs of those less fortunate and did volunteer community service every opportunity that was available. This sensitivity and desire to help others seemed to have been rooted in me from very early on. Perhaps it had something to do with my grandfather. When I was 7, I used to see grandpa pass out, seemingly helpless, and my dad would hold him and prop him up. Grandpa was a heavy drinker and he would get so that he didn't know what he was doing or saying. It seemed like he was always in that condition for he had a craving for alcohol. Then there were times, not as often, when he would be the nicest and sweetest person. I used to think he had a devil in him that possessed him to make him act the way he did. But later I came to learn that ever since grandma was killed in an accident in their home in Holyoke where they had migrated to in their youth to work in the paper mill, grandpa took it hard and turned to drinking, and the drinking got the better of him. My parents went and brought him to live with them and started to look after him, but eventually he lost the will to live and he died. When I was a boy I had also seen many drunken people like grandfather in certain parts of Boston and I could not understand why they got so emaciated, unstable and helpless, and acted like they didn't want to continue living. I swore then that I would never put anything like alcohol into my body.

As I grew older something within me drew me to the priesthood and made me want to give myself in service to help the poor, the downtrodden and the spiritually destitute. This was the only way I felt that my life would have meaning and purpose. I wanted to change people's lives, to be an instrument by which they would learn to love God and to be better human beings. So when I told my parents that I wanted to become a priest they were not surprised, and, in fact, after they saw that I was very serious, they were my biggest supporters. At twenty-two, I pursued my dream and enrolled in St. John Seminary in Boston leading up to the most special day of my life, Ordination Day.

It was a Sunday, June 8, 1975, and the church was filled to capacity. All of the ordinands gathered and were standing before the altar dressed in albs and their diagonally-worn deacon stoles. I could not believe my journey had brought me to this point just a few steps to the priesthood. I had completed my B.A. at Boston College in 1970, graduated from St. John's Seminary in 1974, completed the required one year of deaconry at St. Stephens in 1975 and here I was now, a candidate about to become an ordained minister. My thoughts flashed back to the time I was an acolyte in St. Stephens when I was a teenager and a member of the Youth Program, to my work with the poor and needy, to my desire to help those less fortunate, and to my grandfather's tragedy and others like him. And when I thought about Christ and his work among the poor, and about the saints like St. Francis, and St. Augustus and their work to help the poor and needy, I just knew that this was where I wanted to be.

"Evan Michael," *I heard the bishop call out my name.*

"Present," I responded as I caught myself in time and I approached the bishop.

One by one, in the same way, each of the candidates' names was called until the last name and all were standing before the altar.

"We rely on the help of the Lord God and our Savior Jesus Christ," *said the bishop, "and we choose these men, our brothers, for the priesthood."*

"Thanks Be to God," *the congregation responded.*

As each one approached the bishop he was asked if he is willing to serve Christ and His church as a faithful priest. Then hand in hand with the bishop, each of us candidates in his turn, promised obedience to the authority of the church and to his religious superior.

The bishop knelt and invited all present to pray with him for the candidates. Then the Litany of Saints, perhaps the most memorable moment in the ritual, was chanted while the candidates lay prostrate in the aisles and the prayer of litany invoked God's mercy and the intercession of all the saints to send down the Holy spirit upon them who were soon to become priests.

As I lay there, along with all my fellow ordinands, prostrate in the aisles before the altar, I felt as if the Holy Spirit had entered inside me and I felt a joy that I had never known before. And as the most solemn moment came when the bishop laid his hands upon my head ordaining me as he invoked the Holy Spirit on me, my soul was filled and I knew I would serve Christ faithfully.

The ceremony continued through the vesting by the removal of my deacon's stole and the donning of the symbols of my new office: a priestly stole and chasuble.

Next came the anointing of hands by the bishop with the Oil of Chrism. As I heard the words coming from the bishop: "… May Jesus preserve you to sanctify the Christian people and to offer sacrifice to God," *I thought of the homeless and destitute and the sick and the spiritually lost, many of whom I had seen in ghettos when I was growing up and whom I had read about in other places that were even worse than in the Greater Boston, Mass. area. As a priest, I thought, I could do so* much.

"Accept from the holy people of God the gifts to be offered to Him," *continued the bishop addressing each new priest as each one received the gift of bread and wine (in the form of paten and chalice).* "Know what you are doing, and imitate the mystery you celebrate: model your life on the mystery of the Lord's cross."

'I will be a humble priest; I will be a devoted servant of the Lord; I will be an instrument for His use to bring those most needy to the Lord.' These were my thoughts that shall guide me always.

Now, the ordination ritual itself was ended and as new priests we were called upon to assist in the distribution of communion. But before the mass was concluded, as new priests we gave our blessings to the ordaining bishop then to all of our relatives and friends who had joined in the celebration. The mass was now officially concluded.

A reception followed, which was a very joyous occasion with our families and friends gathered in the reception hall where food and drinks were served.

Evan Michael was now a young Catholic priest, having been ordained before family, friends, other candidates, and numerous fellow priests and church officials. He was on his way now to fulfilling his priestly journey and mission for Christ. But that was not without his personal strife and misgivings. In 1976 he was assigned to a parish in the diocese of Springfield, the parish of St. Joseph in Shelburne Falls, Ma; and although he served there faithfully for almost seven years, performing the sacraments and the required duties in the office of a priest, he came to the realization that the inner need he had carried so long within him for sacrifice, for ministering to the most destitute and downtrodden, to the lost and desperate (like his grandfather), and for converting sinners was not being fulfilled. He was a good priest, and he could continue the same way performing all the duties and requirements as he had been doing for the past seven years at St. Josephs, but it would not be the same. What was this inner compulsion? What was this inner voice that kept driving him and filling him with doubts and plaguing him still at this stage in his ministry? He could no longer ignore it. Had he made the right decision in becoming a liturgical priest? Maybe a vocation was the right thing for him, a monk, or a brother, or a friar, working amidst the poorest and the weakest and the most spiritually starved among us. He felt that he had not heeded the voice within him all these years to do what he could to help save the poor and destitute and broken in heart and spirit.

Here he was in the pristine valleys of the Mohawk, a river valley secluded in the mountains and surrounded by rivers and lakes. It is, to some, a natural paradise, almost isolated from the rest of the world, in the Berkshire Foothills and Mohawk Valley trails. It is a safe place away from the troubles and turmoil of life-and-death struggles of the slums of the big cities. If he was retired from life, this would be the ideal place to be; but his heart was troubled.

One evening in the summer of 1982 he was preaching a sermon and, in the middle of it, he suddenly felt distant and disoriented, as if he no longer belonged there; and the words he was uttering seemed not to come from him and it seemed as if he was losing his conviction. He hastily concluded the service and when it was over, he went into the rectory, gathered his things and left with no particular destination in mind, a behavior totally out of his character. The truth is, for some time he had been troubled and doubted his ministry, and whether he was truly fulfilling his Christly mission. He was going through the motions of a priest hoping that in time eventually the need that was driving him would pass, but he felt a crisis building up inside. He spoke to no one about it, nor sought advice, but kept it to himself. Of course, he prayed to God; he prayed hard for forgiveness, guidance and help; but he reached a point where he did not feel that he was serving the purpose of his calling, and he felt that he was no longer worthy to be a priest if he could not fulfill that purpose, which led him to his sudden decision. It was an act of insanity or desperation or both, but he got into his second-hand Chevy and just drove in the first direction until he found himself on I-95 and continued driving for hours and hours not knowing or caring exactly where he was heading and in what direction and he just kept on going.

Chapter V: An Abandoned Section of Harlem

In a certain part of the city that by all indications seemed abandoned (for most of the buildings were condemned and boarded up), on a certain block stood a house where only outcasts of the city were known to frequent. In fact, only drug addicts, pushers and prostitutes, street bums and drunkards hanged out there and ordinary citizens were reluctant to be seen in or near that neighborhood, especially after dark. Decent citizens called that house "The House of the Lost" because they claimed that everyone who goes in there is doomed to perdition for the multitude of sins they are known for and that they practice there. It is a three story building with the 2nd and 3rd floors a flee-bitten hotel where transients, prostitutes, alcoholics, drug addicts and derelicts occupy and are seen coming and going, and where all kinds of illicit activities take place. On the street level there is a bar, Jimmy's or Bigman's, whose clientele are the same prostitutes, Johns, bums and addicts who are attracted to that neighborhood. It is probably only a matter of time before this area undergoes city renewal and urban redevelopment and an attendant cleanup program to rebuild this part of the city. Until then, however, "The House of the Lost" is a haven for its own unique clientele whose broken compasses in life have abandoned them and they have lost their way.

In the past, this neighborhood was much different. It was once a decent place at the turn of the century, in Harlem's heyday, during and just after the great migration, when hard-working citizens were seen commiserating and conducting their daily lives there. The House of the Lost, therefore, now condemned by Christian-loving people and soon to be, if not already, condemned by the City, was once a respectable hotel and boarding house whose clientele were respectable workers, out-of-town businessmen, and visitors who could find accommodation there when it had a reputation as a decent place to stay. But in the latter half of the century, the neighborhood changed radically, the houses were abandoned and boarded up, and most of the population moved away. To the righteous and religious zealots and crusaders of the city, this building, in particular, is the worst eye sore in the neighborhood, and, to let their condemnation of it be known, they got some street artists to paint the name in large graffiti letters on the building, "THE HOUSE OF THE LOST". The owner, when he discovered what they had done, didn't want to spend the money to remove it or repaint the building - – what for if he didn't even know how much longer he would be able to stay in business — and his clientele weren't bothered by the name anyway, so business went on as usual. As for the bartender, Jim Bigman or Jimmy, who is also the owner of the building, he is no stranger to this town; he grew up here, so did his father when his grandfather had emigrated from down south and brought his family here to live. The house was handed down from his grandfather who owned it in prior years when this part of town was more respectable, then it was handed down to his father who then left it to him. He wouldn't walk away from it because he could still eke out a living from it as long as the government didn't close the place down as yet or tear it down. He knew all the street thugs and outcasts and they never bothered him nor he them. Their money was as good as gold to him.

Now, obviously, the place is not so fancy; but it once had a fine restaurant adjoining the bar where upstanding people used to come and eat. Now the restaurant is no longer operational and that adjoining room is only used if, and when, it is ever overcrowded or when small groups and couples want to drink in privacy — mostly, the room is always empty, except sometimes when a few drunks and drug addicts are seen there strung out over the tables.

In any case, this was the year 1982 and much of Harlem and the South Bronx were already in decay and ruin. Re-gentrification and rebuilding were already on the horizon and would soon take over in the years to come.

On Sunday, June 6, 1982, if you read any of the weekend newspapers, such as the N.Y. Times, The Daily News, The Amsterdam News, New York Post, etc., you were likely to still see headlines like:

1.   Senate extends Voting Rights Act of 1965

2.   ABC champ Larry Holmes scheduled to fight Gerry Cooney for heavyweight title in Ceasar's Palace on June 11, 1982.

3.   Pete Rose is 5th major leaguer to appear in 3,000 games (after Cobb, Musial, Aaron, and Yaz)

4.   Lena Horne, Lady and Her Music is closing at the Nederlander in N.Y.C. after 333 performances.

5.   Israel invades Lebanon to drive out PLO.

6.   Ronald Reagan is in his 2nd year as President of the U.S.A.

7.   Hugh Carey is serving his last year as governor of N.Y.S.

8.   Ed Koch is starting his 2nd term (82-85) as Mayor of N.Y.C.

Yes, but as far as Harlem is concerned, that once black mecca where the black renaissance had flourished, it was now dead or dying.

June 6, 1982 was a rainy Sunday night and very few people were out in the streets except perhaps in this section of town where only the lost or depraved may be seen wandering about. Around 9:30 p.m. a stranger, perhaps from out of town who didn't know any better, was seen making his way into the House of the Lost into Bigman's bar at a time when most of the good citizens of New York City were wise enough to remain snug in their homes or in some drier and brighter surroundings. Inside Bigman's bar, as in the entire House of the Lost, the lighting was poor and no more than twelve to fourteen patrons were there either sitting on the bar stools or sitting at a table or lying on the floor in some corner. The bartender, Jim, was about to serve a drink to the stranger who had just walked in out of the rain. He wasn't a regular and he didn't seem like the usual drunk who hangs out in such places. He looked suspicious at first. You know, Jim was wary of any strangers walking into his bar because he never knew when some undercover agent might be checking the place out or checking up on him.

"You look like a stranger from out of town. I've never seen you around here before," said Jim.

"Yes, I'm just a guy looking for a drink on a lousy night like this."

Jim trusted his instincts and decided he was not an agent or an undercover cop but he was still very cautious.

"What will you have?" he asked.

"Give me a Hennessy and soda," said the stranger.

"Will that be all?"

"That's it. By the way, who's the owner of this establishment?" asked the stranger.

"I am. The name is Jim Bigman. Who are you and where are you from?" said Jim.

"I'm sorry," said the stranger, "my name is Mark Henderson; just came into town from Atlanta where I've been living for a while."

Just then there was a news program on the TV and they both stopped to listen to it. The program was a retrospective on the Vietnam War and the Paris Peace Accord of 1975 that finally ended all official hostilities based on the peace accord agreement. The commentators were discussing the war and criticizing the U. S. for its role in it and for paying such a high price for a war they did not win, and could not have won in the first place. It was a rehashing of the same old story and they were both a little annoyed by the discussion so Jim turned off the TV and turned to the stranger.

"You don't mind, do you? They're always talking a lot of shit, and they don't know a damn thing about anything."

"I gather you have some strong opinions about the War. Are you also a veteran?" asked Mark.

"You're damn right I am," responded Jim. "So many good brothers fought for this country and lost their lives over there and for what? Those people didn't do us any thing; yet we went over there and killed a whole lot of them and a lot of our own young men and women as well! By the way, you sure you're not with the CIA, or the FBI, or the NYPD?"

"No, I am not! I am an angry veteran just like you." Mark replied. He neglected to tell him the real reason he came into the bar, and the burden he was carrying since he left the army.

With the ice broken, though, Jim seemed to trust the stranger a little more and warmed up to him. The conversation began to flow more freely after that.

"By the way, in what unit did you serve?" asked Jim.

"I was in the 199th Light Infantry," responded the stranger.

"What unit in the 199th Infantry?"

"F Company, 51st Infantry (LRRP)."

"That means your outfit was mostly into reconnaissance and patrols, I figure."

"Yes, our unit was patrolling the regions near Pleiku and DAK TO provinces, South Vietnam, months before the first Tet Offensive. We were in the thick of VC territory."

"I was a non-commissioned officer (NCO) in the 2nd Battalion, 3rd Infantry myself," said Jim. "I served under BG Frederick E. Davidson, the first African American to command an Army brigade in combat. The 199th Infantry Brigade saw some serious action near Pleiku, DAK TO, Danang, and Saigon in '67 and '68, especially during the Tet Offensive in '68. I've seen a lot of dead men in Vietnam."

Mark Henderson, the stranger, didn't seem to want to talk too much, but Jim, the bartender was just happy for the chance to talk to someone half-way sober, especially about the war, so he continued.

"In my unit alone, the bloods caught a lot of hell, more than half the soldiers killed and injured during the encounter with the VC/NVA forces south of

Saigon were bloods. The 199th Brigade was later sent to support the invasion of Cambodia in 1970; and, finally, in the fall of 1970, was withdrawn from South Vietnam and deactivated at Fort Benning, Ga. I was glad as Hell to get out of that mess alive; but I know a lot of good brothers who didn't make it. How about you, I'm sure you've seen a lot of action yourself?"

"Yes, I've seen a lot; I saw some things that turned my stomach and that still bother me now sometimes."

"There were some awful atrocities on both sides," said Jim, "like the My Lai village massacre. Were you anywhere near My Lai?"

"No. I wasn't in Charlie Company. In 1967, like I said, I was in Company F, 51st Infantry (LRRP), mostly a reconnaissance and patrol unit, in the central region of South Vietnam near Dak To. But I heard about the massacre in My Lai. (He was a little uncertain about the facts because he was stricken in a coma in '68, although he later read about it and therefore he pretended to be knowledgeable of the incident.) Some U.S. Lieutenant by the name of William Calley I heard led that massacre, and then they tried to cover it up. What the hell were we doing over there anyway killing innocent men, women and children?"

"It was a nasty war, no doubt about it;" said Jim, "and there were massacres on both sides. But if you ask me, I think the Black soldiers, more than any other group, Vietnamese included, suffered the worst from the Vietnam War. The highest casualties were among blacks and yet they got treated like dirt when they returned home to the U.S. You sound to me like you also had a bad time over there so what's your story?" Jim asked, trying to get the stranger to open up.

"It's a long story," said Mark, who, after a moment's hesitation, continued, "I was shot and left for dead, but I guess it wasn't my time. They rescued me and patched me up real good, although I still have some internal damage and some bitter feelings. Don't get me wrong; I don't hate the Vietnamese, even though they were the enemy and I was sent over there to kill them. Sometimes on our own side we've got worse things than Vietnamese."

Jim sensed a personal bitterness in Mark's tone that seemed to go deeper than any hatred for the Vietcong. Something real terrible must have happened to him in Company F, 51st Infantry. Then Mark reached into his pocket and pulled out a picture of his platoon with a circle around the target of his hatred, Dexter Dixon, and was about to show it to Jim when, Just at that moment, at about 11 p.m., a man dressed like a preacher appeared at the

285

entrance of the bar with an umbrella in his hand, wet from the rain, in a black suit and black shirt with a white collar turned around his neck.

Chapter VI: The Convergence of Lost Souls and a Priest

Who Lost His Way

The stranger who entered was indeed a minister; it was Reverend Evan Michael who had driven all the way from Shelburne Falls, Ma. He had not realized how far he had come, nor why to this destination. He had travelled on I-95 south all night, crossed the George Washington Bridge and ended up in Harlem, in this forsaken neighborhood of all places. A faint light that he had seen from a block and a half away led him straight to Jimmy's bar. He opened the door and entered and when he looked inside in the dimly lit room he saw what appeared to be about a dozen or so strange, wasted-looking individuals.

"What kind of place is this," he asked himself, *"and who are these strange-looking people?"*

It was like a page taken out of Eugene O'Neill's The Iceman Cometh, or Dante Alighieri's Inferno, with broken-spirited individuals, remnants of lost and wasted beings who sought the dimness of a place like this for escape and its trough for drowning their pain. He had wandered here that night after driving who knows how long, and after abandoning his vehicle that had stalled in a flooded street a block and a half away. Every one of the inhabitants looked at him strangely as he entered the bar and Jim, the bartender, was the first to speak.

"Father," said Jim, "why…what… are you doing here? Are you sure you're in the right place?"

"I guess I am lost;" responded the reverend, "My name is Father Evan Michael and my car just broke down in a pool of water a block and a half away and I saw the light of this place…"

"Well, come in out of the rain anyway; and don't let these lost souls and drunken has-beens bother you. Hey, Crypt!! Get the hell up from that table and let the Rev. have a seat, and don't try to hustle him, either, or you know what!"

After seating him, Jim asked Father Michael to give him a few minutes, and he will return and try to help sort out his situation. As he turned to go back behind the bar, one of the barflies, Quickie, eased over toward the reverend.

"Hey, Rev., are you looking for some company, or maybe some action tonight? Let me…"

And Jim, looking back just in time, interrupted her.

"You slut, show some respect to the preacher. Go back and sit your ass down!"

"Yeah, show some respect, honey." Said Angie sitting nearby who chimed in. "You want to go to hell? But you're going there anyway, 'cause there's no hope for people like you and me. Best leave the preacher alone...Hi, Rev.!"

"Hello," said the reverend with a smile.

And Crypt, a notorious ex-con and street hustler, who must have gotten a sudden flash of religion, turned to Quickie and admonished her.

"You better pray for forgiveness and for your God-forsaken soul. You can't tell the difference between one of your whoremongers and a man of God? Bitch, you must have lost what little sense you got left!"

"I'm sorry...," said Quickie. "Please forgive me, Rev."

"Never mind, my child... no offense taken." And turning to Crypt, Reverend Michael thanked him for his timely intervention.

Dolly, the ex-call girl turned prostitute, drug addict and drunkard, came and sat down beside the reverend.

"Can I buy you a drink, Rev?" asked Dolly.

"No, thank you," he replied.

"You know father, and I mean no disrespect to you or to the profession, but I knew a preacher once who after preaching on Sundays all day, by Sunday night he was hitting the bottle hard and he went on like that for years," said Dolly.

"What happened to him?" asked Father Michael.

"The same thing that happens to all alcoholics, he went to Heaven...in a bottle." She was testing the reverend.

"That's very sad," said father, "but I have a story, too. I knew a very humble man once who met an alcoholic and said to him, 'God loves you and He loves you because you have something very precious."

Two or three of them leaned close to hear what the reverend was saying for it seemed to have a sweet "savor" to it, and Dolly, most of all, was very anxious to hear his answer.

"And what is that?" asked Dolly.

"A heart that is hurting that wants to be loved. God loves you no matter what; he doesn't care what condition you are in, who you are, or what you have done. He doesn't look down on you; He knows what you are going through every day and every hour and He can help you defeat the demons. He can give you peace and love and make all the broken parts whole again. He knows you can't win the battle by yourself, no one can. That's why He is willing to help you if you will allow Him to."

And they were quiet, for what he said gave them pause for a moment. But not Marvin Hollowman, the ex-gambler and policy runner who was almost killed by the mob for a debt he owed and now had become a druggy and an alcoholic who sometimes has moments of lucidity like the present time when he chose to speak.

"Well, what do you know," said Marvin, "we've got ourselves a real preacher in our midst. Before you know it, he's going to start giving out confessions and trying to save us lost souls. I, for one, am too far gone for that. And look at Crypt there, a.k.a. William A. Smith, acting like he's got a soul. You'd think he's the last one with a soul worth saving, all the evil things he's done already. A North Carolina A & T College dropout journeyed all the way up to the big city to set up an illegal tobacco, liquor, and drug-running business between N.Y. and N.C. till he got sent up to Sing-Sing for five years of hard labor, and now that he is out once again he is into every kind of fast hustle on the streets trying to out slick everybody. And my man over there, what's his name, Charlie, the old timer, he's only forty, but he looks like sixty. He is the most down-and-out of all the down-and-out derelicts I know. He can't even stand up straight. He's got some kind of curse in him, too, always blabbering and mumbling about devils and evil spirits after him, and he sees them all the time, except when he is stone-cold drunk. Half the time, he's laid out like a cold dead fish. If he had a soul, he lost it somewhere.

Then there's the good doctor over there, or used-to-be good doctor (He was referring to Bernard Drew), running away from his past, trying to commit suicide inside a bottle. A man can only fall so low from so high. He's a goner soon, for sure. And you already heard from Miss Quickie over there, a.k.a. Mary Jean, ran away from home in hick town Ohio at fifteen with a drifter. She'll do tricks for favors. Get her drunk and you can take her upstairs for the night. And Ms Angie, a.k.a. Angela Darsey used to be a nurse's aide before she started turning tricks and becoming a drunk. And don't forget Ms Dolly over here interrogating you, reverend, like she wants to take up

289

religion or something, she's a college dropout from Boston, ex-model, ex-call girl busted, turned prostitute, alcoholic and dope addict. Man, what a collection we got here, Reverend. Quite a congregation wouldn't you say?"

"And what's your story... Tell us your story, crack head, you know so much," said Angie who was sitting off on the side with her John.

"Well, well now, Angie, Ms Used-to-be-nurse's-assistant who's turned to tricks and drugs, I am a piece of shit, and I am not trying to hide it. I'll probably be dead in a few days anyhow; but look at drifter Dexter Dixon over there. He's going to go on drifting and drinking and drowning his crimes – God knows how many! The army messed him up good. Made him a monster of some kind, worse than the one he was already, and now he can't even live with himself, so he crawls inside a bottle so as not to face reality. Do you know he was born an Oreo? Yes, Oreo! His father was a white southerner, his mother black. His father's relatives, like all southern racists, hate the idea of mixing the races and look down on black people as inferior. The thought of having a black grandson or grandnephew gives them cirrhosis of the liver, in other words, makes them damn sick and full of devil hate. So his father abandoned both him and his mother when he was born and he grew up in Philly full of self-hate inside. He hates who he is and if he could paint his skin any whiter, he would do so in a minute. He is mixed up psychologically and he prefers whiteness over blackness. Ain't he a mess?"

Dexter Dixon looked like he was just awaking from a stupor when he heard his name called.

"Who...the shlit...just called...my f......g name? Tell the slon-uv- a-bitch...to stop...callin' my name."

He may be a derelict and a drunk, and a monster and all that; but one thing he knows is that if he wants anonymity, somebody calling out his name is not the way to get it.

Well, go back to sleep, Dex," said Marvin, "sorry if I disturbed you. Whoever you hiding from, you ain't worth the effort, cause you've been dead a long, long time ago... and there's no preacher who's going to save you. Ain't that right, Reverend?"

The dozen or so drunks and prostitutes looked at Marvin and then at the Reverend, knowing too well that everything Marvin said about them was true. He had described them down to a "T" with his uncharitable words as a pile of dead or lost souls beyond redemption. How could this reverend or anyone change anything or erase from their lives all the things that Marvin had said. He made them feel hopeless, all of them. Why did they even bother to listen to the Reverend?

But the reverend sensing their pain and their cries deep down for help, looked at Marvin and then looked at all of them with compassion and said:

"Don't be fooled by such bitterness and self-hatred. His voice is a voice of despair. He speaks very desperately from a place of defeat where it is so easy to surrender, as he has done. He tries so hard to kill the terrible pain that is deep within him, but he cannot. He wants you to believe as he does that there is no hope, no way out. Oh, but he is so wrong. He can still be the victor over whatever is hurting him inside the most. It is never too late! Believe what I tell you, it is never too late! You can be the victor, too, if you want to be whole again. The question is never can I be whole again? That is asking the wrong question. The only true question is how? How can I? I wouldn't be a priest if I didn't know there was a way. If I could show you a way, if I could show you a way right now, tell me, wouldn't you take it? If I could show you how to live again without the pain, without the hurt and despair, wouldn't you want that? Wouldn't you want to be whole again?"

You could see that something in the reverend's words or something about him was starting to penetrate the numbness and almost lifelessness that some of them had withdrawn into for so long, and they had not completely lost all their humanity yet so long as there was still a faint glimmer of hope deep inside them that made them desperately want to live and to believe.

While the reverend was speaking and several of them were gathering near him where he was sitting, suddenly, the sinister Daemon, who was sitting in the far dark corner of the bar with his sinister eyes and motives, flicked his fingers like some kind of signal towards Marvin who got up from his bar stool and went over to him like he put a spell on him. Daemon then gave Marvin something and he took it and went straight towards the men's bathroom with it. When he returned, he just sat on his stool motionless for a little while at first, and then, suddenly, he got up and started acting crazy, then he ran for the exit like a bird flying out the door…and he was never seen again.

"Fellow lost souls," shouted Crypt who had to make a comment, "there's a good example of a firecracker that just went off, in his brain, that is. He ran his mouth for a little while talking about everybody else until his demon took over and he went shooting off like a rocket zzzzzzzooooooom. I doubt if we'll ever see him again – maybe for a week or two – maybe never. But the rest of us get to go on in this little dream world with this comedy of ours. Now you can all go back to your favorite past time, getting drunk, and to hell with everything and everybody else…O please forgive me, father, I didn't mean you."

Suddenly there was quietness in the room as everyone sat still, reflecting on what had just taken place.

Chapter VII: The Miracle

Jimmy's Bar soon returned to normal again after Marvin Hollowman's sudden flight and disappearance and the liquor started pouring again. For most of the clients, numbness and oblivion seemed to them to be safe and liquor or anything stronger would fit the bill. But despite everything, for some of them, at least a half dozen including Dolly, Angie and her John, Doc, and to some extent, Crypt, it appeared that the reverend had brought something different into their world. Somehow there was something about him and his words that affected them that the narcotics and the booze couldn't make go away because they had not heard anyone speak like that before. Perhaps, though, they were too afraid to even think it, somewhere deep in their souls they were wishing they could taste some of this hope that he was preaching. The Reverend sensed in them, even in the worst one among them, their deepest pain and feeling of helplessness, and a silent, desperate plea, though they could not express it, for a miracle; and in his heart he wished that he could be a way to give them that miracle.

Meanwhile, Jim and the stranger at the bar returned to their conversation at the point when the stranger, Mark Henderson, was about to show him the photo of himself and the members in his platoon.

"Yeah, where's that photo you were going to show me?" asked Jim.

And Mark handed him the photograph to see if he knew any of the men. It was doubtful he knew anybody except, perhaps, the man Mark had circled. That was the main reason he came here in the first place. He wanted to find that man.

"Check them out," said Mark, "I circled one man in particular who I am trying to find."

"Don't tell me he has something to do with your bitter feelings and with what happened to you in Vietnam?" Jim queried.

"Just do me a favor," said Mark, "look at the picture and tell me if you've ever seen that man."

Jim took one look, and he knew who it was. It was Dexter Dixon, the habitual drunk, the wasted Dexter Dixon whom he had pity

on because he was a veteran like himself and he saw him as a casualty of the Vietnam War, empty inside and tormented by his past battlefield experiences. Jim did not know what had happened in the war between him and Mark, but he couldn't see any point in taking revenge on a man who was already dead. You can't kill a dead man.

"I...I...don't know, Mark," said Jim. "What the hell did he do to make you have it up for him, anyway?"

"He's a murderer, that's what," almost angrily, Mark retorted. "He killed my buddy and left me for dead on the battlefield! I swore I would get even when I caught up with him."

Who wouldn't take sides with Mark Henderson? He saw his closest friend murdered in cold blood, and he, himself, was shot and left for dead. He was sure the killer was Sargent Dexter Dixon. He tracked him down to this God-forsaken place, and now he was going to end it and get his revenge.

"I know how you feel, man, believe me," said Jim, "but sometimes people pay for their crimes in different ways, sometimes worse ways than you or I can imagine."

Just as Jim was trying to get Mark to turn from his intent on revenge, Dexter popped up from the corner where he was and stumbled up to the bar.

"Heyyyy, barrr....ttttender..." he called out, "I'm thirrrsteeee...pooor me... a dammm drink... will ya? ... What the rest... uv you slobbbs ... looking at ... Nnnnever seeeen a mannn ... orrr..derrr a drink ... before?"

They must have sensed what was about to take place. It's a kind of instinct the downcast seems to possess about such things. At the same time that Dexter appeared at the counter and spoke, Mark caught a good look at his face.

"That's the dirty son-of-a-bitch I have been looking for," Mark said to Jim. "I'm going to finish him."

And as he moved toward his target with a gun in his hand, everybody scrambled for cover.

"He's got a gun! He's got a gun!!" They all shouted.

"Dexter Dixon," Mark Henderson called to him, "You S.O.B., get ready to meet your maker; I'm going to kill you for murdering my buddy, Mitchell Goldberg, in Vietnam!!"

Dexter wasn't even sober enough to remember all the evil he had done and had been trying to forget since he took to the bottle. He just stood there like it didn't make any difference to him, and, what the heck, Mark would be doing him a big favor anyway.

Meanwhile, the reverend saw what was about to take place, and he could not stay still and allow it to happen. He got up quickly, stepped in between Dexter and the gunman as the gun went off... BANG... and he took the bullet that was meant for Dexter Dixon.

"Oh my God!" he cried as he fell to the floor.

When Mark realized what he had done and saw the reverend fall, he was filled with so much remorse and guilt that he dropped the gun and ran to the aid of the reverend lying on the floor.

"I didn't mean to shoot you...I didn't mean to shoot you, Rev. Please forgive me! Please!" he pleaded, then he frantically called out, "Is there a doctor, is there a nurse, or anybody who can help?" as others ran over to try to help.

Jim, in the meantime, phoned for an ambulance and called the precinct; but he was not too hopeful.

"In this neighborhood," he said, shaking his head, "who knows when they are going to get here? We got to help Reverend ourselves. We can't let him die."

"Doc, doc," said Crypt, you were a good doctor once, in fact, the best surgeon there was. I used to read about you, man. You got to help the Rev. You got to, doc."

And everyone implored him, all the drunks in the bar.

"I used to be a nurse, too, once," said Angie, "I'll help you, Doc, if you give it a try. Come on, Doc, what can you lose?"

Suddenly the past flared up in Doc's brain, and for a few seconds, he relived everything, his childhood, his broken home, his loneliness as a little boy, his beautiful wife, Mary, how she made him so happy, and the time she was brought to the emergency room, the time he rushed to her gurney in the emergency receiving area and had her taken up to the operating room immediately and would let no one else perform the operation but himself, the best neurosurgeon in the country, with the best nurses and the best-assisting doctors with him in the operating room working frantically, and he still could not save the life of the one he loved. He did everything he could, everything, summoned all his skill and knowledge; but even with all his surgical ability, with all his will, with all his earthly powers, it was not enough – he could not save her life. The hurt and anguish came back… "Why? … Why? …" He never stopped blaming himself, and now, something would not let him be. He heard a voice from deep within him call to him through the countless numbers of benumbing drinks that racked his mind and body and tell him he had suffered enough, that it was time to let it go and to do God's work. The spirit so overwhelmed him that it gave him the strength, somehow, to make an effort.

"Quickly," he said, "there's no time to lose. We've got to move him to a bed or couch to make him comfortable, and, nurse Angie, I need you to get some blankets, some tourniquets, bandages, soap, boiling water, alcohol for sterilization, and, above all, some tools to operate and remove the bullet lodged near his heart. Good God, people, give me the help I need!"

As they carefully transferred the reverend to a bed in a backroom where Jim slept, Jim also remembered that he had some medical tools and supplies that his father, who was a medic, was fond of and that he, Jim, had kept and was hoping to sell to make some money for it. He never got rid of them; now, they would surely be needed. He brought the tools in a bag and gave it to Angie, who sterilized the tools that were needed and gave them to Doctor Bernard Drew, the once famous neurosurgeon who miraculously conjured up from deep down all the skills that he had once known to employ it now and to save the life of the reverend. It may have helped that the impact of the bullet was impeded somewhat and slightly deflected away from his heart by a heavy medallion the reverend wore about his neck. Nevertheless, the situation was a matter of life and death.

They improvised almost everything, extra lighting, water, sterilization, clean blankets, sheets, bandages, gloves, etc., and with a miracle working for them, Dr. Drew successfully removed the bullet, stopped the bleeding and bandaged the reverend up, and had him resting comfortably with an excellent chance of recovery.

By that time, finally, the ambulance arrived. The patient would have surely died if they had waited for them. Good thing it was not the reverend's time, and a good thing, too, the Great Spirit resurrected the lost Dr. Bernard Drew just in time. Of course, the police took statements from those they could get anything intelligible from, and the ambulance took the stricken reverend to the hospital for further treatment and care. The hospital staff was amazed at the emergency care he was already given and praised whoever had done the surgery under such impossible conditions.

Chapter VIII: Conclusion

All of the outcasts in the House of the Lost, except for Hollowman and Daemon, came to the hospital deeply concerned for the reverend. Somehow in the little time he was in their midst, he had meant something to them. He wanted to help them and was willing to give his own life to do so, and they, in turn, were there for him when it counted. Father Evan Michael, after a few weeks of convalescing, recovered fully from his injuries. Of course, there was an investigation and visits from the Boston Archdiocese and the New York Archdiocese when they heard what had happened. Father Michael then made a humble plea to his Superiors, gave his spiritual reasons for making such an extraordinary request, which was granted after the necessary arrangements could be made between the Boston and New York diocesan titular heads, that he be transferred to the Archdiocese of New York City and given permission to join the Order of St. Francis, the Order of Friars Minor (OFM), and become a Friar in the Church of St. Francis of Assisi. At last, he found his true mission there and his calling to the ministry. This is where he was certain he was guided to serve. In one night, he had touched the lives of some of society's lost and most rejected, had offered his own life to save one of these the most wretched among men, was rescued and saved by prostitutes, drug addicts, alcoholics, and a lost neurosurgeon, and, that night, and in the years to come, he was a part of his own miracle and the miracle of the redemption of those whom he came in contact with in the "House of the Lost." This was the life experience that he needed. After that night, he became a great servant and preacher among the neediest and most destitute, and he never again doubted his purpose in life.

As for the others:

Mark Henderson was spared being charged with the crime of attempted murder when, of all people, Dexter Dixon, his worst enemy, agreed to take the fall for the accidental shooting of Father Michael, with which all the witnesses agreed. Mark Henderson was later confessed by Father Michael, who succeeded in convincing him to turn away from his hatred and to forgive his enemy, who must still answer to God for his sins.

Mark thanked Father Michael for helping him to lift the heavy burden of hate and revenge that he had carried in his heart for so long and for forgiving him for accidentally shooting him. Before returning to Atlanta, he went to the PA Veterans Memorial Cemetery located in Indian Town Gap, Lebanon, PA, to visit the grave of his friend Mitchell Goldberg and place a wreath of friendship flowers (yellow roses) near his tombstone. He prayed that he would rest in peace now, knowing that his war buddy did not forget about him. Mark returned to Atlanta, where fortunately, Martha was still waiting and was glad that the man who came back to her was now liberated from his terrible past, at least the ghosts that tormented him, and she was happy to become Mrs. Mark Henderson. Mark, with the influence of Father Michael, became very religious and a dedicated counselor for disabled and PTSD veterans in Atlanta.

Dr. Bernard Drew came back from the dead. After the tragic loss of his wife, for which he blamed himself, and tried to punish and destroy himself for not being able to save her on the operating table, thankfully, the events of that night in the "House of the Lost" happened, and the encounter with Father Michael happened, and a miracle happened. After that, he was able to accept God's will and purpose for him, and a new spiritual awakening cleansed him of his addiction and his sense of guilt, made him regain his practice and become again what he was meant to be, a great neurosurgeon of his time.

Jim Bigman no longer owns "The House of the Lost," a.k.a. Jimmy's Bar and Grill, for its days were numbered anyway, but at least for a while, he was a proud owner who took delight in telling the story of what happened that night of June 6, 1982. It even made the next day's evening news at the time and made Jim Bigman's infamous Bar famous for a short while. The name on the house was painted over and changed from "The House of the Lost" to "The House of Miracles," and, on no less than two occasions, Jim had hosted a reunion of those who were there that night and were still alive, only they held the reunions in a restaurant where no alcoholic beverages were served. Since that night of the incident, with the help of Father Michael, most of the participants had either been cured or had joined AA with his recommendation and were on the wagon for good or well on their way to being rehabilitated.

Maybe redemption is possible for all sinners, even Dexter Dixon. After all, he did take the blame for shooting Reverend Michael. It was probably the most decent thing he ever did in his wretched life. He was sentenced to 10 years in prison for it and, on Father Michael's recommendation, received drug and mental disorder treatments. It is said that before he died in prison after serving only four years, he confessed all his sins, including murder, self-hatred, and hatred for others, to Father Evan Michael, who visited him regularly until his death.

Well, there seems to be no redemption for Quickie, not as yet, anyway. She is still tricking and sometimes can be seen working the streets, but it is certain that she, too, remembers that night. She often confides with her street peers that she plans to quit her life and go back home. Maybe one day, she, too, will find her miracle.

If Angie could change, every street-walking prostitute could. With help and spiritual counseling from her now favorite reverend, Angie cleaned herself up, gave up prostitution and drinking, went back to school, and is now working in Dr. Bernard Drew's hospital as a registered professional nurse. She sometimes speaks at homes for wayward girls and at nursing schools to motivate students. She is a real success story.

Of all the lost souls, Dolly was the one who wanted most to hear and accept Reverend Michael's message. In fact, for a long time, she had been grappling with her problem and wanted to change but did not know how. He gave her hope and the incentive she needed. She was the first one to go into the A.A. group he recommended, and she gave up liquor and prostitution for religion. Like Crypt, she is now a counselor for those seeking a new start in life from life on the streets and from drug and alcohol addiction. With Father Michael's spiritual guidance, she was able to make the transition.

Some people say Crypt should never have been a hustler or an alcoholic. He had the brains and the heart to succeed in anything he put his mind to. Luckily, in the end, he turned from crime and alcohol after his life connected that night with Reverend Michael, Dr. Bernard Drew, and Mark Henderson. He has gone straight and clean ever since and is now an advisor in a program for wayward youth and ex-convicts. He is very successful.

As for Marvin Hollowman, he never returned to Jimmy's that night or any other night. In fact, that night, they found him dead of an overdose of cocaine mixed with alcohol -- a combination that should never go together. It looks like he was right when he said he would be dead in a few days, only it came sooner. Too bad he did not convert before seeing his Maker.

We know very little about Daemon, only that he was a drug pusher and always remained as mysterious as he was that night in Jimmy's. He disappeared and probably ended up just like Marvin Hollowman.

Poor Charlie, he is still a street bum and a drunkard. Guess you can't win them all in this life.

And that's the end of my story.

John Weldon Evans

Author

AMAZING GRACE

Orient Avenue Church of God was filled beyond capacity until there was standing room only in the vestibule, on the stairs, and outside in the street. In fact, to hold such a large crowd, the service would have required a cathedral, but in a small Jersey City community, that was hardly possible.

Inside the church, midway through the service, the organist played a few introductory bars, and the congregation rose and sang, "Amazing Grace, how sweet the sound…" The voices and the music filled the church until the echoes overflowed out into the streets, and those outside joined in with the chorus. After the last verse was sung and the congregation was seated again, the acting pastor approached the pulpit. A solemn, bespectacled gentleman in his late 20s looked out on the audience and spoke.

"Dear family members and friends, brothers, and sisters all, as children of God, we are put here on this earth to do God's will, to live out our days in service to Him so that His work may be fulfilled. When God wishes us to follow a certain path He has chosen for us, He makes a way for us to do so, and it matters not where we find ourselves or in what circumstance. So it was thirty-five years ago when He said to our beloved pastor, "I will make you an instrument for a good work I have for you," and He touched him in a way that only God can do. That was the moment of his spiritual awakening, the beginning of a new life, a life of commitment, dedication, and service symbolized by true humility and compassion for others. We are his beneficiaries. How fortunate we are that God chose him to be our pastor…"

The words rang true in the hearts of everyone, many of whom came from far away to pay their last respects, and there were many tearful eyes as the speaker continued.

"There isn't one person, sitting or standing in this room, whose life he did not touch. Yes, he converted many to the church, and he was a true drum major for Christ. So often, he stood at this very pulpit where I am standing and delivered sermons that stirred our hearts! Many times, too, he gave eulogies for others…only this time the eulogy is for him…"

The speaker went on to tell of the good deeds and charitable works of the deceased Reverend, which could fill volumes. How different would it have been if, 35 years ago, his life had ended or taken a different path? The world would never have been the same.

300

No, the world could not have been the same. Perhaps if men had written the script, but herein lies the mystery of how God works in our lives to serve His purpose. For a better understanding, therefore, we must return some 50 years earlier to a small town in Long Island, N.Y., to a time when two children were growing up, when their souls were just beginning to form impressions of the world around them, and their characters struggled to take shape.

Robert Patterson and Mark Andrews were two boys growing up in the same neighborhood in Wyandanch, Long Island. The bond that developed between them was as strong as if they were the same flesh and blood – they were inseparable. Robert was inclined to mischief, it seems, from the day he was born, for he was a troublemaker from the beginning. He had so much anger within him, along with a streak of wildness and what seemed to be a disturbed nature. Probably he inherited his anger from his father, who was always bitter toward the world, who used to drink a lot, and who ended up taking out his bitterness and frustrations on his wife and son every chance he got. He was a cruel and mean man, and, in return, whatever love might have been in Robert's heart for him was rapidly extinguished, especially after seeing his mother suffer beatings at his father's hands for no reason whatsoever. Eventually, his father got into some kind of trouble...they said he raped a 16-year-old girl in the neighborhood and was put away. The little ranch house they lived in was not much, and they would have lost it then if his mother didn't find work and taken in welfare children to help pay the mortgage. They barely survived.

As far back as Robert could remember, he used to spend most of his time in his friend Mark Andrews' house nearby. There, he was happy playing games, reading comics, listening to the radio, or riding Mark's bicycle. On Saturdays and some weekdays in the afternoons after school, they would both go roaming through the neighborhoods and surrounding woods, searching for all kinds of imaginary adventures. On many of their adventures, they would commit pranks like throwing stones, breaking windows, puncturing car tires, molesting neighbors' guard dogs that were fenced in, ringing peoples' doorbells, and bullying smaller children. Most of the pranks were Robert's idea which Mark went along with. Mark, unlike Robert, was of a gentler nature, always respectful and thoughtful, but he liked Robert, although he was so impulsive and unpredictable. Robert did things that Mark found exciting, but he, himself, didn't have the courage to do them. Each of them was an only son in their families, but unlike Robert, Mark loved his father, who was a deacon in the Baptist church and a devoted husband and father. Sunday mornings were probably the only times when the boys weren't together because Mark spent the time in church. Robert said that his family went to the Jehovah's Witness Church, but in reality, he never went to church. He may have said he did to please Mr. Andrews when he was asked.

Mark and Robert went to Deer Park Jr. High School together, but even in school, Robert got reported for truancy and misconduct quite often. He was suspended once, and Mrs. Patterson had to go to the principal's office to find out about it. That was after his father was put away in prison, and Mrs. Patterson could hardly afford to take time off from her job to go there. She worked in a nearby factory sewing vinyl upholstery. Mr. Sheftel, the principal, said to her, "If your son Robert doesn't change his behavior, I am afraid he's going to be put out of school for good someday." He really meant suspended because Robert was underage at the time, and they had to let him go to school; it was the law! Then there was an incident one day when someone broke the fire alarm box and set off the alarm, which caused a big furor when the fire trucks came for nothing. Everyone knew it was Robert who did it, and he would be suspended or transferred for sure, but it was Mark who took the blame for him and got suspended for three days instead.

By the time they reached the ninth grade, the differences in their characters and reputations began to increase greatly. Robert could hardly keep out of trouble and was barely surviving academically. Mark, on the other hand, was becoming more and more self-disciplined, serious, and successful in his studies. He was also spending more time at the church on Sundays and sometimes during the week. It was amazing, though, that he and Robert remained the best of friends through thick and thin, standing up for each other and sticking together as much as possible. In fact, it was probably because of Mark's influence that Robert softened to a large degree the troubling side of his nature, for, in Mark, he found the only true friend he had, and, in a way, he wished he could be like him, so calm and self-assured. When he felt a rage inside, Robert could always turn to Mark, who understood and who helped him to calm down. He was like a brother and a father all in one. Robert really loved Mark like a brother and would do anything for him. Mark, on the other hand, always had a strong protective feeling toward Robert, as if he was afraid to leave him alone as if his mission was to save him from himself.

By some minor miracle, Robert passed Jr. High, not without Mark's help, of course, and both went on to attend Babylon High School. The next two years, although there was some improvement, did not fundamentally change Robert's nature, and he was no less angry or bitter towards the world, but Mark was always there to help him deal with it. They would talk out their feelings often when Robert would vent some of his anger and disillusionment.

"Mark, school stinks, and life stinks! What's the use anyway? Nothing makes any sense. Why bother to study or follow the rules? Even if you finish high school, it's going to come out the same way. People like you and me are going to get kicked around anyway."

"It's that kind of thinking that will always keep you down and get you into trouble," said Mark, "it doesn't have to be like that. You can be anything you want, so stop talking that way. If you had a little faith, you wouldn't act and speak the way you do!"

"Yeah, listen to St. Mark! I can see you wearing a preacher's robe already!"

"And what's so bad about that? Anyway, you're right. I've been talking with Rev. Rivers at the Church of God on Sundays about becoming a preacher someday, but I'm not worried about me. It's you I'm worried about, you don't seem to have interest in anything. Next year we'll be graduating, and you don't have the slightest idea what you want to do with your life!"

"That's just the point," said Robert, "I don't believe in school, or people, or church as you do, or anything. I only know that I would like to get away from this place, far away from here!"

"You can't run away from yourself, Bob; anyway, where would you go?"

"Join the Army! We'll be close to 19 next year after graduation. Let's enlist! I hear you can learn a trade in the Army and go to school afterwards on the G.I. Bill. You can travel and see all kinds of places."

"Would that really work for you, Bob?"

"Sure! What's two years in the service? We'll be better off for it. You'll still have time to be a preacher if you like."

That was the typical conversation that took place from time to time as the end of their senior year approached. Many seniors were thinking about what college they were going to attend after high school, but Robert's mind was on the Army and seeking something different, at least from the world as he perceived it.

In 1950 the Korean War was heating up, and more and more young men were being conscripted via the draft, but many enlisted in the service before they were drafted. Robert and Mark decided to join up rather than being drafted immediately after graduating in June, and, with their parents, especially Mark's, reluctantly consenting, they went off to basic training in Fort Benning, Ga. By September, they were shipped off to Japan.

When they arrived in Japan, they were confined mostly to Army barracks, for they were to be shipped out to active duty almost immediately. They were given a day of leave, however, which they spent touring downtown Tokyo and visiting a few of the places where G.I.'s frequent. Before being sent over to Korea, they talked about where they were going and the certainty of seeing action. "Mark," said Robert," this looks like the real thing for sure! Isn't it exciting?"

But Mark was skeptical.

"Robert," he said, "Listen to me. Going into combat and the prospect of shooting at real people frightens me. Shooting at targets and dummies was one thing, but I don't know if I will be able to kill real people."

"Now, you had better stop talking that way! You were trained for combat, and you had better get it into your head that you kill the enemy before the enemy kills you!"

Mark thought to himself, "I guess it takes people like Robert to fight this war, people who don't believe in or care about anything, who just take life as it comes, but there's something terribly wrong with war. I wish we were back home in Long Island."

"Hey, Mark, stop looking so depressed. We'll do all right, you'll see!"

Robert and Mark were assigned to the same Corp, same battalion, company, and platoon, and now they were on their way to Inchon, Korea, together. From there, their unit, the 10th Corp, commanded by General Edward M. Almond, was to participate in the U.S. forces' ground action behind enemy lines as part of the U.S. counter-offensive to drive the North Koreans out of So. Korea. The 10th Corps sailed from Japan to Inchon and landed in amphibian boats. From there, they moved north, joining up with the marines under General Walton H. Walker, who had broken out of the Pusan Peninsula perimeter, thus routing the communists and pushing further north toward Seoul, South Korea.

As the 10th Corp and the marines advanced towards Seoul, patrols were sent out from time to time to check enemy positions. Robert and Mark were on a patrol team together. As they penetrated the thick terrain they had no idea that they were surrounded by enemy troops who would just as soon fire on them if they discovered their presence. "Robert," said Mark, "I saw something move in the bushes over on your right!"

"Yes, it's a commie. They're all around us. If they discover us, we're finished! We'd better keep still and wait 'till they are gone before heading back!"

They were both facing east, the direction of the movements, but didn't realize that from the opposite direction, another North Korean soldier had seen Robert and was coming straight at him from behind with a bayonet aimed. Robert must have bent over for a moment to fix his bootstrap and was unaware. Mark, who was crouched down just a few feet away, saw the enemy soldier, but he couldn't shoot his rifle; neither could he allow his best friend to be bayoneted. Doing the only thing he could do under the circumstance, he threw himself between Robert and the bayonet, taking full thrust. Robert by then reacted and knocked the enemy soldier down and finished him off. Then he turned to Mark who was mortally wounded and cradled him in his arms, admonishing him, "Why didn't you shoot? Why didn't you shoot? O God, you should have shot him! You should have shot him!"

Mark replied, "I am sorry, Robert! I'm sorry, but I couldn't! Besides...a shot would have given away our position and brought more commies."

"But you didn't have to do what you did! You should have let him run me through! It's my fault...it's my fault...you don't belong here! You never did!"

"That isn't true...don't be blaming yourself...besides, who was going to watch over you?"

"Instead of a gun, you should be fighting with a bible saving people so they don't have to have wars, killing each other; but you risk your life in this stinking Korea for a wretch like me. What did I do to deserve a friend like you?"

As he cradled him, Mark began to cough and was losing lots of blood. Robert knew he had to get him back behind the lines where he could receive proper medical attention or he would die. He said, "Take it easy, Mark, I'll get you back, I'll get you back somehow!"

In between his coughing, Mark found the strength to speak. "Robert, you know if I should die, only one thing would give me satisfaction, and that is to know that you gave God a chance in your life. It's the only way you'll find meaning in this world. Promise me! Will you promise, Robert? Promise me!"

Robert, seeing that his best friend was slipping away, said, with tears in his eyes, "Yes...yes, Mark, I promise you anything. I promise you; but don't leave me! Don't leave me, Mark!"

"I'll never leave you, Robert," and saying that, he died in his best friend's arms Robert cried like a baby for he had lost the only true friend whom he had loved more than anyone in the world and who had given his own life to save his.

Somehow, he managed to get out of that dangerous situation, and carrying his dead friend over his shoulder, he made it back to camp. He wouldn't let anyone touch him until the company chaplain came and softened his heart the way Mark used to do. He comforted him, took him aside, and told him, "You have to put your trust in God, my son, for all things work for his good, even death. I know you loved your friend. He had great faith and was not afraid to die, for he believed in the Lord and in the resurrection." Then the chaplain handed him a letter he had been holding in safekeeping from Mark to give to him in the event something like this should happen. It read:

"Dear Robert,

I asked Chaplain McDonald to give this letter to you only in the event something should happen to me, and I didn't make it.

I thought about being a preacher many times, and maybe I would have one day, if it were God's will. You probably blame yourself for talking me into joining the Army; but you shouldn't. I have never told anyone this, not even you, but before we decided to enlist, I had a dream that it was God's plan that I should take that step, somehow. I also had a vision of my death; but I don't mind dying, as long as my death is part of His plan. God has spared your life for a reason. He's the only way you will find peace and meaning in this world. Promise me you'll get to know him.

Forever,

Mark"

He tucked the letter into his pocket and prayed with the chaplain. It must have been the first time in his life he had prayed. He then returned to his platoon and went through the motions of a soldier, but he had lost his taste for war.

In 1951 just a few months after Mark's death, another tragedy happened while he was still in the service--he received a telegram that his mother had died. She had taken ill with cancer and, soon after, went quickly. Now, the two persons who mattered in his life were gone, and he was filled with a kind of despair and emptiness worse than anything he had previously felt. What was the point of anything anymore, the stinking war, life, the future? If it was pointless before, now it might just as well be over with. Although he was still a soldier, he was now a zombie-like creature who no longer had a sense of where he was, nor who he was, nor did he care if the next bullet had his name on it. He moved through the lines in and out of the fire, and only by some miracle was he not killed, either by enemy fire or fire from his own troops. It may have seemed that he had no fear, yet it was not bravery, as some of the other soldiers thought, but a total disinterest in survival and an indifference to his own safety and life that drove him, almost as if he wanted to be shot, though he never was. Others were dying on both sides of him, but not one bullet touched him. All this time, he seemed to be searching inside himself for a reason to go on living.

Meanwhile, as the war progressed, which is all history now, the Allies and the Communists fought see-saw battles, with heavy losses on both sides, eventually to a standstill at the 38th degree parallel which became a demilitarized zone after truce talks started in 1951 and were finally concluded in 1953.

By whatever miracle, Robert Patterson survived the war and returned home in 1953 a completely different person from the one who left. Before, his life was empty and meaningless, but something happened after Mark died that had a profound effect on him. He kept his promise and joined the Church of God. He went to see the Reverend Paul Andrews and told him his story, that it was he, Robert Patterson who had died in Korea, that he was ready to give his life to God, that on the battlefield with death all around him, though he wanted to he could not die! God would not let him die! Finally, he came to a place where he knew for the first time what he must do with his life. "Reverend Andrews," he said, "I want to be a minister. Can you help me?"

"There are three things," said the reverend, "that are necessary before you can become a minister, my son. First, you must receive the calling from God. Second, you must know the word inside and out; and third, you must have the gift to preach the word and impart its message. When you have acquired these three things then you can be a preacher of God."

Robert, who was moved by only one desire now, to know and to serve God, was most eager to learn, for he was ready and his heart was open. He went off by himself and prayed. Day and night he prayed and immersed himself in the scriptures. He read everything written by inspired men of God and in his quiet meditations he cried out to God and asked for help and guidance. He prayed and asked to be made worthy, and the spirit within him filled him up and made him humble. He felt closer to God. He had never known such a feeling before of inner peace. Afterwards, he thought of Mark. He remembered Mark's last words, "I'll never leave you." Then the tears rolled down his cheeks as he said, "Thank you, Lord!"

With Reverend Andrew's recommendation and guidance he was accepted by the protestant conference as a candidate and after years of studies, meditation, and prayer, he returned to Pastor Andrews at the Church of God in L.I. Pastor Andrews saw the remarkable transformation in him and said, "Yes, I see you have learned a great deal, and you seem to have the spirit in you, but can you preach the word? That is your third and last requirement."

"How can I," said Robert, "unless I am given the chance?"

"We will see," said Pastor, "after you serve as my assistant. I will teach you what I know; the rest is up to God." He was certified by the District Superintendent to be an Assistant to Pastor Andrews, and in his sixth month of assistantship, he was given the chance to preach his first sermon. The text that Sunday was based on the Gospel according to Luke 15:11-32, the Parable of the Prodigal Son. After the Gospel reading, he stood at the podium, looking out at the congregation, and began to preach: "My dear brothers and sisters, today's scripture reading teaches us a great lesson about forgiveness. That is why I now put to you this question: Should the father have forgiven his wayward son no matter his transgressions? Would you have done so if you were in his place? After all, the son not only squandered his inheritance, but he wasted his life in profligacy and licentiousness as well, and maybe worse. Shouldn't the father have said to him, 'Away with you, you ungrateful sinner! I have no use for such a worthless wretch!' and disown him and send him away, the way that so many are rejected in our society today because of the hardness of people's hearts? How many prodigals are there in the world? Do you know any of them? Who are the prodigals in your lives? Who are the prodigal sons and daughters in our cities? Who are the lost and dead in spirit? We are tempted to say that they are the criminals, the prostitutes, the thieves and all who bear the scorn of society. Their sins are great indeed! But be not quick to judge, for, in truth, we all are prodigals in God's eyes. Long ago we jeopardized our inheritance when we turned away from God, seeking the pleasures of this world, seeking after lust, greed and selfishness, and wandering like lost sheep. And yet God made a wonderful thing to happen. A most wonderful thing indeed, for, we who are the sheep who went astray, have been given forgiveness through the blood of Jesus Christ. What a bountiful table the Lord has prepared for us! O what a feast awaits us, no matter how great our sins! And if Christ can forgive us, who are undeserving, then should we not forgive others? Should we not forgive all of our brothers, our sisters, our neighbors, even our enemies, and rejoice when they drink the cup in Christ's name? We are all children of the one Father in Heaven who loves us in spite of our sinful nature. Yes, we are all prodigal children in the eyes of God, yet the gift of forgiveness is ours through Christ who died for us. Forgiveness, therefore, is a gift that we must give to others if we are to be worthy of the gift that was given to us. It lifts a burden from us so that we may love more fully.

So, my brothers and sisters, if there is anyone in your lives, or anyone around you whom you need to forgive, give them the gift! Open your hearts and let the blessings of Jesus Christ enter there, for he has taught us the greatest lesson of forgiveness. Amen."

The sermon was well received and many were deeply moved by it. Afterwards, Pastor Andrews said he had made a good start; that it looked like he was going to be a preacher after all!

During the next year he was allowed to conduct many more services, and each went well. The congregation responded with a spiritual fervor and awakening to the new celebrant and opened their hearts to him. By the end of the second year Reverend Andrews decided that he could teach him no more. It was time he had his own church.

It was learned that there was a parish in Jersey City in need of a new pastor. With Reverend Andrews' strong recommendation he had no difficulty being appointed. At last he was really going to begin his work in a church of his own, albeit it was far from Long Island, N.Y.

A few days after his arrival, the new reverend gave his first sermon in The Church of God on Orient Avenue to a packed house. It was apparent that most of the parishioners came out of curiosity, to get a first impression of him. Even the once-a-year church goers came in their finest to hear and see the new pastor from L.I. Before the service began, there were whispers and rumors in the pews about his looks and his stature. "He's a young one," someone said. "He can't be more than 36 or 37. Is he married?" "We hope he's a good preacher because we've waited long enough!" etc.

It was a bright Sunday morning in May, 1970. The altar was decorated with flowers, the choir was assembled, the affirmation of purpose of the gathering was said, and the organist played a lovely prelude that echoed melodiously through the hall. During the prelude the processional took place and as it ended and the music slowly died away, Rev. Patterson stood at the altar and began the adoration, the choir sang a hymn, and a prayer of adoration was spoken, followed by the confession with the congregation joining in. The choir sang both before and after the invocation and scripture readings, then the meditation followed during which the choir sang, "He Looked Beyond my Faults." After the gospel lessons were read, Reverend Patterson approached the pulpit to preach the sermon for that day: We Must Be Born Again.

"Unless we are born again," he said, "we cannot enter the Kingdom of God! These words, taken from the scriptures, were spoken by our Lord and Savior, Jesus Christ. They represent the heart and soul of our faith as Christians, the key by which all sinners, no matter what their past transgressions may have been, can come into God's realm.

And yet, Nicodemus, a learned Pharisee, did not understand Christ's meaning, like so many of us today who do not understand that we can be alive in the flesh but be dead in the spirit, or alive in the spirit though the flesh is dead, and, since we can die twice, both physically and spiritually, we can also be born twice, for we can be reborn in the spirit and have a new life in Christ. Yes, we can cast off the old life seeped in sin, evil and wickedness, which only keeps us mired in the darkness; and we can put on a new life, one that shuns the darkness and flourishes in the Light of Heaven. When we accept Jesus Christ as our Savior, we shall be born again, not in the flesh but in the spirit, and, when we do, we will have no more desire to sin, thereby returning to the ways of God. In the beginning, as we well know from the scriptures, when God created Adam and Eve, He made us eternal beings in his own image, but we turned away from Him and we were punished with death of the flesh. Because of original sin we died in God's eyes, and it was through Jesus Christ that we were given the gift of rebirth, that is, salvation, which is ours when we accept Christ as our Savior.

There are too many people in this world today who are dead in the spirit, though not in the flesh, and have turned away from God and will not seek salvation through the Lord Jesus Christ. But I tell you, they are in great danger of eternal damnation, and that is the worst death of all, for if the flesh dies and the spirit also dies, then we are separated from God forever, and that is worse than death! So if anyone has not done so as yet, now is the time for you to give yourself to Christ before it is too late! Come to the supper of our Lord. Give yourself to Christ and become a new person, a new being in Christ and inherit the gift of eternal life."

After the sermon, the congregation was invited to confess their faith and renew their obedience to Christ publicly, then a hymn was sung and the people rose and together affirmed their faith in God. This was followed by the offertory and the offertory prayer, a hymn, the recessional and the dismissal.

The service was well received by everyone, and the congregation assembled afterwards in the basement for a reception in honor of their new pastor. They had a lovely program in which even the children performed, and speeches were made. There was plenty to eat and drink in a very friendly atmosphere. It was a warm reception, and everyone was eager to shake his hands and gain a personal introduction with him that evening. Reverend Patterson knew he had made a good beginning.

As time went by, he immersed himself in the life of the community, visiting the sick and the aged, welcoming the homeless, the hungry and destitute to the church where he ministered to them, feeding and helping them to find permanent shelters. He even visited the prisons and gave sermons there on several occasions. He came to be known by all as a saintly priest, and was loved and respected by everyone. He had a way with him that you could not resist or refuse. He could soften the heart of a stone. No one could resist his appeal for a worthy cause. He appealed to your higher nature, and the power of his gentle persuasion was irresistible. He successfully started fund raising events to build homes for the needy; he enrolled persons of wealth, businessmen, professionals and the entire community in supporting projects to build a children's hospital, a home for the aged, a school for the handicapped, and he helped the poor to find jobs. He got to know every parishioner and every household; and whenever there was a personal tragedy, he was there; whenever a life was in distress, or a soul was troubled, he was there. It was unbelievable how one preacher could make such a difference in the life of a community that seemed to be completely transformed after he came there.

However, while his parishioners were observing him and admiring his indefatigable energies and amazing accomplishments, some of them were concerned that their pastor was still not married and lived alone without a wife and family. After all, he was still in the prime of his youth. Such a fine young preacher and not married! Whenever the ladies church groups met, it was a topic of discussion, and they wasted no time trying to find a suitable candidate, even dropping hints and remarks to him. They made sure that at social gatherings they introduced hand-picked candidates to him; but they needn't have worried about their pastor, for in due time nature would take its course.

As it happened, Reverend Andrews had a niece who lived with him and whom Robert had met when he was his assistant pastor. He had not given any thought to her at the time because he was totally consumed with his studies, his apprenticeship, and his goal of becoming a preacher. As consumed as he was, he did not have any interest at that time in such things as conjugal bliss nor concern about his own personal life. After several years in Jersey City, however, the thought occasionally came upon him. Providence had a hand in it, too, as it developed.

He was visiting Reverend Andrews in Long Island one Saturday morning when he happened to meet Celeste again. He rang the doorbell, and she opened the door. "Why, hello, Reverend Patterson, how nice it is to see you again!" she said.

"Uh…uh…hello…Celeste?" he said, as if half believing it was, her. He should have had no trouble remembering since she used to be very active in the church and she used to help her uncle a great deal with clerical matters as well as certain household chores, and he used to see her there often.

"Yes, it's me," Celeste answered, "Reverend Andrews' niece! Won't you come in? I'll tell uncle you're here."

And as she walked away, he couldn't help noticing for the first time that something or someone other than the church and his priestly duties had captured his attention. It was strange to him that he never even saw her in that way before during the time he served with her uncle. In a few moments the pastor who was once his mentor and teacher came to greet him.

"Hello, Robert, how wonderful to see you again! I have been hearing such great things about your work. But tell me, what brings you to Long Island?"

"I came to the city on some business for my church, and I thought it would be nice to stop and pay you a short visit."

While they were talking, Celeste softly entered the study where they were and asked if they would like a cup of tea. Reverend Andrews invited her to join them, which Robert did not mind at all. During the entire time they did not take their eyes off of each other. Most of the conversation was about the work that he was doing and how much he still had to accomplish, for, as

Reverend Andrews knew, spreading God's Word and helping the needy is a work that never ends.

"Yes, that is true, Robert," said Reverend Andrews, "but you must still find a little time to rest and relax. You're still a young man and you haven't even taken the time to find you a wife. You must do something about that, too, Robert."

And as he said that, Celeste looked at Robert beamingly, and it didn't go unnoticed by him. At this point, Reverend Andrews interrupted the conversation to say that he hoped that Robert was not planning to leave soon because he had to stay for dinner; in fact, he insisted on it and Robert did not turn him down. You could see a sign of relief on Celeste's face when he accepted, for she had long been fond of Robert secretly though he never knew or seemed to co-respond a similar interest in her before.

Celeste herself prepared the meals for them instead of the housekeeper, perhaps to show her culinary skills. The roast beef was delicious, and the apple pie dessert as well. He praised her cooking, and she blushed before him and her uncle; perhaps, at last, another door was opening up for Robert Patterson. Only time will tell.

After dinner while they were sipping some wine, Reverend Andrews told him that one day he would like to come to Jersey to visit his church and see the children's hospital first hand. Robert insisted that both he and Celeste should come soon, for he would love to have them. They talked for a good while but Robert had not noticed how fast the time had passed while they were chatting when he suddenly realized the hour. He explained that, regrettably, he had to get back to New Jersey and must return to New York to the Port Authority to catch the bus for Jersey City. Celeste ceased on the opportunity to offer to drive him into the city so he would not miss his bus. Rev. Andrews said it was a good idea and Robert and Celeste left for New York City together.

On the way, they had a good chance to talk, and, of course, they found the words for many things that were unsaid before. "Celeste," Robert said, "is there anyone in your life? I mean, are you committed to anyone in a serious way? You don't have to answer. If you think I am being too personal or presumptuous, I…"

She cut him off before he could finish.

"No, Robert, there isn't anyone…and you are not being presumptuous!"

"Good," he said, "because I think you would make someone a very good life partner one day."

"Who do you have in mind, Robert?"

Her answer was so direct that it caught him off guard, and he stammered.

"I…I…I suppose it would have to be someone you liked very much to want to spend the rest of your life with that person."

She knew that in the game of words, he was really speaking for himself. He stopped talking for a while as if waiting for his words to take effect or else to catch his breath.

"Don't stop talking now when I am getting so interested in what you have to say," said Celeste.

He was beginning to feel a little awkward as he said the following.

"I, too, wish to continue this discussion, but another time when we can have dinner together, perhaps, and spend an evening together.

"When will that be? You come to Long Island so seldom." She replied.

He quickly responded as if the answer were in his mind before the question was asked.

"Celeste, there's going to be a revival in New York City a week from next Friday. Will you come?"

She said she would not miss it for anything and she looked forward to seeing him there. The rest of the time they talked about their lives, he, about how it was getting harder to manage things alone, and she, how much she would like to work with children, and how much she had learned about running a church since she had lived with her uncle.

By the time they reached the Port Authority Bus Terminal, there was nothing left but to come right out and say they were meant for each other. But without saying it, it was obvious that they both knew that that was the case. Of course, they met again at the revival, and she and her uncle visited Jersey City more than once. Finally, Robert proposed, and Celeste was relieved, for it was what she had wanted all along. The wedding was set for six months later, sometime in June.

One day in April, while Robert was in the rectory reading and preparing his next sermon, there was a knock on the door. The housekeeper opened the door and spoke to an old man who stood there, "Hello, sir, and how can I help you?"

"Is this the residence of Reverend Robert Patterson?"

"Yes, it is, and what business, may I ask, do you have with the Reverend?"

"I would like to speak with him, please. It is very important."

"And who shall I say would like to speak with him?"

"Tell him someone who knew his mother when he was a child. He will understand."

"Very well, just a moment."

The housekeeper went inside and told Reverend, "A stranger, an old man, is asking for you. He wouldn't give his name, but he said he knew your mother. What should I tell him, pastor?"

Whereupon the Reverend was suddenly taken aback, for he could not imagine who it could be. A thought stirred in the recesses of his brain that he could not dismiss, but how could it be possible? He thanked the housekeeper and told her he would take care of it, then he hurried to the door and looked upon the old and haggard face of a man who was like a ghost from the past.

"Come in, sir. It is much warmer inside; you are most welcome in this house!" and he led the stranger into the living room.

As the stranger entered and Robert looked closer into his face, although covered with wrinkles, marks of a hard life, and a beard besides, he knew it was his father. Robert had not seen him since the time he was arrested and sent to prison and had not heard from him in all these years. In fact, years ago, when he was still in high school, he was told that he was dead. He never expected to see him again, not that back then he had cared to, for he had hated his father then because of the way he treated him and his mother. The old man looked at him with a pleading look and a look of contrition with tears in his eyes. Robert reached out his arms and embraced his father, himself taken with emotion.

"It is alright, father. You are home now, and that is all that matters!"

"Please forgive me, son, for all the things I did to you and your mother. Please forgive me," his father pleaded, "I have lived with my sins for all these years; can you forgive me?"

Perhaps the old Robert Patterson could not, but the Reverend Robert Patterson did. He warmly embraced his father and begged him to forgive him, too, for the hate he once had in his heart toward him, but now, how happy he was that he had a father once more!

"It was the hand of God," the reverend said, "that led you to me."

His father cried and said, "I am only sorry your mother is not here for me to ask her forgiveness!"

"But she is, at least in spirit, for she is with God now, and she would be happy to know that you were sorry and asked for forgiveness. She would be happy, too, if you would accept Jesus Christ as your Savior. Stay with me," continued Robert, "and we will pray together. You can ask Christ to lift all your burdens and give you peace, as he has given me."

He brought his father to Christ that evening as they knelt and prayed together, prayed for forgiveness for past sins, and prayed for absolution. Robert felt his heart lift, for he knew his father for the first time as he had never known him, and he thanked God for this day. His father was converted at that time, and he was a different man.

He called Celeste on the phone and told her the wonderful news of the return of his prodigal father, whom he had not seen in all these years, and she was happy for them both. In their previous conversations, he had shared with her many things about his past, including his childhood life. As a teenager, he had been led to believe that his father had died, so he considered it a miracle when he reappeared and was transformed from the man he once was. He and Celeste provided a place for him to live with them in Jersey so he could remain a permanent part of their family after they were married.

In the meantime, on that first Sunday of his father's return, Reverend Patterson preached a sermon with even greater fervor than ever before, for his heart was full, and that which was unresolved from the past was made right at last. Both he and his father visited his mother's grave and placed a wreath there, and from that day, his father kept fresh flowers there and visited her every week until his own death less than a year later when he was buried in the same grave with his wife, reunited in Christ forever. Before his death, however, he was able to know one of the happiest moments in his life when he got to see his only son get married a year before he passed away. It was one of the happiest moments in his life and a blessing that he took with him.

Robert and Celeste exchanged their vows in the Church of God in Jersey City to the delight of all his parishioners who only wanted their pastor to be happy. It was a most joyous occasion with Reverend Andrews performing the wedding ceremony, and even Robert's ex-army chaplain, Rev. McDonald, was there. The whole of Jersey City couldn't fit in the church, but they managed somehow to fit into the garden leading from the basement of the church for the reception. The Reverend and Mrs. Robert Patterson could have had the thrice spacious regal reception hall donated by the wealthy business community, but they wanted to keep it in a more modest place under total control of the parishioners, and it was well managed with everybody doing his/her share.

The honeymooners could only look forward to a 5-day vacation because the Reverend was hard-pressed to be spared from his duties. However, they spent the most glorious 5-day honeymoon in the Bahamas, leaving the Monday morning after the wedding and returning the following Friday. So much for the celibacy of one celebrated pastor! When the Reverend and Mrs. Patterson returned from their honeymoon, they got right into the work of the church, with Mrs. Patterson helping to organize and work with different societies and church groups, of adults as well as children, in planning social events and activities, charities for the sick and the poor. She was a great help to the Reverend and a blissful addition to his household. He had a new cheerfulness to go along with his sublime grace, and you knew that his bride was responsible for the former. He went about his work with an energy and vigor that was enough for two or three priests at least. He served on boards and statewide committees, he was a guest speaker on numerous public occasions, he administered the blessings and prayers at weddings and public functions, and if there was a problem anywhere, a riot in the streets or even in the prisons, he was called in to calm things down. He was like a spiritual guardian over every aspect of the life of the community, such that people only asked for Reverend Patterson, "Send for the Reverend," they would say, and they knew everything was going to be alright. In their prayers, everyone thanked the Lord for giving them such a reverend to watch over them.

The years went by so quickly that they hardly noticed. Reverend and Mrs. Patterson had three lovely children, Mark, Celia, and John, and they grew into their teen years fine and upstanding. Mark, the firstborn, was 18, Celia 16, and John 14, each two years apart. They were brought up in a Christian home with abundant love and kindness, and they loved and, for the most part, emulated their parents. Mark had long decided that he wanted to become a

317

minister like his father and already was following in his footsteps, assisting with the services in any way that he could. Celia wanted to be a schoolteacher and even started to teach Sunday school classes like her mother; John, was probably the most unpredictable of the three, but he wasn't sure as yet what he wanted to do with his life.

When the Reverend had his regular one-on-one talks with his children, John especially, he would ask him, "John, don't you think you should have some idea by now what you want to become when you are a man?" and John would reply, "No, father, I know I don't want to be a preacher, and I don't want to be a teacher, either; I just don't know."

"But why?" asked his father, "Is there something wrong with being a minister or a schoolteacher?"

"No, I didn't mean that. I just don't know what I want to be, that's all!"

His father would hug him just the same and say, "It doesn't matter, son, whatever you decide, I am sure it will be alright."

Robert couldn't help thinking of his own childhood and the period he went through when nothing interested him or had any meaning. The only difference now is that his son did not hate or was not angry and could count on his love and understanding. He would be spared the painful experience of losing his way, of feeling alone, of being unloved, of feeling hopelessness and despair, for he would have the time and all the tenderness and understanding around him that he needed to help him find his way.

As it turned out, several years later, John did show an aptitude for writing and, in fact, became a successful author when he grew up. Mark, of course, became a preacher like his father, and Celeste received her PhD. in Education, married, and became a successful college professor.

In returning to the central thread of the story, the Reverend and Mrs. Patterson continued God's work for more than 30 years, becoming more and more widely known both locally as well as throughout the tri-state region. He was very highly respected among his fellow clergymen, being invited to represent them at the ecumenical councils, and was looked to for leadership and inspiration. He was a true spiritual leader on all levels, in all walks of life.

So it was, until a sudden illness overtook him, and his condition got worse. The Reverend Robert Patterson was not afraid, however, to meet his maker; in fact, he was more than ready, for he had served him well! It was grace that saved him when he was lost almost 50 years ago, and to his dying day, he never forgot what had happened to him on the battlefield. That is why on his deathbed, he made but two requests that the first verse of the hymn, "Amazing Grace," be inscribed on his tombstone and that a certain letter be buried with him. It was the letter from his boyhood friend, Mark Andrews, which he carried with him throughout his life and to his grave.

The funeral service in the Church of God came to an end with the viewing and then the recessional. Afterwards, the pallbearers carried the casket and placed it in the hearse. The trail of cars in the funeral procession stretched for miles and miles, it seemed, as they slowly headed to the interment site.

It is now five years since the Reverend Robert Patterson was laid to rest, and if you were to visit the cemetery near Jersey City where he is buried, you would see the inscription written in gold letters on a marble tombstone. The life it represents is a further testament to the spirit of God in man…Amazing Grace!